Brazil

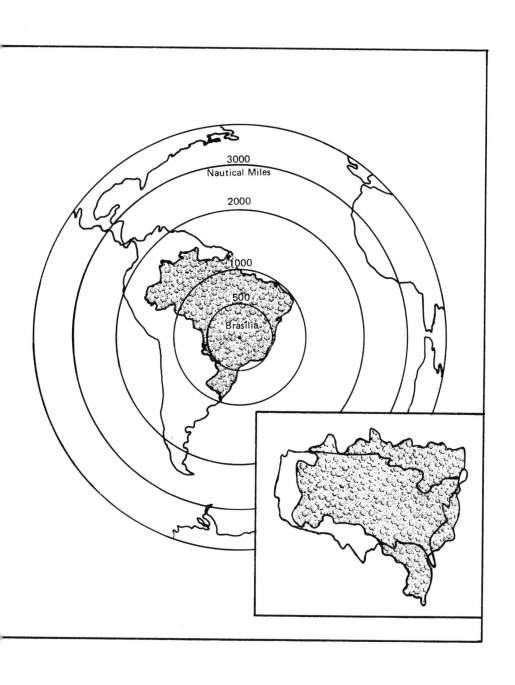

3000
Nautical Miles

2000

1000

500

Brasília

Two Perspectives of Brazil

Westview Special Studies on Latin America

Brazil: Foreign Policy of a Future World Power
Ronald M. Schneider

Brazil is nearing the ill-defined but generally recognized point at which it can claim to be a ranking power—the first Southern Hemisphere star in the world system. As it single-mindedly pursues development strategies within a changing world economic order, Brazil is using its new power and freedom of action to work out more flexible alignments than in the past. The Brazilian government is prepared for an active diplomacy, bordering on a kind of international economic warfare if necessary, to achieve the export growth and access to supplies of goods and credit which the nation's economic progress requires.

This volume moves from a discussion of Brazil's present condition—political, economic, and international—to an analysis of foreign policy and the policymaking process, and finally to an examination of the dynamic factors in the present situation and the prospects for the future. A number of the basic constraints and facilitating factors discussed in general background terms in the first chapter are viewed in the perspective of late 1976 as on-going issues that will weigh heavily on Brazil's future international role and foreign-policy orientation, and future trends and developments are forecast and their implications evaluated.

In addition to addressing thoroughly the issue of Brazil, Dr. Schneider has provided a valuable comparative foreign-policy study, presenting a series of cases in foreign-policy decision making.

Ronald M. Schneider is a widely respected scholar and author in the field of Latin American affairs. Currently a professor of political science at Queens College, he holds a Ph.D. in political science from Princeton University.

BRAZIL

Foreign Policy
of a
Future World Power

Ronald M. Schneider

Westview Press
Boulder, Colorado

Westview Special Studies on Latin America

Published 1976 in the United States of America by
    Westview Press, Inc.
    1898 Flatiron Court
    Boulder, Colorado 80301
    Frederick A. Praeger, Publisher and Editorial Director

Library of Congress Cataloging in Publication Data

Schneider, Ronald M.
    Brazil, foreign policy of a future world power.

    Includes bibliographical references and index.
    1. Brazil—Foreign relations—1930- 2. Brazil—Foreign relations administration. I. Title.
JX1533.S36   327.81   76-28345
ISBN 0-89158-200-2

Printed and bound in the United States of America.

For my parents

Contents

Introduction

Brazil is nearing the ill-defined but generally recognized point at which it can claim to be a ranking power—the first Southern Hemisphere star in the world galaxy and the first new major power to emerge on the international scene since the rise of China after World War II. The surge of energy propelling Brazil upward and outward results largely from economic drives, and the country's concrete objectives are chiefly economic—although Brazilians have a very real aspiration to national greatness, with expectation of success at least by the year 2000.[1]

Under present circumstances, Brazil is steadily moving toward an accentuated nationalism, although both the tactics and the intensity of this movement are likely to vary with changing internal and external conditions. Since, in any case, Brazil's weight in international matters will continue to increase steadily—indeed, the real takeoff point is only now being reached—its foreign policy and policymaking processes merit scrutiny.

In *The Political System of Brazil* (Columbia University Press, 1971) I analyzed in some detail Brazil's internal politics. From that time to the present I have been engaged in an equally painstaking investigation of Brazil's international role and of the links between its domestic politics and its foreign policy. During 1974 and 1975 this effort resulted in a major study within the Department of State's external research program. This book goes well beyond that study in terms of its scope, depth, and time frame. It is intended not only to clarify many key aspects of Brazil's visibly increasing international prominence, but also to provide a framework for intelligently comprehending the changes that will continue to occur in the years ahead.

An additional purpose of this volume is to add some sorely needed substance to the evolving academic field of comparative foreign-policy studies. Surely we must first ask why a certain state acts as it does in a particular situation, and then examine how it responds to changes in this situation, before we can make generalizations about how any state is likely to act in a given situation. Thus, the need for well conceptualized and deeply analytical comparable studies is logically antecedent to sound comparative work.[2]

Recent years have witnessed a marked increase in the attention paid to the comparative study of foreign policies, long a rather neglected field. With a few notable exceptions, such as Michael Brecher's work on Israel, most major studies have been focused on the foreign policies of great powers, while some laudable efforts at regional analysis have struggled to transcend the handicaps imposed by lack of serious and specific research. In either case, most studies have analyzed the substance of policy rather than the processes by which policy is formulated and implemented. If it is to be properly done, such an analysis requires a deep understanding of internal governmental institutions and political dynamics.[3]

To no part of the world are the aforementioned observations more relevant than to Latin America—where the literature on comparative politics is far from adequate and that on international politics still weaker, and where systematic studies of foreign policy and policymaking are all but totally absent. At the present time some work is being done on the international roles of Mexico and Venezuela, but Brazil affords a much more significant case. Neither the rational-choice theory nor the bureaucratic model of foreign-policy decision making, both so much in vogue in recent years, corresponds in any significant way to Brazilian reality; hence they are not utilized in this study. Moreover, my basic approach does not recognize the sharp distinction between internal policy and external policy which holds back much of the research in the foreign-policy field. Here my conceptual position is in agreement with Cohen and Harris, when they observe that the key to dealing effectively with the domestic sources of foreign policy (internal input variables) is the realization that

> the increasing importance of transnational actors such as multi-national corporations, the penetration of many political systems to greater or lesser degree by official and unofficial agents of other states, and the flow of international communications are only some of the factors which make the distinction between domestic and foreign difficult to maintain.[4]

This is particularly true in a country such as Brazil, in which developmental considerations—particularly the pursuit of economic growth— are high-priority matters decided at the top level of a centralized system of governmental decision making in which foreign policy is viewed essentially as being merely instrumental to national goals.

Pursuant to this view, I rely on the concept of constraints and opportunities, as they are perceived by the real policymakers to exist in the domestic environment, as a means for linking consideration of internal variables with the impact of these variables upon foreign policy. I also hold that the conventional distinction between political and economic factors has lost much of its usefulness, and may even inhibit understanding of the policies of a country in which this dichotomy is not important in the minds of policymakers.

While this basic approach heavily conditioned my inquiry,

it has rarely been brought to the forefront of or made explicit in the text. Specialists in this field can see that the framework is there without an elaboration of it which would distress the nonacademic reader. I should like to point out, however, that in my attempt to get at the roots of Brazil's international behavior, the roles and identities of the participants in the policymaking process were not assumed, inferred from the structure of that country's government, or considered to be self-evident. Instead, the essential elements in the process have been established empirically, beginning with that evidence which can be observed clearly—Brazil's actual policies as revealed by actions, not by public pronouncements.

By looking at a given set of foreign policies—in this case those of Brazil under the Geisel administration and its immediate predecessors—and working back to the processes of choice from which these policies emerged, it was possible to uncover the various input factors involved in the making of decisions and to assess the relative influence of these factors. Once this retrospective analysis had been completed in respect to a sufficient number of issues and problems (with a longitudinal dimension going back to 1964, but concentrating on 1970-1976), I could then work toward predicting future policy decisions.

This volume moves from a discussion of Brazil's present condition—political, economic, and international—to an analysis of foreign policy and the policymaking process, and, finally, to an examination of the dynamic factors in the present situation and of the prospects for the future in terms of Brazil's role and position. Thus, Chapter 1 considers Brazil's foreign-policy capacity and stance in the context of such basic aspects of the internal environment of policymaking as the country's economic wealth, the effective utilization of its resource base, the nature of its political system, its level of institutionalization and degree of mobilization, its basis for legitimacy, and the extent of policy-relevant public participation. Chapter 2 assesses the international environment in which Brazilian foreign policy is made and implemented. This chapter includes a brief overview of Brazil's present goals, priorities, development strategies, and security doctrine, as well as a summary discussion of the impact of increased capacity on foreign-policy predispositions and on Brazil's will and ability to move toward increased international status and influence.

Chapter 3 analyzes the roles of the president, the presidency, and the Armed Forces, while Chapter 4 focuses on the Foreign Ministry. The dramatic role expansion of other agencies in the Brazilian government is discussed in Chapter 5, and the roles of nongovernmental actors in Chapter 6. In each of these areas, attention has been paid to organization and staffing role perceptions, objectives, priorities, linkages to other elements of the foreign-policy community, and internal dissension.

Chapter 7 pulls together many of the trends discernible in the preceding chapters and highlights some of Brazil's most important international decisions and engagements. While in a conventional sense providing conclusions to the study, this chapter serves, in addition, as a transition to the forecasting projections that round out this book. To this end, in Chapter 8, a number of the basic constraints and facilitating factors discussed in general background terms in the first chapter are viewed, from the perspective of mid-1976, as ongoing issues that will weigh heavily on Brazil's future international role and foreign-policy orientation. Finally, in Chapter 9, future trends and developments are forecast, and their implications are evaluated.

Most of the factual information in this study comes from an extensive and careful reading of the Brazilian press and relevant specialized publications. I have also benefited from discussions with many United States officials concerned with Brazilian affairs and with a score of individuals involved in the formulation and conduct of Brazil's foreign relations. Elizabeth H. Hyman, G. Harvey Summ, and Mary K. Manzoli played active parts in shaping this inquiry and also served as intelligent critics of the preliminary drafts. Other individuals in the U.S. State Department who have been particularly helpful include David Smith and Daniel Fendrick. Nonetheless, the views expressed and the conclusions reached in this study are solely the author's, and should not be interpreted as representing the opinions of any government employee, much less as reflecting the official policies of the Department of State.

Similarly, while useful perspectives were provided by the comments and observations of the scholars and diplomats assembled by the Office of External Research on April 29 and 30, 1976, to discuss contract studies on Brazilian foreign policy, these individuals share no responsibility for the content of this volume. However, I would like to express my special appreciation to participants Joel Bergsman, Douglas Chalmers, Albert Fishlow, and Ambassador John Hugh Crimmins.

In spite of the fact that we worked separately, rather than in close consultation with one another, I would like to acknowledge the stimulation received from Gertrude Heare, Stanley Hilton, and Wayne Selcher, authors of the other external research papers on Brazil. Indeed, I gave serious consideration to including chapters by Professor Selcher in this book before deciding that his work merited publication in full as an independent monograph.[5]

Finally, I consider myself fortunate in having found in Fred Praeger—my first publisher nearly two decades ago—a true professional who could understand the urgent need to get this book into print without the frustrating delays that generally accompany publication of a scholarly work. Implementation of this desire has been made possible by Westview's highly efficient managing editor, Lynne Rienner. And the reader, as well as the author, owes a vote of thanks to Ann Williams, whose conscientious and intelligent editing has added greatly to the clarity and pace of this work. Once again Marcia Case has done a highly professional job of preparing the index, a difficult, yet essential step in the transformation of a manuscript into a book.

Notes to Introduction

[1]Ray S. Cline, of Georgetown University's Center for Strategic and International Studies, rated Brazil in 1975 as already sixth in the world in

terms of international perceived power, ranking just after China and ahead of Iran, the United Kingdom, Canada, and Japan (which round out the top ten). See his *World Power Assessment: A Calculus of Strategic Drift* (Boulder, Colo.: Westview Press, 1975), p. 130. Dr. Cline previously headed the State Department's Bureau of Intelligence and Research after a distinguished career with the Central Intelligence Agency.

2The best evaluation of the unsettled state of theory in the international field is found in Fred I. Greenstein and Nelson W. Polsby (eds.), *International Politics*, vol. 8 of the *Handbook of Political Science* (Reading, Mass.: Addison-Wesley, 1975). Of greater immediate concern to this study is Bernard C. Cohen and Scott A. Harris, "Foreign Policy," in *Politics and Policy Making*, vol. 6 of the same series, pp. 381-437.

3The foundation for an attempt at formulating a systematically comparative foreign-policy effort is a partial reworking of Howard Lentner's framework as briefly discussed in n. 1, Chap. 1.

4Cohen and Harris, "Foreign Policy," pp. 410-411.

5Professor Selcher, along with Jordan M. Young, Kenneth Erickson, Stefan H. Robock, John M. Cates, G. Harvey Summ, and a number of my associates in the political science department at Queens College, is collaborating with me in a continuing study of Brazil's international relations.

1
Brazil
as an
International Actor

Brazil, one of the most upwardly mobile actors in the current international political system, is moving from a policy of engagement toward one of expansion in international affairs.[1] In terms of foreign-policy capacity, it is an upper-middle power with the potential to move into the ranks of the five great powers that presently occupy a place in the international stratification system below that of the two superpowers, the United States and the USSR. Brazil's continental expanse (it is fifth in the world in area), its population of 113 million (it has overtaken Japan for sixth place among the nations of this globe), its rapidly growing economy (its GNP recently surpassed India's for tenth place), and its expanding foreign trade all underscore its potential for achieving major-power status within a relatively short period. Thus, Brazilian spokesmen such as the former vice-chief of the Armed Forces General Staff, Gen. Carlos de Meira Mattos, are realistic when they say that "Brazil is presently trying to consolidate its position within a framework as a regional power, to which, because of their continental dimensions, only three countries can aspire: China, India, and Brazil."[2]

1

Just as the United States dramatically raised its sights and expanded its international focus after World War I, Brazil has extended its foreign-policy interests to all corners of the globe; these interests now include largescale foreign economic operations. As it singlemindedly pursues its own national development strategies within a changing world economic order, Brazil is using its new power and freedom of action to work out increasingly flexible international alignments. Brazil's identification with the Western countries is gradually fading in the present atmosphere of détente, and economic alliances are largely replacing traditional strategic ties.

The tendency to view Brazil as a significant factor in world affairs is quite recent. A generation ago Argentina and Mexico appeared to be at least on a par with Brazil, which seemed barred by both its economic backwardness and its non-Hispanic culture and society from any international role larger than that of being merely one of the more important Latin American countries. Less than fifteen years ago, unrealistic efforts by the governments of Jânio Quadros (January-August 1961) and João ("Jango") Goulart (September 1961-March 1964) to project an "independent" foreign policy contributed to the decision of the Armed Forces to oust Goulart.[3]

Today, the Brazilian government is well organized and prepared for conducting an active diplomacy (bordering on a kind of international economic warfare, if necessary) in order to achieve the export growth and access to supplies of goods and credit which the nation's economic progress requires. The Brazilian executive has exceptionally wide powers to handle the big issues of policy and to shape Brazil's foreign relations– powers that Western industrial countries customarily grant their leaders only in times of war. The executive can subordinate crosscurrents of private interests, harmonize bureaucratic conflicts within agreed concepts of national security requirements, and generally maximize the impact of the policies that it adopts. As for external constraints, the Brazilian economy has made considerable progress toward buffering and regulating transnational influences that, via control of credit and of investment sources, have traditionally restrained Brazil's freedom to decide its own policies. The external payments situation now constitutes the principal determinant of the rate of Brazil's economic growth.

In rising toward major-power status in the present international order, Brazil has been largely unhampered by the needs to organize massive military forces to provide for its security in global affairs, to seek the protection of exclusive military alliances, or to make other confining political commitments. Brazil can also escape military strategic pressures and keep military expenditures low (about 3 percent of its gross national product) because its military forces are the strongest in South America, and because that region is comparatively free of interstate conflict.

Conflicting pressures create difficult imperatives for Brazil as it moves onward and upward: to please both oil producers and major industrial consumers of energy, to appease anticommunist sentiment within the military establishment which opposes expanding ties with socialist countries, to keep the lid on political dissenters at home while avoiding liberal and third-world accusations of abusing human rights, and to balance the interests of North and South in multilateral affairs. Nevertheless, Brazil is not locked into the complex mesh of political, military, and economic interests–both domestic and foreign–that entangles the policies of many other nations, particularly those that have already reached major-power status.

Since 1974, economic imperatives have increasingly dominated Brazil's foreign policy. After oil prices rose to new high levels, Brazil had to set aside nearly two-fifths of its export earnings to pay for foreign oil. From Itaipu to Bonn to Baghdad, Brazilian economic and diplomatic officials struggled to ease the burden of these energy costs on the national economy. In the process, they stayed closer to energy producers than to the major consumer nations, took an independent road on nuclear-energy development vis-à-vis the United States, dealt with the Soviet Union for turbines, and cast pro-Arab votes in the United Nations. Economic pressures carried Brazil away from its traditional Western industrial partners, made new dealings more attractive, and placed a renewed emphasis on independence in foreign affairs reminiscent in content, if not in style, of the Quadros-Goulart era of the early 1960s. "Responsible pragmatism" has given way to "no automatic alignments" and "other options" as catch phrases of Brazilian diplomacy.

This study focuses on the institutions and individuals responsible for foreign affairs and on the policymaking roles they play in Brazil. Because a country's capacity to engage in and influence international situations is affected by its ability to cope with its fundamental political problems, significant features of the Brazilian political system will be discussed in order to elucidate the internal environment of the institutions making foreign policy. Economic capabilities will also be discussed because development priorities greatly influence Brazilian policy decisions, while other vulnerabilities of the Brazilian economy also impose major constraints on foreign policy. The attitudes and outlook of Brazilian policymakers will be explored, along with the stimuli to Brazil's foreign-policy institutions that come from abroad—for only within its world context can the foreign-policy decision-making process in Brazil, as analyzed in chapters 3-8, be adequately comprehended.[4]

Political Factors

The major watersheds in Brazil's political development have been its declaration of independence from Portugal (1822), the establishment of an elite-dominated republic (1889), the overthrow of that republic by disaffected young soldiers and middle-class civilians (1930), the end of the neo-corporatist regime of Getúlio Vargas (1945), and the seizure of power by the Armed Forces and allied civilian elites which put an end to the country's brief experiment with a populist-leaning administration (1964).

Much of the basic structure of contemporary Brazilian government and politics dates from the Vargas era. Indeed, the 1964 revolution was, in a very real sense, only another link in the tortuous chain of Brazilian political life. This chain extended from the 1930 revolution that brought Vargas to power through the 1945 revolt that ousted him, and on to the *golpe* against him during his second term (1951-1954) which led to his suicide. It threaded its way through the regime of Juscelino Kubitschek (1956-1961), the election of Jânio Quadros in 1960, and the succession crisis of August-September 1961, which was precipitated by Quadros' abrupt resignation and the assumption of the presidency by Goulart.

Mistrust of Goulart, a prominent Vargas supporter who was vice-president under both Kubitschek and Quadros, lay at the root of each of the four military interventions into politics during the 1954-1964 decade. Under Goulart's presidency (1961-1964), the growing forces of the left tried to wrest control from the dominant center-conservative elements, while improved political communications and radical agitation aroused strong desires for sweeping changes in the established order. Although the increase in the number of radical leftists in policymaking positions in the Goulart regime worried Brazilian centrists and conservatives, as well as some foreign observers, the inclusion of the leftists was aimed at redressing a power balance that had long been weighted in favor of the traditionally dominant elites.[5] Peaceful incorporation of emerging groups had helped Brazil avoid violent political upheaval in the past, and the gradual but fairly rapid broadening of the political base (the Brazilian electorate doubled between 1950 and 1962) changed the composition of the policymaking elite. The course of these changes was drastically modified, however, by the military movement of March 31, 1964, that brought down the Goulart government.[6]

A fundamental purpose of the military regime that has governed Brazil since 1964 has been to replace the old "political class"—flawed in the new regime's estimation by the vices of the Vargas-Goulart era—with a new civilian elite possessing "a sense of national security."[7] To date, the new regime has been substantially successful in destroying the old political elite—part purged, part pensioned off, the remainder rendered largely powerless except for those incorporated into the rather artificial biparty system. Three legislative elections, three sets of "revolutionary" governors, and the appointment of almost fifty civilians to cabinet-level posts have so far produced substantial post-1964 leadership cadres rather than a complete new political class. Renovation has been even more gradual in professional career services such as the Armed Forces and the foreign service, where there has been greater continuity. It is in the economic and technical agencies that turnover has been most complete since the military came to power.

Although Brazil has had only four different military presidents since the 1964 revolution, the country has experienced at least twice as many distinct periods in terms of basic political strategy and orientation. Each stage has become significantly longer as the crises that have led to several coups-within-coups have become less frequent. The first such period, in early April 1964, saw an interim junta-type government presiding over the selection of a chief executive for the revolutionary regime. The Supreme Command of the Revolution issued a sweeping Institutional Act under which it purged political figures closely associated with the Goulart regime. The inauguration of Gen. Humberto Castelo Branco as president in mid-April, engineered by the military in conjunction with the governors who had supported the resolution, ushered in an eighteen-month period during which some of the substance as well as the facade of formal democracy was preserved. Relying on a coalition of those elements within each of the preexisting parties which had supported the military's action, Castelo Branco strove to reform the political system in anticipation of the reestablishment of competitive political processes.

Any prospects for ending the supposedly temporary period of military rule were eliminated when the president's efforts to move toward political normalcy by calling partial gubernatorial elections in October 1965 backfired because of voter hostility to the regime in major urban centers and hard-line (*linha dura*) military insistence that the punitive phase of the revolution had not gone far enough. Forced to accept a second Institutional Act which reinstituted the powers of the military to purge and to suspend political rights—powers that he had allowed to lapse—in 1966 Castelo Branco dissolved the existing parties and replaced them with two new parties: the National Renovating Alliance (Arena), representing the proregime political forces, and the Brazilian Democratic Movement (MDB), for the government's critics. The president then reshaped basic legislation and revised the constitution so as to give his successor sufficient authority to act without having to resort to extraconstitutional powers.

Though his nomination was accepted with reluctance by Castelo Branco and his advisers, War Minister Arthur da Costa e Silva was imposed on Arena as the military's choice for the 1967-1971 presidential term. The rules of the electoral game were repeatedly changed and patently manipulated in order to ensure the elevation to chief executive of the general who had headed the revolutionary supreme command and who had mediated the army's intramural conflict in 1965. Costa e Silva's ratification by Congress was followed by legislative elections in which Arena returned a substantial majority for the government; however, that majority consisted mainly of politicians of the pre-1964 political elite and lacked any significant infusion of new elements to balance the purges of leftists and radical nationalists. The artificiality of the imposed two-party system gave rise to a new opposition movement, a broad front (Frente Ampla) that united the ex-presidents purged by the revolution—Quadros, Goulart, and Kubitschek—with the most deeply disenchanted of the original civilian backers of the 1964 coup, among them Carlos Lacerda, former governor of Guanabara. Resistance to the renewal of parliamentary purges led to the temporary closing of Congress, a sign that political normalcy would be long in coming.[8]

The fifth period of the revolution, initiated by Costa e Silva in March 1967, saw the progressive disillusionment of those who had believed that his pledge to "humanize" the revolution presaged a significant liberalization of social and political policies. Instead, the regime's repressive response to student and church manifestations of opposition led to increased polarization. Both lawful forms of criticism and competition with the dominant military-technocratic alliance had been rendered ineffective by the government's often-arbitrary use of the vast powers it had been granted by the 1967 constitution and by modifications of national security legislation. The regime tended to equate resistance to its policies with subversion. With the outlawing of the Frente Ampla and the emasculation of parliamentary opposition, the trend during 1968 was toward increasing violence.

The regime's conflict with radical student elements and with the progressive wing of the Catholic church provided the context for yet another coup-within-a-coup in December 1968, when a behind-the-scenes bid for greater power by rival right-wing military factions was camouflaged by a concerted blow against the regime's critics. Large-scale purges were resumed under a fifth Institutional Act which resulted in the destruction of almost a third of the MDB's congressional representation and the virtual elimination of the liberal constitutionalist wing of the government party. What remained of the Congress was given an indefinite recess that lasted more than a year.

Thus, as 1969 opened, Costa e Silva found himself in a position roughly analogous to that of Castelo Branco at the end of 1965, except that no single powerful figure within the Armed Forces loomed as the heir apparent. His authority compromised by the jockeying of military factions that were looking beyond him to the 1970 presidential succession, Costa e Silva was caught between hard-line pressures for the institutionalization of what was fast becoming a dictatorship and civilian demands for reestablishment of a representative and consultative, if not really competitive, dimension to the system. As the radical opposition turned to using violent tactics, the president's dilemma intensified until his incapacitating stroke in September transferred the problem to other hands.

Under a caretaker junta composed of the incumbent service ministers, a process of consultation and selection within the armed forces resulted in the elevation to the presidency of Gen. Emílio Garrastazú Médici. The Arena majority in

Congress was given no option but to ratify the military's choice, since the government continued to hold in reserve the arbitrary authority vested in the president and the National Security Council by the December 1968 Institutional Act. Torture and repression had become widespread by this time, and, since the radical left was then resorting to bombings, robberies, and the kidnapping of foreign diplomats, the interim government made little effort to curb such abuses. Although the Médici administration took steps to keep repression within limits after the terrorist problem was largely eliminated, the government's position was then based to a considerable extent on calculating whether the costs of officially sanctioned torture—which included criticism from abroad and friction with the church—were commensurate with the security benefits of such a policy. The junta also promulgated a substantial revision of the 1967 constitution, significantly broadening the authority of the federal government to intervene in the states and severely limiting parliamentary immunity.[9]

From the beginning, the Médici regime used the ablest manpower from the earlier military administrations, thus providing maximum continuity in the work of the economic-planning technocrats. In addition, new talent uninvolved in the rivalry between the followers of Castelo Branco and those of Costa e Silva was brought into the government, and the regime's communication with the public was greatly improved. Equally important, the Army Ministry under Gen. Orlando Geisel began to seek maximum military unity; many of the most-politicized mid-grade officers failed to receive promotions and thus were retired from active service. In 1970 basic goals were defined in a National Security Council document entitled "Goals and Bases for Government Action." Elections were subsequently held which greatly strengthened the regime's support in Congress and reduced the MDB to virtual impotence. Hand-picked and generally young governors were installed in the statehouses through further rationalization of the process of indirect election initiated in 1966. Ministerial stability and continuity in major appointive offices lasted through 1974, as the president's political strength and popularity continued to rise.

On January 15, 1975, Brazil's electoral college by a vote of 400 to 76 confirmed the choice, originally made by the Armed Forces and subsequently ratified by the government party (Arena), of Gen. Ernesto Geisel, younger brother of Orlando Geisel, to succeed Gen. Emílio Garrastazú Médici as president. From that day until the inauguration on March 15, all political efforts were bent toward ensuring a smooth transition of power.

The heart of the new government consisted of individuals who had been closely associated with the late Marshal Humberto Castelo Branco during his presidential term. Geisel had served in that administration as chief of the president's Military Cabinet; his own choice for chief of the Civil Cabinet, the key ministerial position on the presidential staff, was retired Gen. Golbery do Couto e Silva, another of Castelo's closest associates. Continuity with the Médici government was provided by Planning Minister João Paulo dos Reis Velloso, while the brilliant young (thirty-nine) economist Mário Henrique Simonsen was brought in as finance minister to replace Antônio Delfim Netto, who had built up an international reputation as the architect of Brazil's dramatic economic growth. Other major appointments included career diplomat Antônio Azeredo da Silveira, then serving as ambassador to Argentina, as foreign minister. Armando Falção, a longtime congressman and justice minister during the democratic government of Juscelino Kubitschek (1956-1961), was picked to return to that position, which in Brazil is chiefly concerned with liaison with the political class.

The selection of new governors for the 1974-1978 period dominated political life from April through July. Much as Castelo Branco and Costa e Silva had hand-picked official candidates for subsequent ratification by the state legislative assemblies in 1966 and 1970, Geisel worked out solutions to the succession question which were acceptable to Arena leaders. The congressional elections of November 15 resulted in a surprisingly strong comeback by the MDB, which scored a sixteen-to-six victory in Senate races and elected 45 percent of the chamber of Deputies. Nonetheless, the government—sobered but not really shaken by the poor showing of its party's candidates—retained a decisive edge in the lower house of the National Congress (204 to 160) and an even bigger margin in the Senate (where holdovers gave Arena 46 seats to the MDB's 20). Moreover, the government party continued to control sixteen state legislatures, although the opposition had majorities in several of the most important states. March 1975 saw both the full functioning of Congress and the installation of the state administrations chosen by Geisel to replace the Médici regime's lame-duck carryovers, and by September new national leadership for Arena had been selected and a new party program formulated.

Gradualism is the basic strategic theme of the Geisel government, much as a team approach characterizes its policymaking style. Having been burned by their experience during the Castelo Branco government, and determined to avoid another breakdown of efforts at political normalization like the failures that occurred in December 1968 and September 1969, the key decision makers have emphasized that their commitment to decompression is intended to strengthen the regime, not to liberalize or democratize it. The process is to be "slow, gradual, and secure," with carefully considered, even cautious, steps. The administration's strategists have considered consistency and coherence—a "firm" sense of direction and determination—to be more important than a rigid timetable. One key minister has said that Brazil must exercise "caution to avoid regression," while his rival for the president's ear has emphasized the necessary risks involved. The regime's position is that, while progress in this direction must be sufficient to justify self-restraint and cooperation with the government on the part of the MDB, changes should not be allowed to build up their own momentum; the impulse for change must remain channeled.

Roberto Campos, perhaps Brazil's leading technocrat/diplomat, believes that since 1964 four vital ingredients have been added to Brazil's development picture: (1) political stability, through an alliance of the reformist-oriented military and the civilian technocrats, (2) an open and "associative market economy," (3) "rational pragmatism" in public and private administration, and (4) a system of mechanisms for mobilizing and channeling internal savings.[10] Escapism, paternalism, and "temperamental" nationalism—the "deforming" attitudes of the populist regime of the early 1960s—have given way to institutional modernization. Although he admits that the government still encounters difficulties in the realm of "popular reconciliation" and political institutionalization, Campos perceives the regime as gradually establishing a political system of "participatory democracy with a strong executive."[11]

Other observers view the Brazilian system in less sympathetic, albeit basically similar, terms. In the eyes of one United States scholar, the system is characterized by

> repressive military leadership combined with technocratic decision making in the political sphere; state entrepreneurship and discipline combined with liberal capitalist incentives in the economic sphere; and emphasis on nationalist symbolism combined with openness to international corporations in the sphere of external relations.[12]

Yet, this student observes, while the military does set basic priorities and possesses a definitive veto power, it does not actually make policy in most fields.

> Most of those who make the day-to-day decisions are civilians. Even longer-range policy is probably formulated in large part by civilians. These decision makers must operate within the limits of a military conception of "national order," just as the military must take care to maintain a "favorable investment climate."[13]

Whether one considers the present regime as an example of "pragmatic Bonapartism" or as "institutionalized pragmatism" largely depends on whether one emphasizes its long-run potential vulnerabilities or its demonstrated short-run strengths.[14] At this time the regime seems to consist of a developmentally oriented alliance of the military with the civilian bureaucracy and the entrepreneurial stratum of the private sector. While critics decry the absence of political representativeness, they reluctantly credit the regime with a high degree of rationality and administrative efficiency.

The successful pursuit of Brazilian foreign-policy goals is in large part dependent upon specific political capabilities and developments, as well as performance in the economic realm. Perhaps the first political requisite for attainment of continental paramountcy and wide recognition as an emerging major power is continued political stability—preferably a stability that primarily depends not on force and on a well-developed repressive capability, but rather on widespread public acceptance of the regime. The current Brazilian political system is characterized by a degree of fragility, and may have serious long-run weaknesses: limitations on participation, lack of a strong political party system, absence of a true ideology, vulnerability to unfavorable international economic trends, and a succession mechanism that does not appear to provide a reliable means for the political opposition to achieve power without resorting to violence. Yet similar conditions prevailed during the periods of the greatest relative political stability in Brazilian history. The Second Empire lasted for nearly fifty years (1840-1889), the Old Republic for more than four decades (1889-1930), and the Vargas regime for more than fifteen years (1930-1945, with a return to power in 1951-1954), despite the absence of anything approximating what contemporary political scientists would consider adequate institutionalization.[15]

At present it appears that the prevailing trend within the Brazilian military (hence one that is likely to be reflected in national policy) leads toward a more populist and pragmatically nationalist stance. Even so firm a critic of the existing regime as Brady Tyson has argued that "the military paternalism as practiced by the 'new professionals' can easily become 'populist.'"[16] In early 1971 Steiner and Trubek noted that "nationalist themes have come to figure importantly in the articulation of the regime's basic programs."[17] This nationalism, which has roots in the military leading back to the Tenentes of the 1920s and the army's role in the establishment of a state petroleum monopoly in the early 1950s, blends well with the developmental orientation of major sectors of public opinion. Nurtured in an earlier generation by Getúlio Vargas, the idea of national development caught on with the Brazilian people during the Kubitschek years (1956-1960). The university youth of the 1950s are now moving up in the professions, management, and government service. In the years to come this cohort will be backed up strongly by members of a new generation whose political socialization has taken place largely under the "revolution." Thus, increased support for the sustained developmental priorities of the military-technocratic alliance is possible, particularly if Geisel and his successors follow through on Médici's tendency to use nationalist sentiment to complement the drive for development. If internal development goals continue to be met and Brazil's position vis-à-vis its continental neighbors becomes increasingly favorable, the next administration (1979-?) should prove able to capitalize on this trend without having to adopt a harshly aggressive tone in international affairs.

The increasing complexity and specialization of structures and roles in the foreign policy–making sphere reflects the significant expansion of Brazil's international involvements during the past two decades, and is closely related to the progressive differentiation of Brazilian governmental policymaking institutions—a development characteristic of all postwar administrations, but one which accelerated as a result of the developmental drive of the Kubitschek period (1956-1960). What has happened is that agencies dealing with security, development planning, finances, economics, and technology have come to the fore—first impinging on, then having an impact on, then influencing, and finally largely determining foreign policy. This tendency, although accelerated under the military governments since 1964, is largely attributable to more fundamental aspects of the Brazilian development process, in particular to the greatly expanded role of the government in the nation's economic life as industrialization and foreign trade have been actively fostered.

Whereas only a generation ago foreign-policy decisions were the preserve of the Foreign Ministry and the president, these decisions are now influenced by a variety of interministerial councils, a half-dozen military-security organs, and at least a score of economic and financial agencies. Concomitantly, the relatively simple organization of the presidential office even during the last Vargas government (1951-1954) and during the ensuing caretaker regime (1954-1956) has been replaced by a complex institutionalized executive and a greatly expanded presidential staff. Landmarks in this transition included the creation of the National Security Council in the early postwar period, the emergence of specialized development agencies as part of Kubitschek's "Program of Goals," the creation of the Planning Ministry by Castelo Branco, the massive role expansion of the Finance Ministry under Antônio Delfim Netto during the Costa e Silva and Médici governments, and the establishment of the Economic Development Council as the single most important decision-making forum by President Geisel.

Economic Factors

As of this writing, economic development remains the government's primary objective, with the result that Brazil's foreign policy is highly conditioned by economic considerations. This is a country which is becoming increasingly urban (already 60 percent) and industrial, in which annual growth rates of 10 percent have almost come to be viewed as the norm, if they are not yet taken for granted. Its gross national product (more than $90 billion in United States dollars, at the end of 1975) has doubled in real terms since rapid economic growth was resumed in 1968; yet its economic growth still falls far short of satisfying the desires of most major sectors of Brazilian society, though their disappointments have not yet been translated into effective demands.

Most members of the present economic policymaking elite basically concur with Roberto Campos' views (see page 11) of the flaws of the pre-1964 regime and of the corrections and refinements that have been made since 1964. Finance Minister Mário Henrique Simonsen has emphasized that the key to the "Brazilian miracle" was the recognition that "in the economic sphere it is impossible to perform miracles"; instead, Brazil had the sense to "use international experience as a focus of inspiration, but not as a basis for imitation."[18] This evaluation was echoed by at least one U.S. observer of Brazilian economic affairs:

> The uniqueness of the Brazilian experience since 1964 lies in the free manipulation by technicians, backed by a strong government, of an economic system which is dominated by the state, but which allows for a sizeable private sector. This manipulation was possible because of the existence of strong and stable governments which ensured that economic policies were fully carried out, regardless of the side effects that they would have on various groups.[19]

Brazil is engaged in a game of forced-draft "catch up" industrialization in which the state plays a leading role, and which bids fair to transform the country, in one generation, nearly as completely as Germany was transformed during the Bismarckian era. Certainly this transformation has been a triumph more for the military-technocrat alliance than for free enterprise, more for the state than for the private sector.

Brazil's pattern of state-entrepreneurial relations might well be called jet-age Bismarckian, in that the government is determined that the private sector pull its own weight in the drive to become an industrial power. The nature of the partnership—which might be substantially different in a politically competitive situation—is fundamentally asymmetrical: the government can exercise leverage on commerce and industry significantly greater than that which these groups can bring to bear on the essentially military regime. The public-sector *técnicos* provide a mediating link; while to a certain extent they may function as brokers, in the final analysis they are most responsive to their military allies, on whom their tenure in office ultimately depends.[20]

To better appreciate the nature of the state-private enterprise relationship, one needs only consider that it is the government that takes measures to strengthen the Brazilian private sector relative to foreign capital. Finance Minister Simonsen, perhaps the most powerful friend the private sector has within the present government, has said he believes that Brazilian private enterprise is relatively weak in comparison with both state and foreign firms, especially in sectors that require massive capital investments. To bolster the private sector's relatively fragile competitive position, Simonsen has advocated moves that would encourage mergers and associations by means of overhauling constraining legislation, stimulating the capital market, and attracting institutional investors.[21] Walther Moreira Salles, a former finance minister (pre-1964) who now heads the powerful União dos Bancos Brasileiros, said in a 1974 interview that he was preoccupied by the fact that Brazil is in large part "statized" and is no longer a market economy. He observed that this situation called for courage and determination rather than despair on the part of the private sector, but explicitly rejected a defiant or recalcitrant attitude since, in his view, "private enterprise and the state must of necessity be united."[22] Similarly, a U.S. critic of the Brazilian economic system admitted:

> Despite the degree to which the state has become, under the military government, an even more formidable economic instrument than it was previously, little or no anxiety has been engendered in the private sector, either foreign or local. Building on the foundation laid by previous nationalists, the military regime has been able to maintain a strong state presence in the economy without appearing to be statist in its orientation. . . . The ideological position of the regime and the concrete coalitions of ownership that have been set up have helped generate support in the business community. . . . The state provides entrepreneurship in the public sector and discipline among those who participate in the private sector. But it does not encroach on areas of profitable private investment and does not threaten the principle of private investment on a cultural or ideological level.[23]

With respect to the political and governmental ramifications of this situation, he concluded:

> The successful symbiosis of the state and foreign firms leaves plenty of room for the national bourgeoisie. They are the essential intermediaries, the lubricant that keeps the gears of the new

coalition meshing smoothly, the cadres that staff both subsidiaries and state bureaucracies. The fact that these roles are not the classic entrepreneurial ones associated with the industrial revolution in England does not make them any less profitable or comfortable for the men who fill them.[24]

The most thorough study of the "present dominance of the state over the Brazilian economy" showed that the public expenditure/gross domestic product ratio, which had reached a relatively high 32.2 percent by 1969, appeared to be continuing its upward trend, while more than 60 percent of loans made by the entire financial system to the private sector was coming from government financial institutions. Moreover, as of 1972, more than half the total employment provided by the twenty-five largest firms came from the seven public enterprises included in this category. An even more striking result was that of the top twenty-five firms in terms of assets, seventeen were governmental, accounting for 82 percent of these firms' total assets. For the hundred largest firms the proportion of assets held by public enterprise was 68 percent.[25] The authors of the study concluded:

> In the process of growing and diversifying its activities, the Brazilian state has vastly increased its present and potential control of the economy. As we have seen, this growth was not planned and imposed for ideological reasons about the proper role of the state in economic activities. It was the result of certain objective conditions; i.e., the desire of the government for rapidly industrializing a still backward economy. With weak private industrial and financial sectors, the choice at various times . . . was between two agents of growth: foreign capital and the state.[26]

Perhaps this tendency has not yet run its course, the authors suggested:

> A continued growth of the state in Brazil's economic activities in the last three decades of the twentieth century is almost inevitable. Brazil's private sector is still relatively small and in no position to play an important role in the country's huge infrastructure

needs or in the most technologically sophisticated industries, which are also the most dynamic—petrochemicals, steel, transportation, equipment, etc. The growth of the state should not be looked upon as a threat to Brazilian private enterprises. It is not a question of taking something away from the private sector but rather a matter of relative rates of growth.[27]

The expansion of the state's direct economic activities gained further headway during the first two-and-a-half years of the Geisel administration. The government petroleum company substantially increased its scale and range of operations, while the state-owned Vale do Rio Doce Co., the world's largest exporter of iron ore, diversified its activities through an array of new subsidiaries. In addition to seeing the creation of Nuclebrás in the atomic energy field and an increase in the scale of government banking and financial activities, the mid-1970s witnessed the establishment of a government holding company to administer Brazil's ports (Portobrás) and the institution of active state trading companies (Cobec and Interbrás). Since early 1975, an energetic press campaign by private entrepreneurs aimed at stemming the "statization" of the Brazilian economy has generated renewed assurances of the regime's high regard for the private sector (along with a cataloging of its shortcomings) and reiteration of the state's commitment to capitalism, but the campaign has had little observable effect upon the government's actions.[28] In fact, since the campaign was launched the state has pushed forward into the fertilizer field on a large scale and has become a major partner in an increasing number of joint ventures with foreign governments and private concerns.

Although there is considerable political sensitivity to the role and influence of the large multilateral enterprises—indeed, the expanded role of the state is often justified as the only way to check and contain these foreign corporations—the Brazilian government is committed to a policy of giving fair treatment to foreign capital while defending and strengthening national enterprise. Considering that an estimated 93 percent of Brazil's capital stock (which then totaled well over

$100 billion) was domestic in orgin as of the early 1970s, the large absolute amount of foreign investment does not seem so impressive in proportional terms. On the Brazilian scene, state enterprises dominate in petroleum and petrochemicals (where Petrobrás holds more than 80 percent of total assets), energy (government firms accounted for 80 percent of electric power generating capacity in 1971), steel (70 percent of total assets), mining, and such areas of transportation as railroads and shipping. With commerce and agriculture as well as the financial market firmly in domestic hands, the foreign presence is most significant in transformation industries and construction. Moreover, the sources of foreign investment are quite diversified: the United States is in first place with about 30 percent, followed by West Germany and Japan, each with more than 10 percent. Having increasingly diversified her foreign trade (with Western Europe accounting for roughly 33 percent and the United States for less than 20 percent), Brazil is in a much less dependent position than are most other developing countries.[29]

The central economic question during 1974 was whether the new administration could continue the economic "miracle" in the face of such adverse international factors as the energy crisis and protectionist tendencies. But the impressive dynamism of the Brazilian economic system, so apparent in the high growth rates since 1968, carried through the year and into 1975. Expansion of real gross domestic product reached a record 11.4 percent in 1973, bringing the average for the past six years to more than 10 percent—a figure that was nearly matched in 1974 as industry ran slightly above and agriculture a little below this mark. The rise in the cost of living, which had been brought down to 15 percent in 1972, began to climb during the final quarter of 1973, chiefly because of soaring oil prices and the corrective inflation that followed the outgoing government's efforts to artificially hold down certain prices in order to meet its antiinflation goals. This trend continued into the new year. By midyear the monthly inflation rates had returned to the 1972-1973 norms, and the average rate of price increases for the entire year came to about 34 percent. In 1975 the rate of inflation dropped to just under 30 percent.

Brazilian exports, which had expanded by more than 55 percent in 1973, continued to grow at a more modest rate during 1974 in the face of negative international circumstances. The export total of just under $8 billion (in U.S. dollars)—up 28 percent, but a full billion dollars less than the original target figure—included $1.26 billion from rapidly growing sugar exports as well as slightly more than $1.02 billion from coffee and nearly $900 million from soybeans and meal (the last two were down from 1973). Exports of industrial goods, chiefly manufactured items, rose to about $3 billion, and iron ore exports brought in another $571 million. Imports, swollen by zooming oil prices, doubled to more than $12.6 billion (FOB) in 1974, leaving a substantial trade gap of $4.7 billion, a current account deficit of $7.1 billion, and a somewhat more manageable balance of payments deficit of just under $1 billion (foreign investment was close to $900 million); import financing, money loans, and credits rose sharply to almost $7 billion in spite of the international economic situation. Since Brazil's foreign-exchange reserves had reached $6.5 billion at the end of 1973—the sixth-highest total in the world—the country was able to cope reasonably well with this deficit situation, in which total foreign debt rose to $17.2 billion against reserves of $5.3 billion for a liquid debt of $11.9 billion.

A few years ago such adverse developments in the international economy as occurred in 1974 would have had a disastrous effect on Brazil's development, but the country's vulnerabilities have been greatly reduced during the past decade. Coffee, which had accounted for more than half of export earnings as late as 1964, had dropped to less than one-fifth by 1973 and just exceeded one-eighth during 1974—although in absolute terms coffee earnings had risen during this period. Yet formidable problems remained. Peter Evans points out the weaknesses inherent in Brazil's development model in relationship to its external environment.

To begin with, it must keep turning over its massive external debt. Any weakening of its good credit rating would be disastrous. Brazil must continue to attract new investment and persuade subsidiaries to reinvest sizable proportions of their profits locally. Sharply rising demands for imports must be counterbalanced by rising exports.[30]

The export target for 1975 was $10 billion (in U.S. dollars), with manufactured goods slated to lead the way at $4 billion (up by one-third), followed by sugar, coffee, soybeans, and iron ore. For the first eight months of 1975 this ambitious goal appeared within reach; the value of exports rose a full 30 percent, while imports were held near the 1974 level. Beginning in September, however, the world economic situation caught up with Brazil, and export earnings fell significantly below the 1974 pace. In early October the government instituted further incentives for exports and placed sharp restrictions upon government imports.[31] For the year, export earnings totaled a disappointing $8.7 billion, while imports were contained at $12.2 billion. This trade deficit of $3.5 billion was nearly matched by a net outflow of $3.4 billion for services (chiefly transportation and remittance of profits), resulting in a deficit on current account of $6.9 billion, almost matching the total of the preceding year. The inflow of new capital approximated that of 1974, as the combination of new financing, loans and suppliers' credits of $6.7 billion, and $830 million in direct investments far exceeded the $2.1 billion paid out for amortization of Brazil's mounting foreign debt. The balance-of-payments deficit of $1.2 billion—only marginally higher than the figure for 1974—left Brazil's foreign reserves just above the $4 billion mark. Although additional incentives were adopted in December along with further import restrictions, continued expansion of Brazilian exports will require all the enterprise Brazil can muster.[32]

Brazil, for example, seeks to go from 11 percent of the world's iron ore market in 1970 to 21 percent by 1980 and 25 percent by 1985. Long-term agreements negotiated during

President Ernesto Geisel's visit to Japan in September 1976 provided for increasing Brazil's iron ore exports from the present level of 17.4 million tons to 37 million tons a year. Also included in the package was the sale of $2.6 billion worth of pelletized ore during the next sixteen years and a massive Japanese investment in a joint venture to produce aluminum in northern Brazil. (Including sales, credits, and direct investments these bilateral accords amounted to an estimated $13 billion inflow to Brazil.) At the same time, Brazil is attempting to reduce imports of steel, and seeks self-sufficiency in steel by the early 1980s. This is a big order, since 1975 consumption was roughly 11.7 million tons with production under 9 million tons; by 1982 Brazil's appetite for steel is expected to demand between 20 and 25 million tons a year. (Steel imports in 1974 were around 4 million tons at a cost of $1.5 billion; the cost dropped to below $1.3 billion in 1975, with only $700 million expected to be spent for this purpose during 1976.) Japanese interests are putting hundreds of millions of dollars into a new steel complex near the ore port of Tubarão; production is estimated to have reached 4 million tons a year by 1980, with further amplification to as much as 12 million tons.[33] Another major new steel plant is being built in Minas Gerais with British financing, and all existing companies are expanding their capacities.

Brazilian planners count on industrial expansion to generate new exports; the automotive field is a prime example. In 1974 the automobile industry—in existence for a little more than fifteen years—produced 861,000 units, of which 517,000 were passenger cars. Between 1969 and 1974 production expanded at an annual rate of nearly 20 percent, but growth of this industry lagged during 1975. In 1976 Brazilian factories were expected to turn out just under a million cars, trucks and buses. The auto industry generated exports valued at some $350 million in 1975, and substantial growth in this industry is likely to occur in future years.[34]

At present a major economic constraint on Brazilian foreign policy is the fact that Brazil must import nearly 80 percent of the crude petroleum it uses; Saudi Arabia is far and away the major source, followed by Iraq, Algeria, Kuwait, and Iran. Venezuela furnishes roughly 2 percent of the oil Brazil imports; Peru and Ecuador provide substantially less. If Brazil has found it prudent to favor the Arab countries in the Middle East crisis, it has also chosen to step up its domestic search for oil and to seek new sources of imports from Africa as well as from the socialist bloc. The continued rise of Brazil's oil-consumption curve—expected to rise to nearly a billion barrels a day by 1977—aggravates the problem, as do the relatively limited possibilities for substitution of other energy sources.

The energy crisis influences Brazil's foreign policy in other ways as well. The Ilha Solteira hydroelectric complex, which will be fully on line by 1980 with a generating capacity of 3.2 million kilowatts, has had some effect on Brazil's relations with Argentina (the issue being the latter country's downstream rights on the same river system). Both the Ilha Solteira project and its diplomatic side effects have been dwarfed by Itaipu, now being constructed on the Brazil-Paraguay border, which will produce up to 12.6 million kilowatts when completed at an expected cost of between $6 billion and $10 billion.

Yet even these massive projects designed to exploit Brazil's vast hydroelectric potential—estimated at more than 150 million kilowatts—will be insufficient to meet Brazil's energy needs; hence, the country has begun a major program for building nuclear generating stations. This move is affecting Brazil's relations with a variety of countries, because the purchase from Germany of a complete nuclear cycle—including uranium enrichment and putonium reclamation plants—raises for some the specter of Brazil's developing a military nuclear capability.[35]

Notes to Chapter 1

[1]The following terms are used in this study essentially as defined by Howard Lentner in *Foreign Policy Analysis: A Comparative and Conceptual Approach* (Columbus, Ohio: Charles E. Merrill Co., 1974):

Engagement characterizes a country's tendency to move from relative international insularity to increasing involvement in less-than-global patterns of interaction in which control over such situations is shared with other nations. *Expansion* encompasses efforts to extend control over international stiuations. The former has marked Brazilian foreign policy since at least the later 1950s; the latter is essentially a feature of the 1970s. Theory in this field is assessed in Stephen J. Andriole, Jonathan Wilkenfield, and Gerald W. Hopple, "A Framework for the Comparative Analysis of Foreign Policy Behavior," *International Studies Quarterly* 19, no. 2 (June 1975): 176.

[2]Carlos de Meira Mattos, in a lecture to some 1,600 Rio de Janeiro secondary-school civics teachers, "O Mundo e O Brasil—Uma visão dos conflictos e das opções—Uma geopolítica de destino," March 26, 1975. An early statement of this basic thesis is in Norman A. Bailey and Ronald M. Schneider, "Brazil's Foreign Policy: A Case Study in Upward Mobility," *Inter-American Economic Affairs* 27, no. 4 (Spring 1974): 3-25. Outside of Europe and North America, only Japan and mainland China exceed Brazil in GNP. See Stefan H. Robock, *Brazil: A Study in Development Progress* (Lexington, Mass.: D. C. Heath and Co., 1975), p. 87.

[3]There is a vast literature on the collapse of the left-populist regime. The most recent relevant works include Hernani D'Aguiar, *A Revolução por Dentro* (Rio de Janeiro: Editôra Artenova, 1976); Hélio Silva, *1964: Golpe ou Contragolpe?* (Rio de Janeiro: Editôra Civilização Brasileira, 1975); and Carlos Castello Branco, *Introdução a Revolução de 1964: Agonia do Poder Civil* (Rio de Janeiro: Editôra Artenova, 1975), and its companion volume, *A Queda de João Goulart.* For an example of the traditional view of equating Mexico and Argentina with Brazil as international actors, see Carlos A. Astiz (ed.), *Latin American International Politics: Ambitions, Capabilities, and the National Interest of Mexico, Brazil and Argentina* (South Bend, Ind.: Notre Dame University Press, 1969).

[4]A scant literature exists in this field. The Foreign Policy Research Institute's *Brazil's Future Role in International Politics* (Philadelphia: FPRI, 1973) contains a preliminary effort along these lines, to which this author contributed chaps. 2, 3, and 5, with Jordan Young's active collaboration, particularly on chap. 3.

[5]These elites included primarily businessmen and bankers, landowners, the bureaucratic middle class, and lawyers closely linked to these elements. Legal representatives of the labor unions, lower-middle-class

workers and peasants won both elective and appointive offices during Goulart's presidency.

6The most comprehensive treatment of these developments is in Schneider, *The Political System of Brazil: Emergence of a "Modernizing" Authoritarian Regime, 1964-1970* (New York: Columbia University Press, 1971).

7"A Doctrina da Segurança Nacional" has been the leitmotif of the post-1964 regime. For full acceptance by the military, a bureaucrat or politician must be viewed by them as having a "sense of national security," which is usually certified by studying at the Higher War College or in the extension courses administered by its faculty and graduates in Brazil's major cities. Some thousands of government officials and private-sector leaders have already qualified in this manner, and the new generation is being inculcated with the doctrine through courses incorporated into the secondary-school and university curricula.

8Each period since 1964 has had its key term or catch word, which, once it took on a negative connotation as a result of disappointed hopes or failure, was thereafter carefully avoided by subsequent administrations. *Normalidade, humanização*, and—to a lesser extent—*renovação* have given way to *distensão*, or "decompression," the form of defensive modernization advocated by the liberal faction within the present government. As of August 1975, *desenvolvimento político* (political development) appeared to be replacing *distensão* as the presidentially approved term, with the former viewed as a prerequisite for the latter (which is thus stripped of its immediacy).

9This is discussed at some length in Schneider, *Political System of Brazil*, pp. 302-304. The most comprehensive collection of constitutional provisions presently in force is Senado Federal, *Legislação Constitutional e Complementar: Com Legislação Citada e Sinopse* (Brasília, 1972). This has been updated by 1973 and 1974 supplements covering Complementary Acts 97 through 99 and Complementary Laws 13 through 20. For perspective, see Osny Duarte Pereira, *A Constituição Federal e Suas Modificações Incorporadas ao Texto* (Rio de Janeiro: Editôra Civilizaçao Brasileira, 1966) and *A Constituição do Brasil 1967* (Rio de Janeiro: Editôra Civilizaçao Brasileira, 1967).

10Mário Henrique Simonsen and Roberto de Oliveira Campos, "Atitudes Políticos-Sociais e Sua Influência no Modelo Brasileiro," in *A nova economia Brasileira* (Rio de Janeiro: José Olympio Editôra, 1974), pp. 39-46.

[11]Roberto Campos, "A Opção Politica Brasileira," ibid., pp. 223-57.

[12]Peter B. Evans, "The Military, the Multinationals, and the 'Miracle': The Political Economy of the 'Brazilian Model' of Development," *Studies in Comparative International Development* 9, no. 3 (Fall 1974), pp. 41-42.

[13]Ibid., pp. 33-34.

[14]The first of these phrases is that chosen by Alberto Guerreiro Ramos to stress the absence of direct popular links, and is expanded on in a paper he presented at Columbia University on January 25, 1973; the second is used by Georges A. Fiechter in *Brazil Since 1964: Modernization under a Military Régime* (London: Macmillan & Co., 1975; New York: Halsted Press, 1976).

[15]The political dynamics of these systems and the processes of their decay are analyzed in Schneider, *Modernization and the Military in Brazil: Political Instability, Institutional Crises and Army Intervention, 1822-1964* (forthcoming).

[16]*The Emerging Role of the Military as National Modernizers and Managers in Latin America: The Cases of Brazil and Peru* (Ottawa: Carleton University Occasional Papers no. 19, 1972), p. 55.

[17]Henry J. Steiner and David M. Trubek, "Brazil—All Power to the Generals," *Foreign Affairs*, April 1971, p. 474.

[18]Simonsen, in his preface to Murilo Melo Filho's *O Modelo Brasileiro* (Rio de Janeiro: Bloch Editores, 1974).

[19]Werner Baer, "The Brazilian Boom 1968-72: An Explanation and Interpretation," *World Development*, no. 8 (August 1973), p. 11.

[20]The most recent book-length effort to deal with the present Brazilian system published in English is Alfred Stepan (ed.), *Authoritarian Brazil: Origins, Policies, and Future* (New Haven: Yale University Press, 1973). Its perspective is that of early to mid-1972, as is also the case with Hélio Jaguaribe's *Political Development: A General Theory and a Latin American Case* (New York: Harper and Row, 1973). His more recent *Brasil: Crise e Alternativas* (Rio de Janeiro: Zahar, 1974) and Celso Lafer's *O Sistema Político Brasileiro* (São Paulo: Perspectiva, 1975) provide useful elements for conceptualizing Brazilian development processes. Creative Marxist approaches include Florestan Fernandes' *A Revolução Burguesa no Brasil* (Rio de Janeiro: Zahar, 1975) and Fernando Henrique Cardoso, *Autoritarismo e Democratização* (Rio de Janeiro: Paz e Terra, 1975). Illustrative of current systematic efforts to

come to grips with the essential nature of the Brazilian system are two papers presented at the sixth national meeting of the Latin American Studies Assn. in Atlanta, March 25-28, 1976: Alexandre de S.C. Barros, "The Changing Role of the State in Brazil: The Technocratic-Military Alliance," and Max G. Manwaring, "Career Patterns and Attitudes in Four Brazilian Military Administrations: Similarity and Continuity, 1964-1975."

[21]See Simonsen's speech upon assuming office, reprinted in *Tendência*, April 1974.

[22]"A Missão Social do Empresario," *Tendência*, August 1974.

[23]Evans, "The 'Miracle,'" pp. 26-30.

[24]Ibid., p. 32.

[25]Baer, Isaac Kerstenetzky, and Anibal V. Villela, "The Changing Role of the State in the Brazilian Economy," *World Development*, no. 11 (November 1973), pp. 23-24.

[26]Ibid., pp. 31-32.

[27]Ibid., p. 34.

[28]The Brazilian government is currently responsible for half of Brazil's foreign trade and plays a major role in capital formation. The minister of industry and commerce, himself a businessman of some substance, has defended the state's expanding role in the economy as necessary to balance the power of the transnational companies, while the minister-chief of the Planning Secretariat has recently explained that the government's policies are keeping the private sector on its feet through massive credits, tax incentives, and even the underwriting of the capital market. See the interviews with João Paulo dos Reis Velloso in *Manchete*, May 1, 1976, pp. 136-137; and *Visão*, April 19, 1976, pp. 41-44.

[29]Only 43 percent of Brazil's exports of nearly $8.7 billion (FOB) during 1975 went to its five leading trading partners. The United States led the way with $1.2 billion or 13.8 percent followed by the German Federal Republic with $700 million or 8.1 percent and Japan with $670 million or 7.7 percent. Brazil's next-best customers were the Netherlands with $562 million or 6.5 percent and the USSR with $397 million or 4.6 percent. Addition of Argentina and the United Kingdom—4.5 percent and 4.0 percent—brings this total to some 51 percent of Brazil's exports, spread among seven countries. Thus, roughly half of Brazil's export trade was with countries whose individual weights as markets for Brazilian goods were quite limited. See *Folha de S. Paulo*, March 18, 1976, for these figures.

30"The 'Miracle,'" p. 42.

31*Jornal do Brasil*, January 22, 1976, p. 23. Brazil's exports and imports were in near-perfect balance for the period 1968-1973, yet increasingly large current account deficits were generated by the roughly 25 percent average annual rise in the negative balance in the services account. Until 1973 these rising expenditures for freight, interest, and profit remittances were more than offset by a positive capital flow which grew from $541 million in 1968 to about $3.5 billion in both 1972 and 1973. Then came the doubling of import expenditures in 1974, with the resulting huge trade deficit. As debt service in 1976 will run well above the $1.8 billion interest and $2 billion amortization of 1975, the balance-of-payments crunch has been officially recognized as Brazil's top-priority economic problem. See also the figures in *Visao*, August 31, 1976, pp. 14 and 80 as well as coverage of the Economic Development Council's decisions in *Jornal do Brasil*, January 15, 1976, p. 24.

32Reflecting the complexity of the governmental machinery in this field, these measures included three decree laws, two presidential decrees, an Economic Development Council decision, two resolutions of the National Foreign Trade Council, two Finance Ministry rulings, six resolutions of the Tariff Policy Council, and six communiqués, four resolutions, and one circular issued by the Central Bank.

33On matters related to steel see *Visão*, September 29, 1975, pp. 43-47; *Manchete*, May 8, 1976, pp. 108-109; *Tendência*, June 1976, pp. 36-40; *Jornal do Brasil*, April 15, 1976; *O Estado de S. Paulo*, April 15, May 7, and July 17, 1976. The Brazil-Japan agreements are discussed in *Visão*, October 11, 1975, pp. 100-105; *Manchete*, October 2, 1976, pp. 4-22; *Veja*, September 29, 1976, pp. 118-119 and September 22, 1976, pp. 14-23; and *Jornal do Brasil*, *O Estado de S. Paulo*, *O Globo*, and *Folha de S. Paulo*, September 11 through 23, 1976.

34See "Automóvel Brasileiro, Ano 20," *Manchete*, June 26, 1976, pp. 75-134, for a comprehensive treatment of this key industry. *O Estado de S. Paulo*, October 20, 1976, places production through September at 736,722 vehicles.

35Consult Norman Gall, "Atoms for Brazil. Dangers for All," *Foreign Policy*, no. 23 (Summer 1976), pp. 155-201. The relevant statements by Brazilian and German officials and the texts of the agreements can be found in *Resenha de política exterior do brasil* 2, no. 5 (April, May, and June 1975), pp. 5-35 and 156-168.

2
The External Environment
of
Brazilian Foreign Policy

In addition to the nature of its political regime and the limitations of its economic system, the conditioning context of Brazil's international relations involves the degree of congruence between the policy elites' conceptions of their country's place in the international order and the manner in which the realities of that global system operate upon an upwardly mobile middle power. The former can be abstracted from the writings and pronouncements of accredited foreign-affairs spokesmen, of which a fairly representative sampling is synthesized in the following section. The impact of external factors can be assessed by comparing the situation presently prevailing in several policy areas with the much greater foreign constraints upon Brazil's freedom of action which prevailed during the 1950s and 1960s. Maritime policy, arms acquisitions, and nuclear energy are the cases selected for specific consideration, but an argument will also be presented that deeper involvement in the international economy does not necessarily mean increased vulnerability, at least when international economic relationships are becoming progressively more diversified.

Brazilian Views of Self and World

Perceptions of national and international reality held by Brazil's policymakers generally correspond to the constraints imposed by objective conditions. Exaggeration of national capabilities is significantly less prevalent in Brazil than in most other upwardly aspiring countries. While Brazilian government and political figures in recent years have tended to use the terms "world power" and "great power" to indicate the goal toward which the nation's energies and resources should be directed, most military and civilian leaders believe that progress toward this objective must evolve from internal development. They see Brazil during the next few years as building the groundwork for movement toward major-power status during the 1980s and 1990s, but they understand that a host of internal problems must be revolved first.[1] Confident that Brazil will have consolidated its dominant position in South America by the end of the present decade, these leaders tend to view the 1980s as the period of Brazil's candidate membership in the family of major powers. One traditional senior career diplomat observed: "Everything indicates that, if we continue the current rhythm of progress, Brazil will be called to assume, in a not-too-distant future, a position among the principal world powers."[2] A younger diplomat emphasized that "only development confers on the state the specific weight it needs to influence the exogenous decisions that can affect its interests and reduce to the minimum the concessions it ought to make in its policies to preserve its fundamental interests."[3] For the moment, he says, "we are an emerging power that can no longer be ignored by the kingmakers of the world political scene."[4]

This view of Brazil as a candidate for world-power status is expressed even more strongly by military spokesmen. The former vice-chief of the Armed Forces General Staff recently declared that "an evaluation of the essential attributes of power as described by many specialists in political science and geopolitics reveals to us Brazilians that we possess all the conditions that enable us to aspire to a place among the world's great powers."[5] With continued internal cohesion, he believes, Brazil can lift itself to the level of the developed nations of the West if it "accelerates production of goods and services and understands and absorbs modern technology in order to quicken the rhythm of social progress, correct income inequalities, absorb the annual increments to the labor force, and achieve tranquility and social peace."[6]

Brazil's foreign-policy objectives are closely linked to developmental goals and considerations of national security. The geopolitical thinking characteristic of the dominant military elements reinforces a widely held belief that the respect that Brazil can command on the world scene (which Brazilians themselves refer to as "projection") depends in large part on its perception by the major powers as the dominant nation in South America. However, cognizant of the failure of Argentina to achieve such projection and still a little embarrassed by the "premature" Brazilian effort to do so under the Quadros and Goulart regimes, the architects of Brazilian policy are determined to keep the developmental horse ahead of the diplomatic cart. Thus, the fundamental objective, frequently iterated by both military and civilian spokesmen, is "to transform Brazil into a developed nation in a single generation." As a first step they agree that during the 1970s per-capita GNP should be doubled, regional imbalances reduced, and the vast Amazon area effectively integrated with the rest of the country. International economic policy should accelerate development without interfering with the control of inflation. To make the development process self-sustaining, Brazil has embarked upon an aggressive quest for foreign markets for its manufactured goods, minerals, and nontraditional agricultural exports. This market search is being combined with a continuing diplomatic campaign against protectionist tendencies in the developed countries.

The Foreign Ministry's most active international negotiator, Paulo Cabral de Mello (he is chairman of the sub-cabinet-level interministerial committee that works out Brazil's position at international trade and financial meetings), believes that as a result of the energy crisis the rich countries, preoccupied with guaranteeing at all costs the maintenance of their high standards of living, tend to forget the fundamental interdependence of the present-day world and to comprehend less well than before the problems of the developing countries and their need for improved access to both markets for their exports and the effective financial and technological cooperation that can only come from the industrialized world.[7]

By way of explaining Brazil's evolving pattern of cooperation with the third world on many international economic issues, Cabral de Mello points out that

The natural result of this situation is the strengthening of solidarity among the developing countries in defense of their common interests, an acute consciousness by these countries of the need to preserve the sovereign use and effective control of their natural resources and the possible political realignments that tend to increase the risks of confrontation between the two halves of the so-called Western world.

Expressing concern about the persistence of Brazil's dependence in the areas of trade, finance, and technology, he articulates the view that

the interdependence of nations in the present-day world is an irreversible process, but there exist two possible forms of interdependence: that which today governs the relations between central and peripheral economies, based on institutionalization of inequities and serving as an instrument of dependency; and that which supposes equity and marks the road to independence. The objectives of effective international cooperation would thus be to facilitate the transition from the first to the second form of interdependency, and this is the only mode of international cooperation that Brazil judges useful in the agitated world of our day.[8]

The view of Brazil's international relations which is promulgated in secondary-school courses is a simplified version of this basic outlook; for example:

Brazil during recent years has created a new image abroad, having progressed and developed, amplifying considerably its diplomatic and commercial frontiers. . . . In the new policy, promotion of exports has absolute priority. . . . The country is reformulating its foreign relations to take advantage of its powers at just the moment when the world is readjusting the terms of political and economic relations. . . . Little by little Brazil stands out from the Latin American complex and increasingly moves away from the Group of 77 (the poor nations), making its own interests prevail as a Nation in search of its rapid realization.[9]

This statement reflects those basic themes of the Brazilian elites' world view which were refined in the pronouncements of the late João Augusto de Araújo Castro (ambassador to the United States at the time of his death in November 1975, a former foreign minister, and head of Brazil's United Nations delegation during the late 1960s), who decried the "new Cult of Power" that took for granted that "force and the use of force are the natural basis for the establishment of a future legal or political situation." Araújo Castro believed that there was no historical evidence to support the "curious" philosophy that power brings moderation and responsibility; to him, any conception of a world order based on "five centers of power" was obsolete and outmoded. He lamented the failure of the international community to implement the 1970 General Assembly resolution—introduced by Brazil—proclaiming the co-relationship of development, security, and disarmament. In his view

> the major industrial nations continue to shirk decisive collective action in favor of the underdeveloped world, thus ignoring and disregarding the principle of collective economic security, likewise proposed by Brazil. . . . It is interesting to note that, although the major industrialized nations insist on the necessity of recognition of a principle for common universal responsibility as regards some problems . . . they are strangely mute, reticent, and noncommittal whenever any country proposes, as Brazil has consistently done, the recognition of a common universal responsibility as regards the problem of development. . . . In other words, sovereignty should be relinquished by the less-developed countries, as regards the policy of utilization of their natural resources without any specific commitment on the part of the major industrialized

nations as regards the implementation of a truly effective system of collective economic security.[10]

Admitting that, as its economy grew and became more complex, Brazil was beginning to face "some of the problems that appear to perplex some developed countries," Araújo Castro credited his country's development success to "some natural conditions and national characteristics that might not prevail in other areas."

Brazilian foreign-policy elites extend their concerns to all regions of the world and seek to use their newfound influence to develop more flexible and increasingly economics-oriented alignments in a changing world. Aware of the constraints on their freedom of action, they are eager to be rid of them; but they realize that it is chiefly through its own development, rather than through skillful diplomacy, that Brazil's vulnerabilities can be minimized. Thus, in the view of one senior career diplomat, Brazil is leaving the "closed, small, and secure world" of its adolescence to enter a "hostile, complicated, and dangerous world, indifferent to our anxieties and our quaint nostalgia, a world where our great hopes and potentialities contrast with our condition as passive objects of history" and where the rationality of Brazil's diplomacy risks corruption by external ideological factors.[11]

Convinced that developed countries will resist any significant redistribution of the world's economic wealth and power and that such a redistribution is now in Brazil's interest, Brazilian policymakers believe that allying with less-developed countries on basic international economic questions is the only effective way to exert leverage upon the industrial powers. Yet such an alliance is not achieved automatically, and—since the continued cooperation of the developed countries is necessary for Brazil's development—on most political matters fundamental cooperation with the industrial powers is still in Brazil's interest. If Brazil's intermediate position constitutes a dilemma, it can also be exploited to maximize freedom of action, which is becoming increasingly important as Brazil moves gradually forward. To exploit Brazil's position requires delicate and sensitive diplomacy, since few matters are neatly divisible into economics and politics. Short-run needs—such as diversifying both financing sources for imports and markets for exports—must be merged with longer-range considerations. The advance to greatness (*grandeza*) must be made irreversible and self-sustaining—a major theme of the Second National Development Plan (IIPND) adopted by the Geisel administration.

The extent of the basic agreement of views between the military elite and the civilian technocrats was apparent during the 1972 Higher War College term. Planning Minister João Paulo dos Reis Velloso, who was selected to give the inaugural lecture (a function which the president had performed in 1970 and the army chief of staff in 1971) took as his theme "New Dimensions of Brazilian Society: National Integration, Social Integration, and External Strategy."[12] Classifying Brazil with India and Canada as the first three of the "intermediate or candidate powers," he stressed Brazilian determination not to permit the developed nations to function as a closed club "on the pretext of pollution and disarmament." Reis Velloso went on to emphasize that it was in Brazil's interest to conduct foreign relations "in consonance with the national development strategy, which seeks the most rapid possible growth, modernization, and greater competitive power of the national economy." Brazilian relations with the United States, he said, should be characterized by an "absence of complexes that obscure objectivity and rationality," adding that although Brazil did not "consciously seek" Latin American leadership, the country would achieve leadership as the natural result of "intensification" of bilateral relations as Brazil fulfilled its potential in the midst of underdeveloped countries.[13]

In international forums Brazilian spokesmen are fond of emphasizing that economic and social development is primarily the "fundamental responsibility" of each country. Multilateral economic cooperation is both complementary to national efforts and essential in order to minimize sacrifices and keep development rates high.[14] In the words of one Foreign

Ministry official, Brazilian policy in this field stems from the need to (1) increase import capacity, (2) expand productive capacity, (3) absorb and adapt foreign technology, and (4) keep foreign debt at a manageable level. The present system of international economic relations is prejudicial to the interests of developing countries—a fact that Brazil has come to recognize. Through UNCTAD and the various new international bodies concerned with these matters, Brazil seeks to "reformulate the mechanisms in order to create conditions that will facilitate its internal development effort." At this stage, it seeks to replace the most-favored-nation policy with a general system of preferences in international commerce, since during the next few years—until the creation of a "great integrated internal market"—it will be desirable for the external sector to "play the strategic role of sustaining the takeoff of the Brazilian economy."[15] Foreseeing "more substantial gains for the developing countries" in this respect during the latter half of the 1970s, this official believes that recognition of the constraining impact of external factors on developing nations leads Brazil to champion

> greater effective participation of developing countries in decisions that influence the behavior of their external sector and, as a consequence, their economic development . . . the objective of economic cooperation ought to be a dynamic international division of labor, oriented toward development, [one that would] lead to a better distribution of income and productivity among the countries of the world.[16]

This broadened scope of Brazil's pursuit of its interests has had an impact on its foreign-policy instruments. Thus, in another address to the Higher War College in 1972, Brazilian career diplomat José Oswaldo de Meira Penna observed:

> In a general way the purely formal and representative phase of our diplomacy is outdated. During recent years we are frankly entering the tasks of negotiation and information. It is enough to point out the role played by economists trained in the school of

Itamaraty in the development of the country, and the role of Itamaraty itself in the expansion of foreign trade, which is our present great success. This preoccupation with economics, a phenomenon so central to the changed diplomatic mentality, reveals the degree of interest in concrete and objective problems that has modified the old tradition of a career of elegance and protocol.[17]

Yet movement toward a larger international role, he pointed out, may bring with it certain negative features. Considering whether great-power status is compatible with Brazil's moral and cultural values, Meira Penna asked:

If Brazil really desires to be a Great Power, and if this implies . . . the potential and concrete exercise of brute force, are we disposed at this level to repudiate a peaceful diplomatic tradition to become engaged in military adventures, which alone, unfortunately, in the cruel world of international relations consolidate the political status of a country?[18]

Seeing a danger in losing sight of the "true characteristics of our development and our desire for security," Meira Penna chose to emphasize qualitative aspects, not merely quantitative goals, citing former Foreign Minister Mário Gibson Barbosa's statement that the "just measure of external application of national power" was the chief task of responsible foreign policy-makers.[19] Both overestimation and underestimation—overemployment or underemployment—of national power, Meira Penna remarked, court disaster, yet Brazil, as the "first example of the viability of Western civilization in the tropics," must take care lest its emergence as a major power "aggravate the social tensions that are causing the modern epoch to become so cruel."[20]

Few members of Brazil's foreign policy elites are so preoccupied with the possible cost of greatness. Unthreatened by large and hostile neighbors (unlike India or China today or Germany a century ago) and located in the lowest conflict area in the world, Brazil need not be burdened by the enormous military outlays that have characterized other nations' rise to major-power status. Then, too, economic power may, to a considerable extent, become a substitute for military power in the world of the 1970s and 1980s. Exclusive and rigid alliances involving the accommodation of powerful partners may not be necessary for a country that is able to simultaneously develop a set of "special" relationships with leading nations in the bilateral sphere and work with influential multilateral bodies in which the distribution of power is quite different.

To keep Brazil's foreign policy in proper perspective one must note that although international considerations are seriously pondered by Brazilian policymakers, major-power aspirations rarely play the most direct or determinant role in policy decisions. Instead, foreign policy is generally viewed in terms of its possible contribution to internal economic development. Majority elements within Brazil's foreign-policy elites, particularly the military and the technocrats, often seem relatively uninterested in policies designed specifically to facilitate Brazil's pursuit of enhanced international power. These policymakers believe that as internal development progresses, and the "economic miracle" is increasingly recognized as such abroad, Brazil's international prestige will rise concomitantly. Until then, they warn, premature efforts to play a more active and influential world role should be curbed—particularly efforts that might be viewed with alarm by Brazil's Hispanic American neighbors. Instead, they recommend that Brazil maintain a fairly low profile in international political affairs until increased trade, backed up by the continued growth of Brazilian industry and the modernization of the nation's military establishment, strengthens Brazil's already dominant position in relation to other South American countries. Vigorous activity in international economic affairs in pursuit of Brazil's interests is viewed as a more effective strategy in reaching the goal of "Brasil-Potência" than are bids for bloc leadership and for prestigious positions in the multilateral sphere.

For most Brazilian policymakers, consolidation of regional supremacy is, in the long run, merely a means of attaining a more far-reaching objective: inclusion in the councils of the major powers; ultimately, potency in world affairs is to be

desired far more than regional hegemony. With this fundamental perspective in mind, a hypothetical agenda of Brazil's
diplomatic interests would include at least the following
items:

● Continued attention to hemisphere affairs, with empha-
sis on developing a relatively equal relationship with the
United States and consolidating Brazil's position within the
South American continent.

● Amplified cooperation with Western Europe, emphasizing closer ties with such major industrial powers as the German
Federal Republic, France, the United Kingdom, and Italy.

● Increased attention to the countries of the Middle East
and North Africa, as Petrobrás' petroleum explorations abroad
lead to more active relationships and Brazilian commercial
ties (initiated to pay for oil imports) develop deeper roots.

● Intensification of the attempt to change what were formerly just listening posts in Africa into centers of commercial
and diplomatic action, with continued focus on the opportunities for becoming the major Western link with Angola and
other former Portuguese colonies.

● Augumented contact with the USSR, stressing broadened economic relations.

● "Qualified" dealings with Eastern Europe—particularly
Poland, Czechoslovakia, and Rumania—with expansion of
commercial relations as the dominant theme.

● Increased presence on a selective basis in Asia, emphasizing a bilateral relationship with Japan based on growing
trade and investment. (A cautious attitude toward the Chinese People's Republic would be tempered by evidence of
significant trade opportunities and conditioned by that
country's international behavior.)

Once Brazilian influence is established on the Pacific coast
of South America—chiefly through developing close relationships with Bolivia and Ecuador, but possibly also by substantially altering Brazil's relationship with the military regime in
Peru—Australia may figure more than marginally in Brazil's
international concerns. Moreover, as general acceptance of its
near-global range of interests as an emerging world power is

achieved, Brazil will begin to pay attention to such countries as India, Pakistan, Indonesia, and Iran, which may also have claims to upward mobility within the international system. By the late 1980s, when Brazil will have attained at least near-nuclear-power status, its presently modest reputation in multilateral forums will have been replaced by that of a nation which is seeking to play a leadership role in regard to selected issues and which is willing to exploit relatively low-risk opportunities for attaining international prestige.

In a world that already contains a near-saturation number of major powers, Brazil's challenge is to identify and assume the role of the leading intermediate country. In terms of geopolitical realities, this role can only be that of the chief industrial nation south of the equator.

Brazil's increased concern with attaining a position of leadership in the southern half of the world dates from its recognition in the 1960s that North-South differences were coming to be more significant in regard to some vital questions related to development (hence security) than were the East-West conflicts dominant during the cold war era. Perhaps the clearest statement of this concern is found in the writings of Lt. Brig. Nélson Freire Lavanère-Wanderley, a former chief of the Armed Forces General Staff and military adviser to Brazil's United Nations delegation who during 1975 was president of the influential War College Graduates' Association. While emphasizing the continuing importance of Brazil's relations with the United States and Western Europe, General Lavanère-Wanderley laid greater stress on Brazil's increasing awareness of being a Southern Hemisphere power.[21] First in size and GNP and second (to Indonesia) in population and military strength among the countries of the Southern Hemisphere, Brazil should, he feels, prepare itself psychologically to take the "necessary measures" to "preserve the Southern Hemisphere from avoidable evils." Already Brazil is the major industrial nation south of the equator, a fact that is likely to be more significant with the passage of time and with further consolidation of this position.

A senior diplomat, the former secretary general of the Foreign Ministry and ambassador to Mexico, Argentina, and Uruguay, elaborated on this theme:

> Driven by an irresistible vocation, Brazil is today launched on the conquest of external markets. Its interests, therefore, not only cross frontiers, but establish roots in foreign lands. We cannot refuse a destiny that, already marked by greatness, imposes responsibilities and tasks of world scope on us. Our interests dictate that we should actively collaborate with other economies to develop resources in friendly lands, in circumstances that would either complement our own economy or generally stimulate the economy of nations whose prosperity and political stability contribute to our own prosperity and security.[22]

The diplomat went on to stress the need for Brazilian financial involvement and direct investments both in neighboring countries and in "overseas territories of geopolitical relevance for us, such as Portuguese Africa."

External Factors and Brazilian Policy

Although Brazil is beginning to have an impact on the policies of certain other countries—most noticeably its small neighbors, such as Bolivia, Paraguay, and Uruguay—it is still substantially more an object of international pressures than a source of them. The impact of external economic factors is substantial; both the energy crisis and the protectionist tendencies fueled by the world economic recession severely limit Brazil's choices, internally as well as internationally. Brazilian policymakers feel that the moves of other international actors, particularly those of the United States and other industrial powers, deeply infringe on, if they do not directly determine, Brazil's behavior. These policymakers believe the United States can change the rules of the global game and sometimes the world itself, and they realize that they must respond—often defensively. Indeed, they frequently feel that they rarely have the opportunity to take positive steps. Araújo Castro says:

> Interdependence is a legitimate and desirable goal . . . it presupposes a previous stage of national sovereignty and economic independence from which mutual concessions will be made and mutual adjustments will be implemented with a view to strengthening international cooperation. Let us move toward interdependence, but let us, all of us, be independent first.[23]

The working of external factors on Brazilian foreign policy institutions and decisions is dramatically illustrated by Brazil's sharp modification of its Middle East policy in the context of the world energy crisis. Yet the evolution of Brazil's maritime policy over the past fifteen years, particularly with respect to the effective establishment of a 200-mile limit for Brazil's seas, is more truly illustrative of Brazil's increasing capacity to cope with external stimuli.

Economic concerns were important in Brazil's decision to extend its territorial seas to 200 miles, but factors relating to national self-assertion and adaptation to changing world conditions also played a part. The issue was joined during the early 1960s in a so-called Lobster War with France over that country's fishing activities off the coast of Brazil's politically disturbed and economically backward Northeast. The vigorous French use of naval power to prevent Brazil's seizure of lobster boats offended Brazilian sensibilities.[24] Following the discovery of a potentially significant location for shrimp fishing off the mouth of the Amazon in 1963, boats from the United States and other foreign countries began to fish these waters. Brazil responded by strengthening its regulatory legislation and augmenting its naval patrol capabilities. Anticipation of important petroleum finds on the continental shelf and increased awareness of the resource potential of the ocean bed reinforced Brazil's determination to protect its offshore interests.

Brazil adhered to the traditional 3-mile limit until November 1966, when Decree Law 44 established a 6-mile limit plus a "contiguous zone" of the same width. In April 1969, Decree Law 553 extended the limit to 12 miles, and less than a year later Decree Law 1098 proclaimed a 200-mile limit for

Brazil's maritime sovereignty.[25] The following year Brazil implemented these nationalistic measures by actively patrolling the shrimping area. As international diplomatic machinery moved ponderously through the protracted series of world law-of-the-sea conferences that have yet to produce a global formula, a pragmatic compromise on the fishing question was reached between Brazil and the United States. This interim agreement limiting the number of U.S. boats permitted to fish Brazilian waters and establishing levels of compensation for the costs of regulation was signed in May 1972 and was renegotiated and extended in 1975.

Closely related to the issue of territorial sea limits was Brazil's desire to reduce the drain on its balance of payments which resulted from ocean freight charges. Here the interests of an emergent developing country and those of the established maritime powers clashed in a classic confrontation. Brazil vigorously insisted on a formula whereby 40 percent of its overseas trade would be carried by Brazilian ships, an equal proportion by vessels of her trading partners, and only 20 percent by third-party bottoms. Patient and persistent diplomacy resulted in a December 1972 agreement that covered most of the northbound trade from Brazil to the United States and embodied the 40:40:20 principle. Meanwhile, the Brazilian navy contracted for purchase and construction of modern fleet units (primarily submarines, missile frigates, and oceangoing minesweepers) with Great Britain and the German Federal Republic, thus greatly decreasing Brazil's dependence on the United States. At the same time Brazil undertook construction of a world-class merchant marine.[26] Brazil's efforts to establish favorable territorial sea limits and maritime policies were facilitated by the aggressive position taken by Ecuador and Peru as well as by widespread international sentiment that time had come for movement on the territorial limit problem.[27]

Brazilian policymakers remain alert to international changes that seem to promise new opportunities as well as a lessening of constraints. Thus, Brazil's positions at petroleum/commodity conferences such as the April 1975 Prepcon meeting in Paris are conditioned by the attitudes and the alignments that emerge.[28] Because Brazil is both a major importer of oil, and an exporter of other basic commodities and raw materials (as well as manufactured goods), the country's pursuit of its international interests is characterized by a substantial degree of ambiguity—a situation that tends to aggravate Brazil's vulnerability to external shifts and changes.

Military assistance is another area in which external factors directly affect foreign policy. Developments in the past decade have greatly enhanced Brazil's ability to procure weapons and armaments advantageously—an area in which, until recently, vulnerabilities and dependence had far outweighed latitude of choice. Brazil's efforts to obtain heavy artillery and other equipment from Germany were interdicted by the Allies in the late 1930s and during the initial phase of World War II. This interdiction was a factor in the decision by Vargas and his military allies to align with the United States and to obtain modern arms and training through participation in the liberation of Europe.[29] After the war, U.S.-Brazilian military cooperation continued and was later institutionalized through the establishment of joint commissions in Rio de Janeiro and Washington.

In the early 1950s, however, offended nationalist sentiment blocked Brazilian involvement in the military operations in Korea and delayed ratification of a military assistance pact between the United States and Brazil for more than a year.[30] Although the veterans of the Italian campaign had regained a dominant position in the military by 1954—contributing to Vargas' fall and suicide and exerting dominant influence in the ensuing interim government—bilateral negotiations with the U.S. during the Kubitschek regime (over an attempt to exchange military hardware for a missile-tracking facility on Fernando da Noronha Island) were made difficult by the Brazilians' attempt to drive a hard bargain in light of what they perceived as the United States' neglect of the traditional "special relationship" between the two countries. Brazil's sensitivities, worn raw by continued U.S. pressure on the petroleum question—even after Petrobrás was set up in 1953 as a state monopoly controlling exploration and exploitation—were further injured in 1956 by Washington's refusal to sell Brazil an aircraft carrier, no matter how small, because of Argentine objections. In a gesture of independence unusual for that time but indicative of future trends, Brazil purchased an escort carrier from Great Britain and had it renovated at substantial cost.

During the late 1950s and early 1960s, Brazil remained largely dependent on the United States for military assistance. Yet by the time of the Costa e Silva government (1967-1969), Brazil's economic strength was sufficient that, when the U.S. refused to furnish F-5 fighters, Brazil could readily purchase Mirages from France. Indeed, between 1968 and 1972 Brazil purchased nearly $500 million (U.S. dollars) in military equipment from European suppliers, while receiving only $76 million in military aid from the United States.[31] Since then Brazil has been able to acquire whatever hardware its rulers consider essential under the most advantageous conditions available in the world market. Thus, the United States was able to get to get back into the Brazilian market with a large-scale deal for supersonic fighters only by making provisions for the transfer of technology and for the eventual production of Northrop F-5Es within Brazil. Successful sale of self-propelled artillery depended on the fact that the U.S. weapons were judged best for the price available. In other cases British, French, German, and Belgian companies obtained large contracts on similarly pragmatic grounds. By the 1970s the international arms trade was a buyers' market, and Brazilians ably took advantage of this situation to do away with the dependence on the United States which up through the mid-1960s had limited their policymaking autonomy. (Indeed, Brazil has become in a modest way an arms exporter, up to the level of small planes and tracked vehicles.)

Brazil's increased ability to cope with external factors—to move to a position of negotiating from strength—is illustrated most dramatically in the nuclear field. In 1946 the International Atomic Energy Agency—then thoroughly dominated by the United States, with the support of the United Kingdom and France—convoked a meeting which also included the Soviet Union and the four countries considered likely to have the world's largest reserves of uranium: Brazil, India, Canada, and Belgium (then still fully in control of the Congo). Determined to implement a decision establishing control over global supplies of atomic minerals which predated the use of the atomic bomb, U.S. representative Bernard Baruch suggested that Brazil give up its radioactive thorium and uranium in order to redress the "injustices of nature" which had put these valuable resources in the wrong hands. Adm. Álvaro Alberto, heading Brazil's delegation, countered with the argument of "specific compensations," which called for reciprocal sharing of the industrialized powers' petroleum and coal reserves—a suggestion deemed not worthy of serious consideration.

In January 1951 the National Research Council was established, and export of uranium was made subject to approval by that body as well as by the Armed Forces General Staff (EMFA) and the National Security Council (CSN), two other recently created bodies with responsibility for Brazil's security and defense.[32] Under pressure to send troops to Korea, the government of Getúlio Vargas (who, when previously in power, had been party to a 1945 secret agreement that in effect consigned thorium sales to customers approved by Washington) decided instead to sell strategic minerals to the United States. An agreement signed in August 1952 provided for the sale of up to 2,500 tons of monazite sands (with roughly 5 percent thorium content) per year for a three-year period. After arranging for this rare earth to be made available in a single shipment, the United States apparently reneged on its commitment to purchase the radioactive tailings as well. In 1954 new negotiations provided for the exchange of 5,000 tons of radioactive minerals for 100,000 tons of wheat.

The narrow limits of U.S. appreciation of Brazil's cooperation were quickly demonstrated. In 1953 Admiral Alberto had successfully arranged the purchase of three prototype gas ultracentrifuges for uranium enrichment from the German Federal Republic.[33] The equipment was destined for Brazil's fledgling nuclear research program, along with a small "swimming pool"-type reactor obtained from France. Delivery was blocked, however, by U.S. occupation authorities (Germany was in transition between Allied military rule and self-government between 1949 and 1953), and this equipment did not reach Brazil until 1956, by which time the German Federal Republic had fully recovered its sovereignty. In the interim, there had been several changes of government in Brazil.[34]

The establishment of the National Nuclear Energy Commission (CNEN) in 1954 marked the virtual end of Brazil's initial effort to develop some form of independent nuclear program, and in January 1955 Admiral Alberto resigned as head of the National Research Council. Brazil then signed an agreement with the United States which provided for very limited training and research technology. A short-lived project for an autonomous nuclear energy effort formulated in 1961 by physicist Marcelo Damy da Souza Santos, head of the CNEN, died with President Quadros' abrupt resignation. For Brazil, the fruits of two decades of "atoms for peace" collaboration with the United States were sparse and disappointing, and the stringent conditions imposed by the U.S. in the early 1970s on the construction plans for Brazil's first nuclear power plant abrogated any hope of significantly increasing the country's technological capacities in this field. (All equipment was constructed in the United States and installed at Angra dos Reis by Westinghouse technicians.)

While in 1953 there was nothing Brazil could do but accept the U.S. embargo and adopt the dependent road to nuclear energy, subsequent developments have made effective longer-run responses possible. The Castelo Branco administration's reservations to the treaty establishing a Latin American nuclear-free zone and the Costa e Silva government's refusal to sign the nuclear non-proliferation treaty kept Brazil's choices open, and late in the Médici regime efforts were undertaken to find ways to import nuclear technology.

Although U.S. companies seeking contracts for future nuclear generating plants agreed to sweeten the pot in regard to the technological benefits of large-scale agreements, the U.S.

position in even so minor a matter as supplying fuel to Angra I, the pioneer installation at Angra dos Reis, appeared to the Brazilians to be excessively restrictive. Then, too, the Brazilian rulers believed that the United States had used or could use Brazil's dependence as a lever in other bilateral dealings with Brazil or even as a curb on Brazil's position in multilateral bodies. Painfully aware by 1974 of the limitations placed on foreign policy by petroleum import needs, Brazilian policymakers were more than a little loath to increase the country's vulnerability to external pressures in the energy field. For example, once Brazil had begun to generate a significant amount of electricity with nuclear reactors, as it hoped to do by the late 1980s, the ability to withhold fuel elements for the reactors would pose a major threat to the economy. This anticipated vulnerability led policymakers to continue exploring avenues for nuclear cooperation with European countries and Israel. When the United States backed away from a long-term commitment to furnish fuel for Angra II and Angra III, this exploration was intensified.

Brazil's nuclear breakthrough began with the 1974 visit to Brasília of Germany's former defense minister, Franz Joseph Strauss, along with the Federal Republic's vice-minister of foreign affairs and secretary of technology. Following a secret visit by Mines and Energy Minister Shigeaki Ueki to Bonn, the Brazilian government decided to build a nuclear program on the foundation of the German-Brazilian Technical and Scientific Agreement of 1969.[35]

After some internal debate about the most advantageous approach to the task, on December 16, 1974, Brazil created Nuclebrás, whose task was to "establish in the country a heavy industry to make reactors and to encompass all stages of the so-called combustion cycle, to provide a growing electrical energy capacity."[36] During the following month, Paulo Nogueira Baptista, a senior career diplomat who had recently finished a tour of duty as minister counselor in Bonn (and who, as head of the Foreign Ministry's Economic Department, had accompanied the planning and mines and energy ministers on their recent trip to the Middle East, arguing along the way for the importance of nuclear independence), was appointed to head Nuclebrás and to assist Mines and Energy Minister Ueki and Finance Minister Simonsen with the final delicate negotiations that would assure Brazil's access to nuclear technology while guaranteeing Germany a reliable source of uranium for its own rapidly expanding nuclear-energy needs.[37]

Reinforced by discoveries of significant uranium deposits within its own boundaries precisely when awareness of the possibility of a serious shortage of that strategic mineral was coming to the attention of the United States and other industrial powers, Brazil was in a position to deal effectively with strong criticism from the United States of its multibillion-dollar agreement with the German Federal Republic (signed on June 27, 1975). Brazilian commentator Murilo Melo Filho extolled the agreement as proof that "we are no longer a junior partner; we are a nation with sufficient political and mental maturity to feel justly ambitious in world terms and not merely in terms of Latin America."[38]

General Meira Mattos, after documenting the superpowers' persistent efforts to keep Brazil from exploiting its uranium and thorium resources in its attempt to obtain nuclear technology, expressed Brazil's determination not to accept any "unjustifiable limitation on our initiative and creativity in the field of nuclear energy production for ends required by our development and scale of [international] power."[39] In fact, on February 24, 1976, astute Brazilian diplomacy won International Atomic Energy Agency approval of the safeguards against diversion of fuel or technology to nonpeaceful purposes agreed to by Brazil and the German Federal Republic, thus removing the last obstacle to full implementation of the June 1975 accords.[40] (It might be noted, however, that these restrictions were unusually stringent, reflecting heavy pressures upon Bonn and Brasília from both the United States and the European industrialized powers.)[41]

The question of fundamental economic dependency remains to be dealt with. At this point it is sufficient to show that sophisticated dependency theorists admit that Brazil's ability to cope effectively with pressures from foreign governments has increased significantly.

> The tendency toward dispersion of the origins of direct investment parallels the tendency toward the dispersion of imports and exports, and, since exports and imports are increasingly transactions between different parts of multinational firms, the two tendencies probably reinforce each other.

> The result of dispersion is to give the Brazilian state increased maneuvering room. There is no longer a single hegemonic power standing behind foreign capital. Any U.S. efforts to protect foreign capital through political or military action would be protecting capital that was about 60 percent non-U.S. No single European power has a sufficiently predominant interest to take over the U.S. role. Furthermore, any single power which enters into direct conflict with the Brazilian state would risk prejudicing its own capital relative to that of the other center countries. In short, while the multinationals can obviously count on political support from their home countries, support is likely to be limited.[42]

Then, too, it is one thing to depend for export earnings on a single commodity for which world demand is often quite weak in relation to supply—as was the case with Brazil and coffee until recently—and quite another thing to be a major exporter of a variety of foodstuffs, minerals, and manufactured items. The world market for each of Brazil's major exports may move sharply up or down, but the drop in demand for some items is normally offset by rising prices or by an increase volume of sales for others.

In sum, while external factors are still important in Brazilian policymaking, they are not disproportionately important; and external pressures impose less-effective constraints upon Brazil's foreign policy than they imposed in the past. In at least some policy areas, Brazil is experiencing increasing freedom of action and discovering viable options.[43]

Notes to Chapter 2

[1]The CSN's 1970 codification of *Metas e Bases de Ação de Govêrno* [Goals and Bases of Government Action] called for measures to build "an effectively developed, democratic and sovereign society, thus assuring the economic, social and political viability of Brazil as a great power" by the year 2000. Policy since that time has been consistent with these goals. See also Carlos de Meira Mattos, *Brasil: Geopolítica e Destino* (Rio de Janeiro: José Olympio, 1975).

[2]Geraldo Eulálio do Nascimento e Silva, "A Diplomacia e o Poder Nacional," *Segurança e Desenvolvimento* 150 (1972): 91-99.

[3]Regis Novais de Oliveira, "A evolução da política exterior e Brasil em face das transformações do equilíbrio de forças," *Revista Brasileira de Estudos Políticos* 37 (September 1973): 104.

[4]Novais de Oliveira, "Evolução," p. 105. The first half of the present five-year National Development Plan is titled "Development and Greatness: Brazil as an Emergent Power." (See República Federativa do Brasil, *II Plano Nacional de Desenvolvimento PND (1975-1979)*, Brasília, December 1974, pp. 21-78.) Basic goals include $100 billion GNP by 1977 and a per-capita GNP of $1,000 by 1979.

[5]Meira Mattos, *Brasil*, p. 72.

[6]Meira Mattos, "Uma geopolítica" (see n. 2, Chap. 1), p. 14. It is informative to compare the self-assured tone of this presentation with the author's significantly more tentative formulation four years earlier in "Nossa Viabilidade para Grand Potência," reprinted in *Jornal do Brasil*, March 31, 1971.

[7]Paulo Cabral de Mello, "O Brasil e os Problemas Econômicos Mundiais," *Revista Brasileira de Estudos Políticos* 42 (January 1976): 150-151.

[8]Cabral de Mello, "Problemas," pp. 155-156.

[9]Arnaldo Niskier, *Nosso Brasil: Para Estudos de Problemas Brasileiros* (Rio de Janeiro: Bloch Editores, 1973), pp. 212-213.

[10]João Augusto de Araújo Castro, "A Brazilian View of a Changing World," lecture presented at Temple University, Philadelphia, on November 17, 1973.

[11]José Oswaldo de Meira Penna, "A Diplomacia e o Poder Político Nacional," lecture presented at the Escola Superior de Guerra [Higher War College] on July 5, 1973, p. 18.

[12]João Paulo dos Reis Velloso, *Novas Dimensões da Sociedade Brasileira*, Rio de Janeiro, 1972.

[13]A good example of the meshing of technocratic and private-sector thinking with respect to the developmental underpinnings of international status is found in Eduardo Celestino Rodrigues et al., *Brasil Potência*, São Paulo, 1972.

[14]Alvaro Gurgel de Alencar Netto, "A ONU e os Interesses do Brasil no Campo do Desenvolvimento," *Segurança e Desenvolvimento* 154 (1973): 133-140.

[15]Alencar Netto, "Interesses do Brasil," p. 136.

[16]Ibid., p. 139.

[17]Meira Penna, "A Diplomacia," p. 17. This Brazilian ambassador has written extensively on matters relating to these themes. See, for example, his *Política Externa, Segurança e Desenvolvimento* (Rio de Janeiro: AGIR, 1967) and *Psicologia do Subdesenvolvimento* (Rio de Janeiro: APEC Editôra, 1972).

[18]Meira Penna, "A Diplomacia," pp. 26-27.

[19]Ibid., p. 29.

[20]Ibid., p. 30.

[21]Nélson Freire Lavenère-Wanderley, "Hemisfério Sul," *Revista Militar Brasileira* 58, no. 4 (October-December 1972): 19.

[22]Manuel Pio Corrêa Júnior, "Empresas Multinacionais e a Mobilização Nacional," *Segurança e Desenvolvimento* 154 (1973): 151. (Reprint of a lecture delivered at the Higher War College on August 1, 1973.)

[23]Araújo Castro, "Brazilian View," p. 8.

[24]In English see Michael Morris, "Trends in U.S.–Brazilian Maritime Relations," *Inter-American Economic Affairs* 27, no. 3 (Winter 1973), pp. 3-24. On the Brazilian side see Carlos Calero Rodrigues, "Relações Internacionais do Brasil: Interesses Marítimos," *Segurança e Desenvolvimento* 152 (1973): 91-102. (Reprint of a War College lecture of May 15, 1972.) E. D. Brown cited the desire to exclude Soviet research vessels as a basic reason for the Brazilian decision to assert a 200-mile limit. See his "Latin America and the International Law of the Sea," in Ronald G. Hellman and H. Jon Rosenbaum (eds.), *Latin America: The Search for a New International Role* (New York: Halsted Press, 1975), p. 261.

[25]Marcello Rafaelli, "Mar Territorial e Problemas Correlatos," *Revista Brasileira de Estudos Políticos* 37 (September 1973): 62.

[26]See Décio Mauro Rodrigues da Cunha, "A Expansão da Marinha Mercante" (mimeographed) March 20, 1974, pp. 19-35.

[27]There is a rapidly burgeoning literature on this question. A convenient brief introduction is C. Richard Bath, "Latin American Claims on Living Resources of the Sea," *Inter-American Economic Affairs* 27, no. 4 (Spring 1974): 59-84.

[28]See Paulo Cabral de Mello's speech in *Resenha de política exterior do brasil* 2, no. 5 (April, May, and June 1975): 95-97.

[29]Consult Frank McCann, *The Brazilian-American Alliance, 1937-1945* (Princeton, N.J.: University Press, 1973).

[30]See Moniz Bandeira, *Presença dos Estados Unidos no Brasil* (Rio de Janeiro: Editôra Civilização Brasileira, 1973).

[31]Luigi Einaudi et al., *Arms Transfers to Latin America: Toward a Policy of Mutual Respect* (Santa Monica, Calif.: Rand Corporation Report R-1173-DOS, June 1973), p. 13. Also useful is Stephen S. Kaplan, "U.S. Arms Transfers to Latin America, 1945-1974: Rational Strategy, Bureaucratic Politics, and Executive Parameters," *International Studies Quarterly* 19, no. 4 (December 1975): 399-431.

[32]Much useful material is contained in "O Brasil na Era Nuclear," *Manchete*, April 24, 1976, pp. 75-97; and Meira Mattos, *Brasil*, pp. 92-97. See also Gall, "Atoms for Brazil."

[33]In addition to the sources cited above, see "Energia Nuclear: Uma forte nação pacífica," *Veja*, July 2, 1975, p. 22.

[34]"25 Anos de Luta pelo Átomo," *Manchete*, July 5, 1975, pp. 16-19. See also *Veja*, May 14, 1975, pp. 16-21, and June 11, 1975, pp. 18-21; as well as "Política Nuclear: Os projectos, as alternativas e o mistério," *Visão*, September 9, 1974, pp. 25-34. A Brazilian nationalist perspective is Moniz Bandeira, *Presença*, pp. 354-372.

[35]Also of use in reconstructing events are "Política Nuclear: Um acordo tamanho quarenta," *Visão*, June 23, 1975, pp. 23-24; and "Depois da victória política, o desafio talvez mais dificil," *Visão*, July 7, 1975, pp. 12-22.

[36]See Ueki's statements in "A Riqueza que Vem do Átomo," *Manchete*, October 18, 1975, pp. 32-34. The law establishing Nuclebrás was No. 61894, December 16, 1974.

[37]See "O Poder Nacional precisa do Poder Atômico," *Manchete*, June 21, 1975, pp. 14-15.

[38]Ibid., p. 15.

39Meira Mattos, *Brasil*, pp. 99-100.

40See *Veja*, March 24, 1976, p. 27. The specifics of the Brazil-GFR nuclear cooperation are discussed in Chap. 5.

41Gall, "Atoms for Brazil," pp. 158-159.

42Peter B. Evans, "Continuities and Contradictions in the Evolution of Brazilian Dependence," *Latin American Perspectives* 3, no. 2 (Spring 1976): 47.

43In a recent essay on Brazilian foreign policy, Dr. Brady Tyson supported this view: "To the degree that Brazil has become a more dynamic and powerful actor on the international scene in the last few years, her foreign policy has become a better instrument for attaining national goals—a function of national development policy—and relatively less responsive to external political events." In Harold Eugene Davis and Larman Wilson (eds.), *Latin American Foreign Policies: An Analysis* (Baltimore, Md.: Johns Hopkins University Press, 1975), p. 225. This is quite consonant with President Geisel's own formulation in his March 1, 1976 address to the opening session of the Brazilian Congress, which stressed that "freedom of action in the international sphere should be conditioned by national interest." See *Resenha de politica exterior do brasil* 3, no. 8 (January, February, and March 1976), p. 7. This theme is spelled out in greater detail in Foreign Minister Silveira's speech on "The View that Brazil has of its Place in the World," ibid, pp. 73-77.

3
The President,
the Presidency,
and the Armed Forces

As Brazil's foreign policy needs have become more complex and its leaders' understanding of the interrelationships among external factors has deepened, the institutional aspects of the country's foreign policy process have become more sophisticated. Almost every ministry, most significant elements of the executive branch, and many autonomous agencies are involved in the conduct of Brazil's foreign affairs, and each has its own ideas about both formulation and execution; thus a great many "actors" intervene to initiate, provide authority for, veto, advise, guide, direct, modify, mobilize support for, provide resources for, implement, coordinate, and administer foreign policy. Moreover, the roles of these institutional actors vary according to the specific issue or policy under consideration, and the influence of each often depends on the identity of its department head, his relationship with the president, and his alliances with other influential persons within the policymaking process.[1]

The individuals and institutional actors who determine foreign policy in Brazil include the president, the several advisory and staff agencies attached to the presidency, the military establishment, the Foreign Ministry (Itamaraty), the Finance Ministry and related economic agencies, and closely related organs of the business community. Except in very special circumstances, a narrowly circumscribed role is played by Congress and the political parties, the communications media, the academic world, the church, and labor organizations. The next chapters will examine the changing roles of each of these actors in the policymaking arena.

The President

The tradition of strong presidential government is firmly rooted in Brazil, and presidents have generally had considerable influence on foreign policy. In the postwar period this was true of Vargas (until the eve of his suicide in 1954), of Kubitschek, of Quadros during his brief regime in 1961, and even of Goulart. The tradition of a strong presidency has been accentuated since 1964 because military presidents have operated relatively untrammeled by Congress and essentially unhindered by considerations of political reaction or public opinion. This generalization is perhaps least true in regard to Castelo Branco, who made heroic efforts to keep Congress and the two-party system functioning under extremely difficult conditions. Yet it was Castelo who, operating in the immediate aftermath of the military's ouster of Goulart, made the most substantial changes in Brazil's foreign policy vis-a-vis the United States, and who reversed the 1961-1964 trend toward a strategy of confrontation.[2]

While Castelo was preoccupied with domestic problems, a substantial consensus on foreign policy among the relevant elites came into existence during his presidency; the leading foreign policy dissidents had been purged, and the remaining left/liberal critics of the United States had been made impotent or muzzled. During this time the idea of a center-conservative partnership with the United States—an outlook previously identified with the National Democratic Union (UDN) party—came to predominate.[3] Career diplomat Roberto de Oliveira Campos, minister of planning (a newly created post), influenced the president on questions concerned with both international affairs and internal policy. During this period, the presidency as an institution grew substantially and became increasingly specialized in order to cope with the significant expansion of its foreign-policy role.[4] The evolution continues to the present day.

During the Costa e Silva administration, foreign policy lived largely on accumulated capital. Good relations with the United States were inherited from the Castelo Branco administration, but by 1968 there had been substantial reassessment on both sides. Few Brazilians then foresaw that the financial policies of the Castelo government, if continued without fundamental modification by his successor, would lead to dramatic and sustained economic development. As Brazil's internal political problems became more acute, its key decision makers felt less concern about U.S. reaction to their policies, although Brazil's image abroad continued to be of some interest to them. The political problems that threatened Costa's survival in power diverted his attention from foreign policy matters. Economic concerns vied with domestic politics for the government's attention with the result that the Foreign Ministry became something of a sideshow under nondiplomat José de Magalhães Pinto. All important national policy decisions were in the military's domain, and the aggressive hard-line faction generally defined the issues in terms of narrow national considerations. Finance Minister Antônio Delfim Netto emerged as a major influence on development policy and was able to sufficiently exploit the erosion of the president's authority to become a major force in the foreign policy realm; it did Delfim no harm that the economic successes of 1968-1969 contrasted dramatically with the regime's political failures.

Perhaps the most significant foreign policy dispute during the Costa e Silva government concerned the proper role of the Foreign Ministry in nuclear policy. The Goulart regime, with the urging of Foreign Minister Affonso Arinos de Mello Franco, actively espoused the concept of a Latin American nuclear-free zone during 1962-1963. Castelo Branco, although harboring substantial reservations about potential limitations on Brazil's freedom of action, did not fully reverse this policy. At Mexico City in November 1964 Brazil was instrumental in the establishment of the Preparatory

Commission for Latin American Denuclearization, but did little to accelerate its work. In September 1965 the president took the position that denuclearization of Latin America was acceptable only if all nuclear powers and countries with Western Hemisphere colonies or territories pledged to respect it and if all Latin American countries, including Cuba, were bound by it.[5] Ambassador Sérgio Corrêa da Costa, who took over as assistant secretary general for international organizations in February 1966, conceived the formula of "positive reservations" which was embodied in the text of the treaty. This clause, however, could be waived by those countries that so wished; the treaty took effect only when all interested parties had fully accepted the obligations involved.

When Costa e Silva acceded to the presidency in March 1967, Corrêa da Costa was elevated to secretary general under banker-politician Magalhães Pinto as foreign minister. Deeply interested in nuclear questions, Corrêa da Costa labored to develop an image of expertise in this field among Brazil's diplomats.[6] With Corrêa's urging and against the background of several ultranationalist campaigns against U.S. exploration for Brazilian atomic minerals in the years preceding 1964, Foreign Minister Magalhães Pinto (a major political figure who then still harbored presidential ambitions) perceived that advantages might accrue to both Brazil and himself if he advocated that Brazil move toward an independent nuclear capability.

While Corrêa's position appears to have enjoyed considerable support within the ranks of ambitious young foreign service officers, it conflicted with the prevailing view in the 1950s that development in the nuclear energy field could best be expedited through participation in the United States' "atoms for peace" program. Mines and Energy Minister José Costa Cavalcanti, a retired army brigadier general and former congressman, favored the latter position. Along with important military elements, he believed that the foreign minister's efforts to mobilize nationalist sentiment in support of a confrontation with the United States over this sensitive issue could jeopardize the cooperative program. In October 1967, scarcely a half-year into Costa's term of office, the National Security Council decided that the Foreign Ministry should retire from the policymaking arena and limit itself to conducting international negotiations.

During the last year of his abbreviated presidency, Costa seems to have been unaware of potentially serious problems in Brazil's relations with the United States, especially after the December 1968 coup-within-a-coup that led to the recess of Congress and the reinstitution of massive purges. Preoccupied with his ultimately unsuccessful efforts to find a viable path between civilian pressures for political normalization and military demands for increasingly authoritarian measures, the president was not well informed about either the further reduction of aid from the United States after the December 1968 fifth Institutional Act or the subsequent hiatus in discussion of new projects. Moreover, the political decay preceding the government's demise was not conducive to effective foreign-policy initiatives on Itamaraty's part.

The Médici administration appears to have taken a broader view of Brazil's prospective international role than had its predecessors. Dedicated to building up Brazil's economic might so as to help the nation assume its rightful place on the world scene, Médici generally favored—though not in any slavish or automatic way—cooperation with the United States. The predominant rational and calm tone became more confident as the "economic miracle" continued and gained international attention. As consolidation of the administration in Brasília limited inputs from outside the government, this period saw increasing centralization and concentration of policymaking authority. Major decisions were made by a relatively small group in what Rio de Janeiro and São Paulo observers viewed as the not-so-splendid isolation of Brasília. Foreign policy issues remained essentially the province of specialized elites, while public interest remained generally low and intermittent. The government was still basically inward-looking—concerned above all with development and security—while Brazil–United States relations remained the chief focus of its foreign-policy concerns. Increasingly, however, the hunt for export markets to sustain the industrial center of Brazil's economic growth became important.

Following the eclipse of the nationalist faction headed by Gen. Albuquerque Lima (Médici's chief rival in the army's internal selection of its presidential candidate in September 1969, who was forced into retirement the following year), the military moved toward a strict orthodoxy that narrowed the field of acceptable options during the first part of the Médici government. As Army Minister Orlando Geisel strove vigorously to reduce factionalism within the military, foreign service officers attempted to adjust to the current line of national security doctrine. Their dilemma was reflected in a 1970-1971 debate on policy toward Chile; those who stressed the distance between the two countries and doubted that the Allende regime constituted even a remote threat to vital Brazilian interests realized that they were becoming dangerously out of line with approved thinking on the subject, and thus tended to keep quiet. An intransigent position on Cuba, a wary attitude toward augmented relations with the USSR, and continued sympathy toward Israel—these were the foreign-policy views approved by the military. (The position of the military had thawed considerably by the midpoint of the Médici administration, as the government's stability had been increased by the virtual elimination of internal security threats and by a major government victory in the November 1970 election.)

In marked contrast to the situation during Costa's thirty months in office, presidential advisers were influential in policymaking during the Médici years. Civil Cabinet head Leitão de Abreu, a former university professor, emerged as a competent bureaucratic infighter. The National Intelligence Service (SNI), under Gen. Carlos Alberto Fontoura, exerted significant influence over Brazil's policy toward such neighbors as Paraguay, Bolivia, and Uruguay, while the Foreign Ministry under Gibson Barbosa seems to have had its way on matters that other, more powerful agencies did not view as significant either to national security or to economic development. Even when Itamaraty began to carry the ball (as it did regarding the bilateral fishing agreement with the United States, when the navy wanted the U.S. boats out), power shifted to the National Security Council, with instructions from the president to resolve the dispute promptly without too much concern for the views of the Foreign Ministry. When his foreign and finance ministers engaged in a public dispute over policy toward Africa, Médici stepped in to censure both.

Médici was inclined to delegate considerable authority—but then to hold his ministers strictly accountable. When the necessity for a decision arose, he would give the problem to whoever he felt might solve it best irrespective of established bureaucratic lines—a situation that often worked to the advantage of Delfim Netto, who had been kept on as finance minister and who was gaining an international reputation as the author of Brazil's "economic miracle." Matters began to change during Médici's final year in office, as the president became more involved in the succession question and Delfim attempted to keep the lid on the economic situation in order to keep his mystique (and his carefully unstated political ambitions) alive. Under the pressures of growing world inflation, the international oil crisis, and the country's economic boom, domestic inflation had again increased by late 1973, and the president's faith in Delfim—whose own popularity with the military had declined—began to wane. Gibson Barbosa sought new foreign-policy initiatives; but as a lame duck with consequently limited authority, he was unable to accomplish anything of lasting importance. Indeed, the international policymakers of the several ministries went very much their own ways during these months.

Although Petrobrás president Ernesto Geisel was the frontrunner almost from the time the dust had settled after Médici's elevation to the presidency, Geisel's selection as chief executive for the 1974-1979 period was far from assured, much less automatic. Early favorites—military as well as civilian—are often burned out by the crucial stretch drive in Brazilian politics, and several other senior generals were available. Médici himself seemed to prefer retired Gen. Adalberto

Pereira dos Santos, who had been army chief of staff when he was first promoted to general officer rank. Civil Cabinet Chief Leitão de Abreu promoted the candidacy of former Army Minister Aurélio de Lyra Tavares, his brother-in-law, who had presided over the military junta that had chosen Médici for the presidency in October 1969. Orlando Geisel, who as Médici's army minister favored his own younger brother's candidacy, was himself preferred by a significant group of officers. General Fontoura, the SNI head, and Gen. Dirceu Nogueira were opposed to the choice of Ernesto Geisel to the very end; while the nationalist wing—which, behind Albuquerque Lima, had challenged Médici for the nomination and which was reported to count four-star generals Artur Candal da Fonseca and Rodrigo Otavio Jordão Ramos among its ranks—clearly would have preferred someone more of its own stripe than the *Castelista* Geisel.[7]

Both straight continuism (staying in power indefinitely) and a limited extension of the incumbent's mandate were discussed within the administration's inner circles as alternatives to endorsing Geisel, but such discussion has become a rather standard ploy to offset erosion of the president's authority as he nears lame-duck status. In the end, much as Castelo Branco had accepted Costa e Silva as his successor in 1967 to avoid deep division within the military, Médici chose Ernesto Geisel as the government's candidate, but forced him to accept Adalberto as his running mate.

A longtime staff man who had served as Military Cabinet chief under Castelo Branco, Ernesto Geisel has involved the presidency much more directly in the decision-making process, it is now the central executive agencies rather than the ministries which most often handle difficult problems. As it affected the institutional side of foreign policy-making, the transition from the Médici regime to the Geisel administration necessitated some changes in personnel and consequent shifts in relationships among key decision units. The changes were facilitated and to some extent rationalized by limited modification of relevant governmental structures. In terms of goals and perceptions, officials held over from the preceding administration adapted to the changed situation, especially to the threat presented by the energy crisis. The need to shift toward the Arab side in the Middle East conflict, the need to respond to fast-moving events in Portugal, new opportunities with regard to China, and changing hemisphere attitudes toward Cuba's continued exclusion from the inter-American system—all these called for rapid presidential response.

In the collegial or team approach adopted by the Geisel administration, policy questions are assigned to interministerial committees in an orderly manner; in cooperation with these comittees, the Civil Cabinet and the Planning Secretariat carry out systematic studies and coordinate working papers for the president. The concentration of economic policymaking in the hands of the finance minister has been eliminated; final decision-making power has been centralized in accordance with this new style, and the president is the final authority. While discussion of policy matters is more broadly diffused than it was under Médici, there is significantly less delegation of decision-making authority by the chief executive. No longer do the SNI head and the Civil and Military Cabinet chiefs together decide many foreign policy–related matters on authority delegated by the president, as appears to have been the practice in the preceding government. And certainly there is no superminister, such as Delfim Netto (or, before him, Roberto Campos), who might take advantage of high-priority economic concerns to expand his influence far beyond economic matters.[8]

The Presidential Advisers and Staff

After the president, the most important departments of the executive office which concern themselves with foreign affairs include the National Security Council (CSN), Civil Cabinet, Planning Secretariat, Armed Forces General Staff (EMFA), National Intelligence Service (SNI), High Command of the Armed Forces, and Economic Development Council. The key personality in this structure is Golbery do Couto e Silva, chief of the Civil Cabinet. A retired army major general, Golbery organized and headed the SNI under Castelo (when Ernesto Geisel was serving as chief of the Military Cabinet). While Golbery is best known as one of Brazil's—indeed, Latin America's—leading geopoliticians, he has so far concentrated his attention chiefly on domestic matters, particularly decompression and the rational fitting together of Brazil's internal policies. And although (unlike his predecessor, João Leitão de Abreu) Golbery has no foreign-policy specialists on his staff, he and Geisel have been close in their basic international outlook for many years, and the president usually consults with Golbery on significant foreign-policy questions. A liberal within the context of Brazilian military politics, Golbery is the chief target of hard-line critics, who seek to undercut his influence and undermine his authority.

Perhaps next in influence is the minister-chief of the Planning Secretariat, João Paulo dos Reis Velloso (planning minister in the Médici government). Like Golbery, he meets daily with the president—a privilege other ministers do not have—and functions as the secretary general of the Economic Development and Social Development councils. With Delfim out, Reis Velloso represents the maximum continuity within the government (he has been part of all the post-1964 administrations and a minister in the past two governments). Reis Velloso does not, however, appear to initiate foreign policy; rather, he coordinates and facilitates efficient operation of the policymaking machinery. While the Planning Ministry, from which the secretariat descended, was clearly in the shadow of the Finance Ministry during the Médici years, it did constitute Brazil's primary contact with several international financial agencies and organizations—notably the Inter-American Development Bank and IBRD, the World Bank, though not the International Monetary Fund. While Reis Velloso thus spoke for Brazil abroad on a number of significant issues, he did not really make policy independently.

The National Intelligence Service is headed by João Baptista de Oliveira Figueiredo, a three-star general who served as chief of Médici's Military Cabinet. Under Médici the SNI, which he had headed for most of the Costa e Silva administration, became involved in foreign intelligence reporting in competition with the Foreign Ministry and the military attachés. While the SNI has since concentrated on internal security matters, there are indications that Figueiredo is little loath to resume poaching on the foreign-policy preserve, particularly with regard to such neighboring countries as Paraguay, where he enjoys a close personal relationship with President Stroessner. Now a rather large agency with its own training school (the ESNI, established in May 1972), the SNI has become a policy adviser on a wide range of issues ("national security" is very broadly defined in Brazil) as well as an evaluator of the effectiveness of many organizations and programs.

The role of the National Security Council—made up of the president, vice-president, all ministers, the chiefs of the Civil and Military cabinets and of the SNI, the chief of the Armed Forces General Staff, and the chiefs of staff of the three services—has diminished under Geisel (its secretary general during the Castelo government); the smaller, more specialized councils have largely replaced the CSN in policy formulation. However, its staff still studies matters affecting national security and maintains representatives in each civilian ministry to provide it with data.

The Economic Development Council, headed by the president, brings together the ministers of finance, agriculture, interior, and industry and commerce as well as the minister-chief of the Planning Secretariat, who serves as its secretary general. While not directly charged with foreign affairs, this council makes decisions that are crucial to international economic relations. The foreign minister at times is invited to attend its meetings.

The newest of these key councils is the Political Development Council, established at the beginning of 1975. Unlike the others, it is not exclusively an interministerial body, including as it does the presiding officer of each house of the Congress as well as the respective majority leaders. This council represents an expansion of the informal group consisting of the president, the minister-chief of the Civil Cabinet, the minister of justice, and the president of Arena which has met frequently to map political strategy since the beginning of Geisel's presidency. This council has so far been kept flexible so as to be able to adjust to changing political circumstances, and its decisions may be used to gauge political reactions to major policy shifts.

The Military Establishment

The basic goals and limits of foreign policy are set, in a fundamental sense, by the military. While, to a marked degree, military influence is made effective through the president, as the four-star general selected for the dual role of chief executive and leader of the revolutionary movement of March, 1964, the Armed Forces has other official channels of expression as well as various informal means of influence. The military does not in the normal course of affairs, directly veto, provide authority for, guide, or revise foreign-policy decisions. Except in situations where security considerations predominate, the military is not usually involved in specific policy decisions; the carrying out of foreign policy is, with very rare exceptions, left to agencies with greater international legitimacy and acceptability.

The military is clearly the president's basic constituency; it is the group whose reactions to significant developments and policy initiatives are most assiduously sought out and anticipated by other groups and individuals. Yet the Brazilian Armed Forces comprises a complex and varied set of organizations, not all elements of which are likely to be satisfied by any given policy or government priority. With military interests so diverse, the administration cannot make a consecutive series of decisions designed primarily to satisfy this most crucial power factor; other considerations must also be taken into account. Most administrations have sought to follow reasonably consistent policies in regard to objectives valued by important sectors of the Armed Forces; at the same time, they have taken prudent steps to avoid the dangerous buildup of organized backlash within the military in response to measures the government has deemed necessary, even if such measures are offensive to some officer factions. Foreign policy is generally of less importance to the military than are essentially domestic political questions such as the gradual decompression of authoritarianism. Indeed, each of the several serious conflicts between the executive and the military which have occurred since 1964 has in some central way involved the military's resistance to moves designed to normalize political life by encouraging an increased role for or tolerance of the opposition. Perhaps the most dramatic and sweeping example of military-sponsored change in foreign policy was the Castelo Branco government's turnaround on policy toward foreign investors and on relations with the United States in general.

While the military clearly constituted the government's power base during the Médici administration, the military did not control all important decisions, especially those related to foreign policy. The Armed Forces did, however, set the tone and limits to foreign-policy debates, even if it did not always take a specific position on policy questions. Chosen to preside over the nation by the Armed Forces, Médici functioned as the final arbiter in policy disputes. For much of his term a considerable gap existed between the military's view of the world and that of Itamaraty, particularly when the latter saw advantages for Brazil in forcing limited confrontations with developed nations in order to extract concessions from them.

The position of President Geisel as political leader of the military has become increasingly solid as he has put his stamp upon promotions. He has met with substantial success in establishing his supremacy—as when he faced down the army minister after the November 1974 elections—but he has found it difficult to reduce the role of the Armed Forces after a history of continuing role expansion. Geisel has used what he calls "responsible ecumenical pragmatism" with some effect in an attempt to disarm the remnants of the hard-line, but these ideological guardians of the revolution must still be taken into account, at least to the extent that they still constitute islands of resistance entrenched within the security apparatus.[9]

Perhaps the most significant aspect of the transition from Médici to Geisel is the fact that military inputs into foreign-policy decision making are now more ad hoc and less generalized than was the case prior to March 1974. The president, by temperament more a centralizer than Médici, relies less on the National Security Council, where the military's input was great at the secretariat level (the chief of the Military Cabinet is the secretary general of the CSN), and places greater emphasis on the advice of specialized councils that bring together four or five ministers with common interests (e.g., the Economic Development Council and the Foreign Trade Policy Council). These councils are presided over by Geisel himself and serve as forums for real policymaking debate. Such large and formal bodies as the CSN, the Council of Ministers (cabinet), and the Armed Forces High Command meet only rarely, and then usually for ceremonial purposes.

To say that the military's impact on the foreign policy is increasingly ad hoc, however, is not to say that its influence has become less potent. On matters related to security the military has a very distinct weight—it can and does rule out certain policy choices and veto some Foreign Ministry proposals. The military is primarily concerned with nuclear policy, interdiction of movement of subversives, Brazilian policy toward Argentina, and, sporadically, matters related to the potentially delicate situation with respect to Peru, Chile, and Bolivia. Relations with Portugal have become a militarily sensitive issue, while maritime law is of concern to the navy, which also has an interest in relations with the countries of Southern Africa.

The nature of decision making within the army's high command and the manner in which its decisions influence foreign-policy matters through the National Security Council is not clear to outside observers; however, the most important link appears to be the president. Through a variety of channels and mechanisms, including—but not restricted to—the service ministers, the chiefs of staff, the military cabinet, the SNI, and the Armed Forces General Staff, Presidents Castelo, Costa, Médici, and Geisel have all kept in close touch with the views of the military.[10] Consensus views are effectively, if at times informally, communicated to the chief executive, particularly in situations that might become critical. As a general rule, however, if the officer corps is satisfied with the president's handling of domestic affairs, it generally accords him a good deal of leeway in foreign affairs. When the military is dissatisfied with international policy, it is likely to focus its hostility on the foreign minister.

The Armed Forces High Command is the military equivalent of the Economic, Social, and Political development councils. Composed of the service ministers, their chiefs of staff, and the minister-chief of the Armed Forces General Staff, this council can be used by the president to structure and channel military input into the setting of priorities and the making of basic decisions. During this administration the Armed Forces High Command has met with the president at least twice: first on June 6, 1974, to consider how to reconcile military reequipment programs with the foreign-exchange crunch and the desirability of building up domestic industry; then again on January 20, 1975, to review the world situation. Basically, this council deals with policy problems of general concern to the Armed Forces.

The Armed Forces General Staff is, by contrast, a continuously functioning body responsible directly to the president and concerned with military power and efficiency. Headed by a four-star general, with a three-star officer as his deputy and with flag-rank officers from each of the services assigned to it, the EMFA is a potential nucleus for a future defense ministry. Its chief has ministerial standing, and even now the EMFA has its own foreign service in the form of Brazil's military attachés. The Brazil–United States Mixed Military Commission and the Higher War College function under its supervision, as does the recently created war materials industry (Imbel). The minister-chief of EMFA, currently General Moacyr Potyguara, has the authority to call meetings of the Council of Chiefs of Staff (Concem), and is gradually gaining increased powers of coordination over the individual services. EMFA is concerned with planning for the future, while the Armed Forces High Command deals with current problems.

The Brazilian Armed Forces constitutes a large and far from monolithic, albeit essentially hierarchical, institution. The army—with an authorized peacetime complement of 183,000 men and an actual strength of more than 170,000— contains some 15,500 commissioned officers and 49,000 career noncoms in addition to volunteer enlisted men and conscripts. These forces are dispersed throughout Brazil under a complex command and administrative structure that is continually being modified. There are four field armies headed by four-star generals and twelve military regions commanded in most cases by three-star (divisional) generals.[11] Even more senior generals occupy posts in the Army Ministry and the Army General Staff (as well as in the bodies previously discussed in this section). The full generals as a group with the exception of the EMFA chief and the ESG commandant, constitute the Army High Command, which is frequently convened by the minister—thus bringing the army commanders into Brasília from Rio de Janeiro, São Paulo, Porto Alegre, and Recife.

The army contains a number of major branches and specialized services, and each of these specialties tends to develop its own distinct outlook; for example, the construction engineers are mainly concerned with the problems of the underdeveloped interior, while the coast artillery's domain is the Rio de Janeiro area and its more international milieu. For the senior officers, the resulting differences in perspective are tempered by a two-year study period at the General Staff and Command School and by a year-long course at the Higher War College, as well as by the large amount of time they spend in staff assignments.[12] In sum, the size and diversity of the Brazilian officer corps are such that generalizing about its views on policy matters, particularly on those related to foreign policy, is hazardous. This conclusion can be validated by reading the army's major house organs: *Segurança e Desenvolvimento, Revista Militar Brasileira, Nação Armada, Revista do Clube Militar,* and *A Defesa Nacional.* The same observation holds true for the navy and air force; the former numbers some 3,500 officers among its 49,500-man complement (which includes a marine corps of some 13,000 men), and the latter has more than 5,000 officers and subofficials out of a total strength of nearly 45,000. Thus the military officer corps in Brazil numbers some 24,000 individuals, without taking into account the officers who command the more than 185,000 men in the full-time paramilitary forces maintained by the twenty-one states and by the burgeoning security forces and militarized police forces.

In both foreign and domestic affairs the army is dominant; the air force does not appear to play a distinct role in these areas. Such is not, however, the case with the navy, whose role in foreign-policy questions is closely tied to the issue of the 200-mile territorial sea limit. Although this issue has long been of interest to certain elements within Itamaraty, for many years the navy felt that the institution of such a limit would carry with it a policing and enforcing responsibility beyond its existing capacity. After the navy shifted its stance in the late 1960s and became willing and even eager to assume the role of enforcer, Brazil moved quickly and effectively to set territorial sea limits. Recent major discoveries of petroleum on the continental shelf have been used by the navy as justification for expansion of its already ambitious building program. Younger navy officers seem increasingly drawn toward a southern cone–oriented foreign policy wherein the navy's potential mission is more dynamic than that of simply helping the United States protect the South Atlantic from the Soviet fleet. Not surprisingly, the navy has evinced substantial interest in Antarctica, a continent that most other Brazilian foreign policy agencies have ignored.

When the military feels that national security is involved, military opinion is decisively expressed. The relevant views and probable reactions of the Armed Forces are usually anticipated by the civilian rulers—certainly by the president and his chief advisers, who since 1964 have been ranking military men. For this and other reasons, a definable military input distinct from presidential opinion is often not easily identified even by local observers. Moreover, a somewhat unusual situation now prevails in that Army Minister Sílvio Couto Coelho Frota was not Geisel's choice for the post; Frota reached that position almost by happenstance after the sudden death of Gen. Dale Coutinho during the early months of Geisel's tenure. Furthermore, General Frota is widely considered to be an adversary of presidential right-hand man Golbery, whose active-duty military career ended at the level of regimental commander in 1961. Thus, Frota does not play the role that Orlando Geisel filled so effectively in Médici's administration. Following Frota's eventual replacement (he was transferred to the reserves in March 1976), the president probably will select as army minister someone who enjoys his greater confidence. At present, however, the army minister is not likely to present foreign-policy views directly to the president unless an issue were to arise on which he could speak for a sudden surge of opinion on the part of a discontented officer corps.

The military, as a consequence of its acceptance of development as the most appropriate and effective means of effecting enhanced power status for Brazil, has gone along with the general thrust of Brazilian foreign policy. To a large degree it has accepted the shifts in policy adopted by the government as a means of dealing with the increased priorities of economic imperatives as a result of the changes that occurred in 1974-1975. At times, however, the military's compliance has seemed to imply temporary acquiescence rather than permanent support. The still-developing questions associated with Angola have strained the military's confidence in Brazil's diplomacy and raised doubts about the desirable limits of third world alignment. The Armed Forces' reaction to the Foreign Ministry's moves during Angola's struggle for independence suggests that the military may be inclined to place restraints on pursuit of an "independent" foreign-policy line in regard to areas considered strategic to Brazil's security interests. Yet, significantly, military discontent has not reached the level at which the government has felt compelled to modify its policy.

The Foreign Ministry, having discovered that favoring the Afro-Asian countries is essential to any formula for achieving diplomatic gains in the fast-changing world of the 1970s, appears to have instigated Brazil's decision to recognize the Soviet-backed Popular Movement for the Liberation of Angola (MPLA). Although this decision may have been, in part, a reaction to the price Brazil paid as a result of the delay in recognizing the Marxist-Leninist regime in Mozambique, the country's move to legitimatize the MPLA was viewed as underscoring Brazil's identification with black Africa. From a diplomatic viewpoint, the controversial decision provided an opportunity for Brazil to gain points with a large number of other countries as well as to forge an early alliance with the group most likely to be governing Angola during that new nation's formative years. Moreover, the move could be rationalized as a recognition of the government in control of Luanda when the Portuguese withdrew, rather than as a preference for one contending faction in a civil war.[13]

The Brazilian Armed Forces became disturbed about both the degree of Soviet and Cuban military involvement in Angola and Russia's plans to build a naval base on the South Atlantic almost directly opposite, and only 4,500 kilometers from Brazil's eastward bulge. Many officers subscribed to the strategic view that

> the moment that a military power hostile to Brazil occupies the Atlantic coast of Africa, at any point—from Morocco to South Africa—we will begin to feel a climate of uneasiness and of war-like pressure in our country without precedent in our history. This is because, today, even a base of intermediate-range rockets installed on the West African salient could easily threaten a long strip of our Northeast bulge.[14]

At the end of December 1975, in the presence of President Geisel, the admiral commanding the Naval War College declared, "Our most legitimate interests would be affected if the control of the South Atlantic should come to belong to a superpower traditionally foreign to the ocean area contiguous to our territory."[15] Brazil's "special representation" in Angola was raised to embassy status (no ambassador was immediately named to head it, however). Although the president's year-end speech commented favorably on the good relations that had been established with Portugal's former colonies in Africa, few observers believed that Angola would cease to be a troublesome issue within decision-making circles.[16] After the victory of the MPLA, the government not only named an ambassador to Angola, but also filled the corresponding post in Mozambique. If the trade prospects in the area turn out to be as promising as those projected by the March–April 1976 special mission to Africa, the Foreign Ministry's position that Brazil needed to "arrive" ahead of the Middle Eastern and African countries on at least one Portuguese African decision may well be validated.[17]

In the ultimate analysis, the influence of the Brazilian Armed Forces on foreign policy is derived from its political role as the president's essential constituency. It is this role, rather than the global defense function on which the U.S. military's influence on foreign policy rests, that determines the range and character of the military's international interests and policy impact. However, while the combination of its expanding security interests and its enormous political influence does give the Armed Forces a substantial voice in the basic orientation of Brazil's foreign policy, the Brazilian military lacks the interlocking leverage achieved by the U.S. military as a result of its massive and worldwide role. Although the Brazilian Armed Forces has begun to furnish material aid and limited training to several smaller neighbors, it is still primarily a recipient of military aid—chiefly from the United States, through the latter's scaled-down but still significant military assistance program.[18]

Although there does not seem to be much formal communication between the military and the Foreign Ministry in regard to policy matters, Itamaraty policymakers, through their family and social connections with the military, appear to have a fairly accurate general view of the military's position on foreign-policy issues. Some members of the military, however, perceive certain diplomatic personnel as being not sufficiently Brazilian in their outlook—in other words, as being striped-pants cosmopolitans. Foreign service personnel, for the most part—while perhaps resenting military overseeing of their activities—appear to accept this imposition as a fact of life.

Notes to Chapter 3

[1]The documentary data available on substantive policy is not matched in the realm of policymaking studies. Roger W. Fontaine's dissertation, "The Foreign Policymaking Process in Brazil" (Johns Hopkins University, 1970), does not deal with the last two governments and is light even on the 1964-1969 period. His *Brazil and the United States: Toward a Maturing Relationship* (American Enterprise Institute for Public Policy Research, 1974) adds relatively little to his previous work. Few other studies even touch upon this subject. In addition to data from published sources and limited field research undertaken during eleven trips to Brazil in the last seventeen years, this composite picture of foreign policymaking during the past four governments relies on a score of interviews held with U.S. foreign-service personnel with relevant experience in Brazil during the period since 1964. Where interpretations of these observers differed, varying weights were assigned their views on the basis of length of service, level and scope of responsibility, and frequency, intensity, and range of contacts with the Brazilian foreign-affairs community as well as of congruence with findings from other sources.

[2]See Luíz Viana Filho, *O Governo Castelo Branco* (Rio de Janeiro: José Olympio Editôra, 1975), pp. 428-451.

[3]These matters are reasonably well covered in Keith Larry Storrs' Ph.D. dissertation, "Brazil's Independent Foreign Policy, 1961-1964: Background, Tenets, Linkage to Domestic Politics, and Aftermath" (Cornell University, 1973). Critical Brazilian treatments include Carlos Estevam Martins, "Brazil and the United States from the 1960s to the 1970s," in Julio Cotler and Richard R. Fagen (eds.), *Latin America and the United States: The Changing Political Realities* (Palo Alto, Calif.: Stanford University Press, 1974); and Moniz Bandeira, *Presença dos Estados Unidos no Brasil* (Rio de Janeiro: Editôra Civilização Brasileira, 1973).

[4]Castelo's presidential decision-making style is discussed in Viana Filho, *O Governo*, pp. 496-521.

[5]Ibid., pp. 446-451. Participants in the September 1965 decision, in addition to the president, included Gens. Ernesto Geisel and Golbery do Couto e Silva (chief of the Military Cabinet and director of the National Intelligence Service, respectively), the chief of the Armed Forces General Staff, the heads of the National Nuclear Energy Commission and the National Research Council, Ambassador José Sette Câmara Filho (Brazil's representative in the nuclear negotiations), and Corrêa da Costa as the Foreign Ministry's responsible official at the assistant-secretary level.

[6]Corrêa da Costa was deeply concerned with restrictions which might have had the effect of curtailing technological development as well as infringing upon Brazilian sovereignty, a position which during the Castelo Branco administration was not viewed with any noticeable sympathy by Planning Minister Roberto Campos, a professional diplomat who had entered the foreign service at the same time as Corrêa da Costa (in 1938) and an advocate of close cooperation with the United States where he had served as ambassador prior to 1964. As assistant secretary general for International Organizations, Corrêa da Costa organized a course on nuclear technology for thirty-five Brazilian diplomats (with the blessing of then-minister Juracy Malgalhães). Subsequently, as Pio Corrêa's successor as secretary general in 1967-1968, Corrêa da Costa brought Paulo Nogueira Baptista—who would later become the first head of Nuclebrás—into a staff position where he could develop into the ministry's ranking nuclear expert. Corrêa da Costa personally believed that Brazil's peaceful nuclear needs might go as far as some important "geographic engineering" projects such as the opening of a canal connecting the Amazon and River Plate basins. His near crusade in carrying the nuclear question, not only into university and military institutions, but also to television audiences and professional groups, raised Brazilian consciousness of scientific backwardness and the need for transfer of technology. It also brought him under heavy press attack, particularly from those newspapers under greatest U.S. influence. In May 1968 he was named ambassador to the United Kingdom, where he remained throughout the Médici government and into the initial stages of the Geisel administration.

[7]Reconstructions by political journalists have become substantially more complete after the fact than was the case during the actual decision. (See, for example, "Retrospecto e Perspectivas da Sucessão Presidential," *Visão*, March 22, 1976, pp. 18-22.) President Médici's public pronouncements during his first year in office are collected in *O Jôgo da Verdade*

(Brasília: Departamento de Imprensa Nacional, 1970), *Nova Consciência de Brasil* (Brasília: DIN, 1970), and *A Verdadeira Paz* (Brasília: DIN, 1971).

[8]An analysis by a longtime Brazilian political observer stressing Geisel's concern with keeping informed on all matters and avoiding complete or exclusive delegation of authority is David Nasser's "Delfim e Simonsen, um soriso, uma lágrima," *Manchete*, April 24, 1976, pp. 54-57. The antecedents of Geisel's councils may be found in Castelo's "sectoral meetings" with the inner group on economic and financial affairs of the 1964-1967 period (now institutionalized as the Economic Development Council). Viana Filho, who was minister-chief of the Civil Cabinet under Castelo, implies that there might be less of the Eisenhower type of temporizing from Geisel than was the case with Castelo. A series of conversations in Brazil during July 1976 underscored President Geisel's increasing tendency to make decisions personally, with close attention to details.

[9]Historical divisions within the Brazilian military are discussed at length in this author's *The Political System of Brazil: Emergence of a "Modernizing" Authoritarian Regime, 1964-1970* (New York: Columbia University Press, 1971), and in Alfred Stepan, *The Military in Politics: Changing Patterns in Brazil* (Princeton, N.J.: Princeton University Press, 1971). A brief treatment can be found in Fontaine, *Brazil and the United States*, pp. 72-93.

[10]It is clear, for example, that Castelo maintained an active correspondence with lower-ranking officers who had served as his aides and encouraged them to express their personal doubts and reservations concerning his policies in a frank manner (even though he would not allow such leeway in public utterances even by the same officers). See Viana Filho, *O Governo*, for evidences of this tendency.

[11]Consult Schneider, *Political System of Brazil*, pp. 299-300, for a fuller description of the command structure. Legislation of November 1974 set the number of active-duty general officers at 129 (10 four-star, 37 three-star, and 82 at the level of general of brigade). Also authorized were 550 colonels, 1,380 lieutenant colonels, 1,800 majors, 4,500 captains, and 7,000 lieutenants. Sergeants were limited to 35,500 along with 132,000 corporals and privates. In addition to the chief of staff and the commanders of the four field armies, active-duty four-star generals head the five major departments of the Army Ministry. The army minister is most often an active-duty general, but need not be by law. The EMFA and ESG heads are usually active-duty four-star generals, so there may be as many as 13 in this category at any one time. Nearly half the

three-star generals command military regions or army divisions; 10 or 11 others serve in the Army Ministry and six on the Army General Staff. It is customary for other officers at this level to be assigned as the president's Military Cabinet chief, the deputy commandant of the ESG, director of the SNI, and vice-chief of the EMFA. Consult *O Estado de S. Paulo*, March 5, 1976, for a complete listing, including the posts for two-star officers.

[12]Schneider, *Political System of Brazil*, pp. 244-257.

[13]*Veja*, January 14, 1976.

[14]Meira Mattos, *Brasil*, p. 75.

[15]*Veja*, December 31, 1975, p. 23.

[16]*Veja*, January 7, 1976, pp. 29-30.

[17]See *Visão*, December 8, 1975, pp. 28-30. The Brazilian trade mission was headed by Minister Paulo Tarso Flecha de Lima, chief of the Trade Promotion Department of Itamaraty, and included representatives of the Planning Secretariat, the Foreign Exchange Department of the Central Bank, the Brazilian Coffee Institute, and Petrobrás' newly launched trading company. See also *O Estado de S. Paulo*, March 25, 1976.

[18]Through fiscal years 1950-1973 the United States trained 7,883 Brazilian military personnel (fifteenth place in terms of such U.S. programs); of those trained in the United States, the total of 7,001 Brazilians ranks thirteenth. See Ernest W. Lefever, "The Military Assistance Training Program" *The Annals of the American Academy of Political and Social Science* 424 (March 1976), p. 87.

4
The
Foreign
Ministry

The Foreign Ministry (generally referred to as Itamaraty) is not particularly prominent within the inner councils of the Geisel government. Not surprisingly, the Foreign Ministry— and especially the foreign minister himself—tends to respond somewhat defensively to the suggestion or even the implication that it is not the central actor in the Brazilian foreign-policy process. (There has been talk in Brasília about the possibility of establishing a foreign policy council, which would of course include the foreign minister—but also, at least the ministers of finance, industry and commerce, and mines and energy, and probably the chief of the Armed Forces General Staff. Itamaraty personnel appear divided on the question of whether the formal recognition of these rivals' voices in foreign policy would nullify the benefits gained by including the foreign minister in a policymaking body chaired personally by the president.) While Itamaraty is involved to some degree in all aspects of foreign-policy formulation, it does not have the deciding voice on major issues. This is particularly true with respect to fundamental decisions stemming from development imperatives that, although originally rooted in domestic considerations, profoundly condition or limit foreign-policy options. During the Médici period—particularly during 1970-1973, when the president was not over concerned with foreign policy and Foreign Minister Mário Gibson Barbosa had considerable political clout—Itamaraty frequently initiated specific proposals in the realm of political relations—but only when important economic or strategic considerations were not involved. Silveira during 1976 seems to have brought the Foreign Ministry back to at least this position—an improvement over the initial phase of the Geisel administration, when its autonomy appears to have been more restricted—perhaps because he has survived in office longer than many expected.

The Foreign Ministers

Gibson Barbosa, as Itamaraty's secretary general under José Magalhães Pinto during the second half of the Costa e Silva administration, had been able to move his men into many key positions within the Foreign Ministry. When he became minister in the Médici government, he ran a tight ship; decisions flowed from above and there was relatively little flexibility at the working level. He tried to convince the military that he was sincerely concerned with national security in order to gain the latter's acceptance of policies that involved some degree of confrontation with the United States, because he was aware that if the military perceived him as unreliable or "soft" in security matters, it would not trust him.

Ambassador to Argentina from 1969 to March 1974, Antônio Francisco Azeredo da Silveira was selected by Geisel as head of Itamaraty in order to dramatize the priority he planned to afford Brazil's relations with her neighbors, particularly Argentina. As Brazil's chief delegate to the United Nations agencies in Geneva from 1966 to 1968, Silveira had taken a strongly nationalistic stance on the nuclear nonproliferation treaty, a position initiated by the Foreign Ministry secretary general, Sérgio Corrêa da Costa (who subsequently became ambassador to Great Britain and, later, head of Brazil's mission to the United Nations in New York). When Costa e Silva failed to secure military approval for Silveira's nomination as secretary general of Itamaraty, Silveira embarked on a relatively long stint in Buenos Aires, where he had served in 1949-1950. Because he had spent so much time in Latin American posts (he also served in Cuba from 1945 to 1949), and had not served in the United States (except as a very junior official in San Francisco from 1937 to 1941), Silveira's perspective differed from that of most other senior career diplomats. During his tenure as head of the Foreign Ministry's Department of Administration from 1963 to 1966, some diplomatic observers noted that he was one of the few senior Itamaraty officials who did not trim their sails in conformance with the abrupt change in governmental orientation after Goulart was replaced by Castelo Branco; indeed, Silveira continued to advocate such advanced policies as recognition of Communist China.

The appointment of career diplomats to the Foreign Ministry is a rather recent development in Brazil. While the Baron of Rio Branco (December 1902–February 1912) was a highly effective diplomat, he was a politician rather than a career diplomat. The choice of relatively major political figures for the post of foreign minister was the rule during the Vargas era, and this pattern continued through the Kubitschek, Quadros, and Goulart periods. Francisco Negrão de Lima (1958-1959) subsequently served as governor of Guanabara; his successor, Horácio Lafer (1959-1961) was a São Paulo businessman-politician; Affonso Arinos de Mello Franco (albeit a former diplomat and son of a former foreign minister) was best known as a scholar and legislator, as was Francisco Clementino de San Tiago Dantas (who served from September 1961 to August 1962, when Affonso Arinos briefly resumed the post). Changes during Goulart's presidency were particularly frequent; lawyers Hermes Lima and Evandro Lins e Silva headed Itamaraty for only nine months and two months, respectively, after San Tiago Dantas' ten-month tenure and Affonso Arinos' two-month reprise. A career ambassador, João Augusto de Araújo Castro, was brought in to hold things together during the last seven months of Goulart's ill-fated regime.

The military also turned first to a career diplomat, Vasco Leitão da Cunha (April 1964–January 1966), before bringing in two political figures, Juracy Magalhães (January 1966–March 1967) and José Magalhães Pinto (March 1967–October 1969).[1] Ambassador Mário Gibson Barbosa served as foreign minister throughout the Médici government, with Ambassador Antônio Azeredo da Silveira succeeding him in March 1974. Thus, since the military took power at the end of March 1964, career diplomats have headed Itamaraty for all but three years and nine months (1966-1969).

Three of the four career men to head the Foreign Ministry had had previous experience as secretary general, the Brazilian equivalent of deputy secretary of state. The one exception is the present incumbent, Silveira, whose nomination for the latter office in the late 1960s was vetoed by important military elements who did not care for his brother's leftist political affiliations. Yet Silveira did hold the post of head of the Department of Administration, Itamaraty's closest equivalent to deputy under secretary of state. This precedent would lead one to believe that the field of future candidates for foreign minister might include the following diplomats: Sérgio Corrêa da Costa, chief of Brazil's U.N. delegation and former ambassador to Great Britain; Jorge de Carvalho e Silva, now ambassador in Rome; and Ramiro Elysio Saraiva Guerreiro, the present secretary general. Both Manuel Pio Corrêa Júnior, who served as secretary general under Juracy Magalhães, and the former's predecessor, Antônio Borges Leal Castello Branco Filho, appear less likely to reach the top spot in Itamaraty, although they might be included in the list of potential candidates. Another possible candidate, Roberto de Oliveira Campos (now ambassador in London), has an atypical background: he headed the Planning Ministry throughout the Castelo Branco administration. Another dark horse is Ambassador José Sette Camara Filho, who served as chief of the Civil Cabinet during Kubitschek's presidency and as governor of Guanabara.[2]

The Inner Circle

The inner circle of Itamaraty is composed of a half-dozen individuals in daily personal contact with the foreign minister. Most prominent among these is the secretary general; next is the minister's chief of staff (*chefe do gabinete*), along with his immediate deputies. Then comes the chief of the Department of Administration, a position somewhat analagous to that of our under secretary for management. It is this small group, rather than the corps of geographic and functional department heads (who correspond to the assistant secretaries in our State Department), that plays a leading role in policymaking at the ministerial level. At present this core group, which is characterized by an unusual degree of economics expertise, is somewhat cool toward the United States, believing that the two nations' interests frequently do not coincide.

Secretary Gen. Ramiro Elysio Saraiva Guerreiro, fifty-seven, a senior ambassador who served as head of Brazil's Mission to the United Nations agencies in Geneva, works closely with the foreign minister's chief of staff, Luíz Augusto Pereira Souto Maior, a forty-nine-year-old minister first class who was his minister counselor in Geneva. The foreign minister's special adviser is Geraldo Egydio da Costa Holanda Cavalcanti, forty-seven, a rapidly rising minister second class whose most recent assignments were in New York (where he represented the Brazilian Coffee Institute from 1967 to 1970) and Hong Kong. The Department of Administration is headed by Dário Moreira de Castro Alves, forty-eight, a minister first class who was *chefe do gabinete* for Silveira's predecessor.[3] Also in the inner circle is Economics Department chief Paulo Cabral de Mello, fifty-one, a minister first class who was Silveira's minister counselor in Buenos Aires. Having earned a master's degree in economics at Harvard, Cabral de Mello is frequently Silveira's choice to head Brazilian

delegations to international meetings where economic considerations are paramount. Gilberto Coutinho Paranhos Velloso,
José Nogueira Filho, and Luíz Felipe Palmeira Lampreia, all
relatively junior counselors (promoted to that rank during
1975), round out the minister's personal staff. The first, with
the title of deputy chief of cabinet, deals primarily with
those elements of the ministry involved with Europe and
Africa. Nogueira is political adviser for Latin American affairs, while Lampreia is the minister's economic and commercial adviser.

Representing Brazil at many international meetings is Ambassador George Alvares Maciel, now following in the foot-
steps of Silveira and Saraiva Guerreiro as Brazil's representative to international governmental organizations in Geneva.
Ambassador to Peru in 1969-1970 and subsequently head of
Brazil's delegation to the OAS, this fifty-five-year-old economist appears to be Silveira's man in Western Europe (where
both Campos in London and Delfim Netto in Paris enjoy a
high degree of relative autonomy). Another senior diplomat
linked fairly closely to the Itamaraty inner circle is Miguel
Alvaro Ozório de Almeida, fifty-eight, a minister first class
who finished a long stint in Brasília in January 1975. Personal
adviser to Magalhães Pinto on science policy, technology, and
similar matters, he stayed on under Gibson Barbosa as policy
planner, a position he held through the first ten months of
Silveira's stewardship. Formerly economic counselor to Brazil's U.N. mission, Ozório has a reputation as one of the most
aggressive nationalists among Brazil's senior career diplomats.

The Institution

Silveira and his lieutenants preside over a ministry organized geographically into departments for the Americas, for
Europe, and for Africa-Asia. There are, as well, a number of
functional departments such as those dealing with economic
affairs and trade promotion. Three divisions of the Department of the Americas deal with South American affairs;
another covers all of North and Central America, including
the United States and the Caribbean. This last organization

manifests the latent friction within the ministry between Silveira's men, who are largely Spanish speaking, and the U.S.-Western Europe oriented officers, who disapprove of the emphasis placed on relations with Hispanic America. During the most recent transition within Itamaraty, considerable confusion was generated by Silveira's insistence on placing his own men in important positions with the result that many career officers routinely returning for tours in Brasília had to be immediately reassigned abroad.

Brazil has had a rigorously professional career-diplomatic service since well before World War II, with entrance determined by examination and promotions awarded essentially on merit. A 1951 law requires two-to-three years of service in the Foreign Ministry after every four-to-six years abroad; hence Itamaraty is staffed by foreign-service officers who have had recent field experience and who expect to go overseas again soon. Since 1949 some 6,000 candidates have taken the rigorous entrance examinations for the Rio Branco Institute, Brazil's foreign-service academy, and about 600 graduates now constitute the bulk of the nearly-700-member diplomatic service.[4] The policymaking positions within the ministry as well as ambassadorial posts overseas are held by the 72 ministers first class and 96 ministers second class. The average minister first class is almost fifty-eight years old and has thirty-four years of diplomatic experience, while ministers in the latter classification are about seven years younger and have correspondingly less experience. Candidates for this elite group are found among the 110 career diplomats, average age forty-six, who hold the rank of counselor (*conselheiro*); in addition, a few of the 120 first secretaries hold administrative positions which permit them to help shape specific policies. Since the typical first secretary is just under forty with roughly fifteen years of diplomatic service, the impact of any changes in recruitment policies would be considerably delayed. The 134 second secretaries and 154 third secretaries (the equivalents of FSOs 5, 6, 7, and 8 in the U.S. foreign service) are at least ten years away from policy-level positions.

Although in recent years there has been a slow broadening

of its traditionally narrow social and geographical base of recruitment, the Brazilian diplomatic service still is an elite body that has a good deal of generational and familial continuity. Its rigorous foreign-language requirements and its demand that applicants obtain a university education before taking the entrance examinations for the Rio Branco Institute give a decided advantage to candidates from the upper classes. Only very limited provisions exist for bypassing the institute by direct examination, and only now is Brazil broadening the base from which it recruits students into its essentially elitist educational system; hence the Foreign Ministry is likely to draw its career officers from the upper classes for some years to come.[5] In conjunction with the deeply rooted preference for an evolutionary and incremental approach to change which has characterized Brazilian diplomacy for decades, Itamaraty's elitist recruitment policies encourage an environment in which

> the system of recruitment and discipline, plus the institutional aura of respect for tradition and the "spirit of Itamaraty," has produced a distinct foreign-office outlook on international affairs. It is nationalist, but more pragmatic than romantic. It is oriented toward Europe and not America. It emphasizes perservation of good relations with old friends, but not at the expense of making new ones. It entails a desire for a larger Brazilian role on the world scene, but it does not exaggerate the nation's present prospects for world power.[6]

United States diplomats who have served in Brazil frequently comment on the "Itamaraty ethos," the widely shared common outlook of Foreign Ministry decision makers. Seriousness of purpose and a desire to advance Brazil's interests characterize this basic outlook, which some U.S. observers see as a "less-developed-countries, left-nationalist" stance and which others see as "an increasingly independent view expressed in generally nonconfrontational ways." A major feature of the Itamaraty ethos seems to be a fundamentally confident nationalism that has little need for stridency. (As Brazil nears major-power status, its nationalistic posture is shedding most remaining traces of defensiveness.) The commonality of outlook among Brazilian diplomats, which often is ascribed to shared experiences at the Rio Branco Institute and to the clublike nature of Itamaraty, also seems related to the recruitment and socialization processes within the foreign service. Given the fact that other good jobs are readily available in Brazil's expanding economy, officers who are disgruntled or frustrated are likely to leave the service; other mavericks may be passed over for promotion and weeded out, thus increasing the homogeneity of this somewhat corporative body. (It should be noted that Silveira has appreciably improved conditions of pay and life for career officers in Brasília.)

Role in Major Policies

Brazilian diplomats are able to learn from experience; they are prone to engage in a continuing reassessment of the opportunities and challenges presented by changing international conditions, all the more so if the president leads the way. Thus, Brazil's substantial shift toward alignment with the Arab world in 1974 represented a modification of traditional policies so as to serve national interests; vital economic concerns took priority over traditional political considerations. The fact that this policy change was instituted at a time when the foreign minister was trying to appear more nationalistic than other ministers, while actively resisting encroachments by the powerful finance minister, makes this case one that affords important insights into Brazilian foreign policy-making.

The tipping of Brazilian policy toward the Arabs in the Mideast conflict closely coincides with the escalation of the worldwide energy crisis. Gibson Barbosa's trips to Egypt and Israel in February 1973 seemed to presage a continuance of Brazil's equidistant stance; he reaffirmed Brazil's "evenhanded" policy of impartiality as late as October 1973. Just three months later, however, he was publicly expressing sympathy for the plight of the Palestinian refugees—after the Arabs had indicated, in late January 1974, that such support would be required if Brazil wished to continue receiving Middle East oil.[7] The pro-Arab trend picked up steam with the change of administration, as Silveira quickly moved to express Brazil's agreement with Arab views on occupied territories and Palestinian rights.

However, the balance of policymaking power as well as the content of policy changed as Petrobrás and the full range of economic agencies participated in a concentrated effort to multiply Brazilian exports to the Middle East. Their goal was to attract Arab investment dollars to Brazil, thus stemming the increased outflow of Brazil's currency reserves. More than any other ministry or agency, the Mines and Energy Ministry, under Shigeaki Ueki, benefited from these developments, as Braspetro and the Vale do Rio Doce Co. expanded their role in foreign-policy concerns. Thus, in November 1974, Ueki and Reis Velloso, not Silveira, headed a special mission to Saudi Arabia and Kuwait; a followup delegation in December included representatives of the Finance Ministry, the Bank of Brazil, and the National Economic Development Bank as well as Itamaraty officials.

If the steady erosion of the Foreign Ministry's once-central role in policy formulation has put Itamaraty on the defensive, Silveira has been trying to regain control and prestige by devising such strategies as calling periodic ministerial-level meetings on bilateral matters under his aegis. (The United States recently agreed to participate in a series of such meetings.) On occasion, he has invoked the image of Henry Kissinger to underscore the need for a powerful and prestigious central figure who would personify the country's international policies. His success has been limited, however; obviously he is swimming upstream against a strong current. Both recent history and current events appear to be working against Silveira's efforts to expand Itamaraty's role in making the major decisions that define Brazil's objectives in the international arena, although the picture is somewhat more promising with respect to questions of more narrowly circumscribed policy.

The nuclear field offers an important example of Itamaraty's waning impact on decisions that vitally affect foreign policy. Although the Foreign Ministry substantially influenced Brazilian nuclear policy during the last stages of the Castelo Branco government and the first months of the Costa e Silva administration, at the time the basic nuclear issue was clearly related to foreign policy: Would Brazil subscribe to a Latin American nuclear free zone, which its diplomats had championed prior to 1964, or would it pay a potentially high diplomatic price in order to maintain its freedom of action? With a determined policymaker, Corrêa da Costa, willing to put his career on the line, the Foreign Ministry carried the day. But when the focus of the issue shifted away from international treaties and toward nuclear energy policy for Brazilian development, Itamaraty's role was sharply curtailed—first by the October 1967 National Security Council ruling, and subsequently by Gibson Barbosa's decision to replace Corrêa da Costa. By 1968, the Foreign Ministry's attempt to promote an independent stance in the development of atomic energy technology had been effectively rebuffed by the military and by Mines and Energy Minister Costa Cavalcanti.

Brazil did, however, refuse to sign the nuclear nonproliferation treaty in order to maintain its freedom to seek a nuclear capability, ostensibly for peaceful purposes.[8] Technical assistance treaties in the atomic field were subsequently negotiated with Canada, Germany, France, and Israel, in addition to the United States, and Brazil's plans to obtain nuclear power plants went forward.[9] Because the October 1967 National Security Council resolution had established independent nuclear energy capability as a Permanent National Objective, the highest level of goals in Brazil's National Security Doctrine, the question was no longer whether, but rather how best to accomplish this. It was within this context that Magalhães Pinto and Willy Brandt signed a scientific and technological cooperation agreeement on behalf of their two governments on June 9, 1969, and in April 1971 the National

Nuclear Energy Commission (CNEN) entered into a cooperative accord with the Julich Nuclear Research Center.[10]

During the Médici government the Brazilian Nuclear Technology Co. was established in 1972 under the CNEN. Both
were headed by Hervásio Guimarães de Carvalho, an advocate
of close cooperation with the United States in this area.
These agencies decided to go ahead with the Westinghouse
project for Angra I in 1972. Subsequently, the Nuclear Technology Co. was replaced by Nuclebrás during the Geisel regime, with Paulo Nogueira Baptista (former chief of the Economic Department of Itamaraty) as its president. Although
Nuclebrás enjoyed a certain degree of autonomy, it is under
the supervisory purview of Mines and Energy Minister Ueki,
perhaps Geisel's favorite young technocrat.

The foundation had already been laid, but the decision to
go all out for a comprehensive program in alliance with the
German Federal Republic was not made until the latter half
of 1974. First the new administration of Ernesto Geisel
dropped the idea of importing the reactors for Angra II and
Angra III from the United States, in light of that country's
perceived violation, in July 1974, of its commitment to provide the enriched uranium fuel the reactors would require.
Behind "walls of caution and discretion," negotiations with
the Bonn government went forward. Much of the initiative
came from Mines and Energy Minister Ueki, with the approval of the president and the National Security Council, while
the Foreign Ministry provided effective "logistical support."[11] Events moved swiftly following the high-level
Strauss mission to Brasília; by February 12, 1975, a half-year
later, basic agreement had been reached on the dimensions
and terms of the deal. Even after this point, debate within
the Brazilian government was limited to a select group, with
Congress excluded until after the accords were actually
signed. Faithful to their gentlemen's agreement with the German government, Brazilian spokesmen maintained a restrained silence in the face of rising international clamor.

In sorting out the roles of the several actors involved on
the Brazilian side, it seems clear that Ueki was the key figure
who helped engineer a compromise between the advocates of

a "dependent" road, requiring continued cooperation with the United States and its close North Atlantic allies, and partisans of the "independent" route to nuclear self-sufficiency.[12] Moreover, it was Finance Minister Simonsen who negotiated the major purchase agreements in West Germany (although the embassy in Bonn had done a good deal of spade work).[13] Electrobrás, a state corporation under the supervision of the minister of mines and energy, had projected a need for 50 million kilowatts of installed generating capacity by 1985 and 70 to 80 million kilowatts by 1990. Given the lack of suitable hydroelectric potential near some major population centers and the prohibitive cost of fuel oil, Brazil's top policymakers chose to purchase complect power plants from Germany with favorable provisions for the significant transfer of nuclear technology. The West German pressurized-water reactors with enriched uranium fuel and light water, it was envisioned, would meet the need for power while enabling Brazil to gain mastery of first-generation reactors, develop some production capability, and participate in the development of a new enrichment process.[14] The plan also called for the training of nearly 10,000 scientific and technical personnel for this new industry, at a cost of several hundred millions of dollars.

While Itamaraty won a minor victory in January 1975 when a career diplomat was named to head Nuclebrás, on the whole the Foreign Ministry has had little say in decisions with important foreign-policy ramifications. The truth of this statement can be verified by a glance at the recent history of Brazil's armaments and weapons acquisitions: Itamaraty appears to have had only a limited voice in decisions related either to arms sales to neighboring buffer states or to other actions taken by the military in regard to these countries. In many ways, however, the limitations on Itamaraty's role are even more significant in the economic realm.

Economic Policymaking

As more and more aspects of Brazil's international relations come to center on technical and technological considerations, the relative lack of expertise in these areas evidenced

by Brazil's professional diplomats has resulted in the elevation of internationally oriented technocrats in other ministries and agencies to key positions in policymaking and international negotiations. Although Itamaraty is actively seeking
to remedy its technological shortcomings, its progress is
bound to be slow unless significant provisions are made for
the lateral entry of experts into the foreign service at mid-
grade or senior levels.

The Brazilian foreign service has valued representation and
negotiation more than other skills; hence the curriculum of
the Rio Branco Institute does not include advanced economics, and its entrance examination and admission requirements
demand competency in foreign languages and a liberal education in the British tradition. During the 1950s and early
1960s Itamaraty's few good economics specialists—most of
whom had purused graduate studies on their own initiative
while assigned to Washington, New York, London, or Paris—
were siphoned off to agencies directly concerned with economic matters. Among the economists diverted by this si-
phoning-off process were Roberto Campos, Edmundo Barbosa da Silva, José Maria Vilar de Queiroz, and Marcilio
Marques Moreira (who subsequently enjoyed a meteoric rise
within the financial hierarchy of the state of Guanabara before moving into the private sector). Thus, it has been a major problem to retain as well as to recruit and develop economics specialists within Itamaraty. Compounding the problem is the increasing tendency of junior officers with economics training to leave the foreign service for the higher pay
and more rapid advancement offered by the private sector.
Then too, with advances in economics training in Brazil, the
quality of competitors in other agencies keeps rising, thus
canceling many of the foreign service's gains in this respect.
Moreover, many of the qualified economists in the Brazilian
foreign service are needed to staff embassies abroad, and
Itamaraty does not wish to go outside its ranks to appoint
economic counselors from economic agencies independent of
the Foreign Ministry; rather, it prefers to increase the capabilities of its career diplomats by giving them experience in such

positions. Paradoxically, the foreign service finds itself—in relative terms, at least—becoming less important, not more important, at a time when foreign affairs is really beginning to matter for Brazil; its loss of importance stems from the fact that Brazil's expanding international role has been keyed to economic goals rather than to diplomatic goals.[15]

While the Brazilian delegation to the Working Group on Science and Technology Transfer, which met in Brasília in June 1974, was composed almost entirely of Itamaraty personnel rather than technology users, it appears that so many government agencies were interested in this matter that all could not possibly be represented within the Brazilian delegation. Therefore, all were placed on call as advisers, thus avoiding the bureaucratic rivalries that might have resulted if a few had been included and others excluded. Such a compromise was suitable for a conference held in Brazil; however, it clearly would not work for meetings abroad. Thus, the Brazilian delegation to the September 1974 world energy conference included numerous representatives of private and mixed companies as well as representatives of public agencies; fifty-three individuals represented twenty-three organizations.

Perhaps another clue to foreign-policy decision making is to be found in the range of agencies holding discussions with important foreign delegations that visit Brazil. When Venezuelan Planning Minister Gumersindo Rodrigues came to Brasília at the beginning of April 1974 to boost his proposal for a Latin American economic system (SELA), he met with all six economics-related ministries, the head of the National Economic Development Bank, and Reis Velloso as well as the foreign minister and the president.

It appears that Brazilian institutional and representational arrangements in bilateral dealings with the United States have tended to be influenced by the pattern Washington adopts. If the United States prefers functional lines, Brazil will nearly always follow this lead; if the United States chooses to negotiate through diplomatic channels, Brasília is likely to do the same. In multilateral arenas Brazil looks to what the major powers are doing as a measure of what is appropriate.

Otherwise, when a high degree of diplomatic negotiations seems to be involved, Itamaraty is likely to get the nod; but when the agenda seems to call for technical expertise or international prestige, the president may well ask one of his several cosmopolitan functional ministers to represent Brazil. Moreover, since the appointment of Roberto Campos, the dominant figure of the Castelo government, as ambassador to the United Kingdom and the naming of Delfim Netto, the superminister of Costa and Médici administrations, to head Brazil's embassy in Paris, these two men have been available for international conferences in Western Europe.

Itamaraty Approach

Brazilian officials generally take a common-sense approach to broad policy questions; they try to retain flexibility and avoid frozen positions. While Foreign Ministry personnel may at times appear somewhat more ideological, if not dogmatic, than other Brazilian negotiators (who are generally intent on the practical outcome), this is partly the result of their desire to maintain overall consistency in Brazilian international policy. Their training and experience afford Itamaraty officials a keen awareness of the limitations of Brazil's present world role; this awareness makes their approach appear relatively traditional in comparison with some economic technocrats and military planners, who may display more enthusiasm about grand schemes and new departures. Yet these "traditional" diplomats have been able to minimize the significant or lasting adverse impact of controversial or even confrontational Brazilian initiatives such as the establishment of a 200-mile limit for its territorial seas. Indeed, as a result of their relatively supple and flexible diplomacy, the Brazilians have developed considerable skill at responding to foreign pressures. Many U.S. officials rate them as capable negotiators, especially skillful at playing off one country against another, to Brazil's benefit.

In recent years Itamaraty may have wished to demonstrate to the military that it can effectively foster as well as protect Brazil's national interests. Certainly the Foreign Ministry has been quick to pick up, if not originate, such slogans as "responsible pragmatism," "ecumenism," "no automatic alignments," "a Brazilian neither satellizing nor satellized," and the recent "horizontal interdependence, yes; vertical interdependence, no!" Beyond merely mouthing slogans, however, Brazilian negotiators have given operational content to these concepts.

In general terms, Itamaraty officials and those in related agencies seem to enjoy little greater freedom of action than do their U.S. foreign service counterparts. The fact that working-level officials in Brasília seem to spend a good deal of their time in meetings with superior officers seems to suggest that they do not benefit from broad delegation of authority by the responsible policymaking officers (who are at least the equivalent of our assistant secretaries of state). This observation is consistent with the fact that the Foreign Ministry does not primarily initiate policy, at least on major questions, but rather tries to effectively implement goals set collectively—except to the extent that it can attain some degree of autonomy over essentially technical "diplomatic" matters of representation and negotiation. But with Brazilian foreign policy largely viewed as merely an adjunct to broader considerations of security and development, even the latter task is difficult.

Role in Communist-Country Relations

A look at the establishment of diplomatic relations with the People's Republic of China provides useful insight into foreign policy-making. The recognition accorded the Peking regime on August 15, 1974, reflected a combination of factors: desire for economic benefits, reaction to perceived international changes, and inclinations toward greater independence in foreign policy, concomitant with Brazil's upwardly mobile or maturing position in international affairs.

The evolution of Brazilian policy on this question began in 1971, when businessman Horácio Coimbra was provided with an "unofficial" Foreign Ministry escort on his trip to the Canton Trade Fair (a move he checked out first with the SNI director).[16] Representatives of the Association of Brazilian Exporters subsequently made visits to mainland China in 1972 and again in April 1974. On the April trip, the private-sector trade delegation headed by Guilite Coutinho was accompanied by Carlos Antônio Bettancourt Bueno, chief of Itamaraty's Asian division, as well as by representatives of the planning minister and the Ministry of Industry and Commerce. (Bettancourt Bueno had published an article favoring relations with China in the December 1973 issue of *Revista do Clube Militar*.) Meanwhile, Communist China had emerged as the second-largest purchaser of Brazilian sugar during 1973, diplomatic relations with the East German Communist regime had been established in October 1973, and Brazil had experienced a change of governments on March 15, 1974. Moreover, the United States' proposal for détente with Communist China, in conjunction with President Nixon's highly publicized venture in personal diplomacy, had helped thaw the attitudes of Brazil's most influential policymakers.

It appears that the outgoing administration had made no firm decision to send an official delegation to accompany the Brazilian exporters, although such a move may have been advocated by Ambassador Miguel Alvaro Ozório de Almeida, chief of Itamaraty's special advisory staff and one of the few key officials held over from the Médici government. A China expert by way of an earlier assignment as consul general in Hong Kong, he was given a new deputy in the person of Geraldo Egydio da Costa Holanda Cavalcanti, who had been recalled from Bonn to serve as an adviser to the new foreign minister. (Holanda Cavalcanti, Brazil's most recent consul general in Hong Kong, had escorted the original trade mission to mainland China in 1971.) At the same time that Itamaraty apparently convinced the president of the value of giving official standing to the trade mission, an interministerial committee including representatives from the Ministries of Finance, Planning, and Industry and Commerce examined the relationship between increased trade possibilities and diplomatic recognition of China. During the delegation's stay in China, the Foreign Ministry's report recommending the institution of diplomatic relations was considered by the presidential staff and by the SNI, and it is possible that the CSN may have been consulted as well. Brazil would have preferred to trade with China without committing itself to formal recognition, while the Chinese hoped to use the lure of trade opportunities as a way of obtaining recognition.

Events moved quickly in August, following the arrival in Brazil on August 7 of an eleven-man Chinese delegation headed by China's vice-minister of foreign trade, Chen Chieh.[17] When the Chinese officials strongly implied that significant growth of commerce would accompany diplomatic relations, the president reportedly consulted with top army commanders before giving his final approval. Whether he actively solicited the military leaders' advice or merely informed them of his decision is not yet ascertainable with any degree of assurance, but there is some evidence that even many hard-liners agreed with this step as an indication of Brazil's new major-league status. The signing of the agreement on August 15 was implemented by the arrival in Peking on April 1, 1975, of Ambassador Aluísio Napoleon de Freitas Rego, a senior career man who had been appointed to the Peking post the preceding December, at just about the time when the Chinese chargé d'affaires arrived in Brasília. By this time Ozório de Almeida had moved on from Brasília to be ambassador to Australia, a post from which he could work actively to promote closer ties between these two large and relatively well developed Southern Hemisphere powers. (Australia reportedly is also considered to be a significant factor in the diversification of Brazil's international interests.)

A brief examination of the process that led to the reestablishment of relations with the Soviet Union is also instructive. Reestablishment of Brazil's diplomatic ties with the USSR (severed in late 1947 as a result of Russia's disparagement of Brazil's contribution to World War II) began with an unofficial trade mission to Moscow in late 1959, a move that was reciprocated by the Soviet Union in 1960; these initial gestures were followed by an official Brazilian commercial delegation the next year and a return mission by the Russians.

Diplomatic relations were formally renewed in November 1961. This process was begun under Kubitschek, accelerated by Quadros, and completed by Goulart. Brazil's motivations for resuming diplomatic ties with Russia were similar to those that led to the decision to recognize Communist China: a desire for increased trade, a wish to demonstrate national maturity in the international realm, and a realistic appreciation of the changes that had recently occurred in the relations between the Soviet Union and the United States. (In the Soviet case, Eisenhower's "spirit of Camp David" played a role analogous to that of Nixon's visit to China.)

For more than a decade after the 1962 exchange of ambassadors, the fruits of Brazilian-Soviet relations were quite limited; however, the combined impact of the energy crisis and increased U.S. protectionism (exemplified by the levying of countervailing duties on Brazilian shoes) encouraged Brazil to seek substantially increased trade with the USSR in 1974-1975. This move effectively enhanced Petrobrás' role in foreign policy, as that agency's operating arm, Braspetro (created in 1972), was assigned to negotiate the sale of shoes to the Soviet Union in an attempt to offset Brazil's new large-scale purchases of petroleum from that country. The Soviet bloc's demand for coffee has been relatively inelastic; sales increased to nearly 2 million sacks after the 1975 harvest, but in the future may not surpass that figure by much. Brazil must depend on other exports; several hundred thousand pairs of shoes figure in the deals that will bring several million tons of Soviet crude oil and diesel fuel to Brazil, thus diminishing the latter's dependence on Middle Eastern sources. (Brazilian purchases from the USSR in 1974 were approximately $170 million, with exports of nearly $100 million; both sides of this exchange rose sharply during 1975, when Brazilian exports neared $400 million.) The substantial surplus in Brazil's favor was a significant boon, given that country's global trade deficit. In recent dealings with the Soviet Union, Itamaraty has played only a supporting role—in marked contrast to the leading part it played in an earlier period, when diplomatic questions were clearly central.

At present a combination of factors related to economics, security, and diplomacy influences Brazil's attitude toward Cuba. Itamaraty's pragmatism is evident in the Geisel administration's policy shift: Spanish American sentiment has changed, and Brazil would like to avoid isolation within the OAS. Brazilian military opposition to the readmission of Cuba to the inter-American system has been neutralized to the degree that the United States has seriously entertained the idea of readmission. Thus Silveira has been able to move Brazil away from a hard-line stance and toward a cautious attitude that advocates delay and collective study of the question. Brazil abstained when the readmission of Cuba became a yes-or-no question at the OAS foreign minister's meeting in Quito in November 1974, and abstained again even when sixteen countries voted to lift sanctions at San José at the end of July 1975. The Brazilian elites remain divided over how readmission would affect such matters as national security and the market for Brazil's growing sugar exports (which exceeded coffee as a foreign-exchange earner in 1974), in addition to Cuba's potential as a market for Brazilian manufactured goods. This lack of agreement enables Itamaraty to make headway with the argument that, if readmission is going to happen anyway, Brazil should not risk incurring the diplomatic costs of holding out against a growing hemisphere consensus; moveover, Itamaraty believes, Brazil should consider the benefits that might be realized in its dealings with third world countries should it modify its conservative image.

Itamaraty has a major voice in narrow questions of diplomatic relations and international law; however, its ability to function in these areas may be chiefly reactive, and may be restricted to issues that are not subject to military veto. Furthermore, much of the Foreign Ministry's role is formal and instrumental. Thus, for example, the burgeoning of Japanese trade and investment during the early years of the "economic miracle" involved Brazilian economic agencies, rather than Itamaraty. Separate visits to Tokyo were made in 1971 and 1972 by the Brazilian ministers of industry and commerce, planning, and finance. Delfim returned to the Japanese capital in early 1973, along with the head of the Bank of Brazil and other economic officials, to hold a seminar on investment and commercial opportunities, and the ministers of industry and commerce and mines and energy followed in October and November. This procession of Brazilian cabinet members to Tokyo ended in March 1974 with a visit by the minister of communications. Prime Minister Kakuei Tanaka's trip to Brazil in September of that year and the visit to Brazil in August 1975 by Deputy Prime Minister Takeo Fukeda were concerned with economic matters, in particular with Japan's role in the $3.4 billion project for developing the rich bauxite deposits of the Rio Trombetas near the mouth of the Amazon, and with Japanese investment in the Tubarão and Itaqui steel mills. In the face of clear signs that Japanese and world economic conditions were delaying, if not placing in jeopardy, these massive projects Ueki went to Tokyo early in 1976. After Ueki's visit, the bauxite and aluminum project was reconfirmed (in view of Brazil's determination to go ahead on its own with the massive power dam and other infrastructural investments), as was the Tubarão steel mill, while the other project was postponed. A major sale of soy products and a state visit by President Geisel were also discussed in Tokyo by the Brazilian mines and energy minister.[18]

Although protocol arrangements for the September 1976 presidential trip were handled by the Foreign Ministry, matters of substance remained in the hands of the economic ministers. In addition to Silveira, President Geisel was accompanied to Tokyo by the ministers of industry and commerce, mines and energy, and planning, as well as the minister-chief of the Military Cabinet. The president personally played a central role in completing negotiations which established the foundation for the multiplication of bilateral trade several times over by the early 1980s.

Silveira's persistent efforts to gain a greater voice for Itamaraty in decisions related to foreign policy led to his presentation of a proposal for diversifying Brazilian trade with the Middle East to a meeting of the Economic Development

Council in late August 1975. (The meeting was devoted to exploring ways of increasing exports and attracting further foreign investment from such countries as Japan and Iran.) However, Silveira does not appear to have played a major role in the council's subsequent decision to permit foreign concerns to explore for oil under service contracts. (Ambassador Roberto Campos' decisive influence on this controversial issue stemmed from his advocacy of such a measure a decade ago as planning minister.) Indeed, by some accounts, Silveira was one of only two cabinet members to oppose this measure.[19]

Notes to Chapter 4

[1]Castelo reportedly was ready to replace Leitão da Cunha as early as June 1965, but left him in office long enough to cap his long diplomatic career by presiding over the Second Extraordinary Inter-American Conference, which, although scheduled for May 1965 in Rio de Janeiro, had to be postponed to November because of the crisis over the Dominican Republic and the U.S. intervention there. The conference's secretary general was Silveira. See Viana Filho, *O Governo*, pp. 430-437.

[2]Not all experience as secretary general is of equal importance. There is, first, a substantial difference between serving under a fellow professional diplomat and serving under a political appointee. Thus, Corrêa da Costa's role under Magalhães Pinto—even more than was Gibson Barbosa's in 1968-1969—was quite different from Carvalho e Silva's subsequent function under his old classmate, Gibson Barbosa. In the former instance, with Magalhães Pinto still hoping to become finance minister in a cabinet reshuffle (which never took place) and spending considerable time tending to his business and political interests in Belo Horizonte, Corrêa da Costa was frequently responsible for foreign-policy decisions. Coming directly to the minister's chair from a stint as secretary general, Gibson did not leave nearly as much policy space for his deputy to occupy. Pio Corrêa served under a nonprofessional, but Juracy Magalhães felt a significant degree of competence based upon his two years' service as ambassador to the United States. Moreover, he possessed a sense of hierarchy carried over from his earlier military career. On leave since 1968 as head of the German Siemens electrical-electronics company's Brazilian subsidiary, Pio Corrêa would seem to be out of the running for the foreign minister's job, while Castelo Branco, as ambassador to the Vatican, appears also more likely headed toward retirement than up to the cabinet.

[3]Holanda Calvalcanti is considered to possess the "best brain" in Itamaraty, at least in the view of several qualified observers. An example of Souto Maior's thinking can be found in "A Política Externa do Brasil," *Revista Brasileira de Estudos Políticos* 42 (January 1976): 175-197. He stresses the "indivisibility" of foreign policy from internal realities and the inseparability of economic and political factors as well as the "brutality" of international power relationships. In the prior administration, two of the nominal subordinates of the *chefe do gabinete* were considered to be brighter idea men, and they may have had greater influence on policy than Castro Alves himself. Biographic data can be found in Ministério das Relações Exteriores, *Anuário do Pessoal, 1974* (Brasília, 1975). Also useful on career patterns is the *Lista de Antiguidade na Carreira de Diplomata em 28 Fevereiro de 1976,* put out by the ministry.

[4]These are current figures. For a solid, if somewhat dated, discussion of the Brazilian foreign service, consult Fontaine, "The Foreign Policy-making Process in Brazil," pp. 276-368; Fontaine, *Brazil and the United States,* pp. 55-72; and H. Jon Rosenbaum, "A Critique of the Brazilian Foreign Service," *The Journal of Developing Areas,* April 1968, pp. 377-392. Also of interest are A. F. Azeredo da Silveira, *Organização do Ministerio das Relações Exteriores* (Rio de Janeiro, 1966), and Geraldo Eulálio Nascimento e Silva, "Organização diplomática brasileira," *Revista do Serviço Público,* 1956, pp. 53-69.

[5]This is not to say that, in absolute terms, the foreign service is as elitist in recruitment as it was in the past generations. Certainly the December 1938 class, the first with the Brazilian Civil Service Commission (DASP) in charge of the entrance examination instead of Itamaraty itself, was drawn from a broader social stratum than were previous cohorts. The question is really whether admission to the foreign service has kept pace with changes in Brazilian society and its stratification system. Comparison with the economic agencies of the federal government might be revealing.

[6]Fontaine, *Brazil and the United States,* p. 67.

[7]This statement was made at a reception for the Lebanese foreign minister in Brasília on January 31, 1974.

[8]Former Foreign Minister Araújo Castro, who served from 1967 to his death in 1975 as Ambassador to the United Nations and then as Ambassador to the United States, repeatedly stressed the NPT as the keystone of the superpowers' efforts to "freeze" the present stratification of

international power. See his "O Congelamento do Poder Mundial," *Revista Brasileira de Estudos Políticos* 33 (January 1972): 7-30. See also H. Jon Rosenbaum and Glenn M. Cooper, "Brazil and the Nuclear Non-Proliferation Treaty," *International Affairs*, January 1970, pp. 74-90.

9See the discussion in Fontaine, *Brazil and the United States*, pp. 103-112, as well as John R. Redick, *Military Potential of Latin American Nuclear Energy Programs* (Beverly Hills, Calif.: Sage, 1972).

10"Depois da victória política, o desafio talvez mais difícil," *Visão*, July 7, 1975, pp. 12-22.

11"Política Nuclear: Um acordo tamanho quarenta," *Visão*, June 23, 1975, pp. 23ff.

12See *Latin America*, March 14, 1975, pp. 82-84.

13The Westinghouse reactor at Angra dos Reis is to be producing power for commercial use in 1977, with nine others to be functioning by 1990. These are planned to have a generating capacity of 10,000 megawatts, or the equivalent of 400,000 barrels of oil a day (over twice Brazil's present production of crude petroleum). Twenty-five other nuclear generators are to be started after 1984 to come on line by the mid-1990s. Before that time Brazil hopes to be well into building reactors and exporting them to other Latin American countries. The agreements with the German Federal Republic involve the reactors and fuel element fabrication plant for eight of these nuclear power plants as well as an experimental jet nozzle-type separation process for a fuel enrichment plant. The most controversial aspect of the accords is for a factory to reclaim plutonium from the spent fuel elements, since this could then be used for explosive devices. The agreements were approved by the German parliament in April 1975, with Silveira signing a formal treaty on June 27. At the same ceremony in Bonn, Ueki and his West German counterpart signed agreements providing for a variety of joint firms to carry out the cooperative provisions of this nuclear partnership. The Brazilian delegation included more technocrats than diplomats, even counting the Brazilian ambassador and his minister counselor, who were already resident in Bonn. See "O Brasil na Era Atômica," *Manchete*, July 12, 1975, pp. 4-12, and *Jornal do Brasil*, May 5, 1976.

14See the interviews with Ueki and Paulo Baptista Nogueira in *Manchete*, April 24, 1976, pp. 76-77 and 90-92.

15An illustration of Itamaraty's diminished role in foreign affairs is provided by the following table showing the memberships held by the three key ministers in policymaking bodies.

Body	Minister-Chief of Planning	Minister of Finance	Foreign Minister
Economic Development Council	Secretary General	Member	——
Foreign Trade Council	Member	Member	Member
National Monetary Council	Vice-Chairman	Chairman	——

[16]*Visão*, August 19, 1975, pp. 15-16.

[17]The relevant documents are in *Resenha de política exterior do brasil*, no. 2 (September 1974): 17-26 and 71.

[18]On Ueki's trip see *Visão*, February 23, 1976, p. 86. Brazilian trade with Japan reached $1.65 billion in 1974 with a deficit for Brazil of over $538 million. In 1975 this trade grew to $1.78 billion with the deficit dropping to $436 million (FOB) but $587 million if imports are valued CIF. Iron ore sales of $290 million made up 45 percent of Brazil's exports to Japan, while steel purchases of nearly $540 million comprised over 42 percent of Brazil's imports from Japan. See *O Estado de S. Paulo*, September 11, 1976. The agreements arrived at during Geisel's visit would help balance trade in the short run through increased Japanese purchases of iron ore, Brazilian exports of pelletized ore, and substantial sales of cellulose and foodstuffs. By the early 1980s Brazil would be exporting substantial amounts of aluminum and steel to Japan as a result of that country's heavy investments in the Albrás/Alunorte aluminum project and the Tubarão steel mill. In current prices Japan would purchase $23 billion in steel between 1982 and 1996 along with roughly an equal value of aluminum. Combined with the iron sales already contracted for and the probable expansion of grain exports, these facts tend to bear out Japanese Minister of Industries and Foreign Trade Toshio Komoto's prediction of annual bilateral trade of $12 billion by 1985. Moreover, both on a visit to Brazil in July and during Geisel's stay in Tokyo, he estimated up to $20 billion in Japanese investment in Brazil during the next ten years. See in particular *Manchete*, Sept. 25, 1976, pp. 48-50 and Oct. 2, 1976, pp. 4-22; *Veja*, Sept. 1, 1976, pp. 86-87, Sept. 15, 1976, pp. 21-23, Sept. 22, 1976, pp. 14-23, and Sept. 29, 1976, pp. 118-119; and *Visão*, Sept. 13, 1976, pp. 70-80 and Oct. 11, 1976, pp. 100-105.

[19]See *Veja*, September 3, 1975, p. 81; Murilo Melo Filho, "A Sofrida Decisão," *Manchete*, October 25, 1975, pp. 12-13; and *Veja*, October 15, 1975, p. 22. Severo Gomes was the other.

5
Foreign Trade
and the
Economic Technocrats

The sources of the final word on Brazilian foreign policy—
the president and the Armed Forces—have already been
examined, as has that part of the government occupied full
time with international affairs. Yet some key actors remain
to be discussed, including several ministers whose views often
outweigh those of the foreign minister, and various agencies
that conduct many of Brazil's most important international
transactions. The Finance Ministry will be analyzed first, followed by the many bodies involved in foreign trade and international finance, and finally by those institutions in the field
of energy and transportation whose activity in foreign affairs
continues to rapidly expand.

The Finance Ministry

If the role of the Foreign Ministry in the formulation of
major foreign policies is smaller than might be expected, that
of the Finance Ministry is substantially greater. Finance was
particularly strong from 1968 through 1973, and friction between these two ministries has become a prominent feature
of intragovernmental politics in Brazil.

During the Castelo Branco administration the Finance Ministry was in the shadow of Planning Minister Roberto Campos. Similarly, during the Costa government, Delfim's influence—at least in the foreign-policy realm—was not as pronounced as it later became under Médici. Under Hélio Beltrão, the Planning Ministry (albeit playing a greatly diminished role from the one it played in its heyday under Ambassador Campos) still enjoyed some residual clout. A substantial part of Delfim's subsequent influence was linked to his strategy of colonizing other agencies with his men—a process that was not well under way until 1969 and which flowered only in the Médici years, particularly before the succession question became prominent in 1973. Key figures on Delfim's team included, in addition to members of his own ministry with its Assesoria Econômica (containing the bright boys of his personal brain trust), the presidents of the Bank of Brazil and the Central Bank, along with the planning minister and the minister of agriculture. Even agencies nominally under the supervision of other ministries, such as the Brazilian Coffee Institute, were subject to Delfim's masterful orchestration.

During the Médici years, the frequent power and policy struggles between the Foreign and Finance ministries nearly always ended in favor of Delfim, rather than Gibson Barbosa. The finance minister exerted the dominant influence on such matters as loans, terms and sources of foreign lending, investment policy, and export promotion (he was backed up in the last by the Ministries of Industry and Commerce and Argiculture). In these areas the Foreign Ministry was all but bypassed.

José Maria Vilar de Queiroz, a career foreign service officer "borrowed" from Itamaraty by Roberto Campos, is thought to be responsible for those provisions of Decree Law 200 (February 25, 1967) which accorded the Foreign Ministry only "participation in," rather than coordination of or control over, "commercial, economic, financial, technical, and cultural negotiations with foreign countries and entities." Shortly after the law was passed, Vilar de Queiroz became chief of the international advisory office of the Finance Ministry and a key architect of Delfim's successful plans for making inroads into Itamaraty's sphere of operations. Indeed, it was Vilar de Queiroz who announced, in February 1972, that Brazil would thereafter concentrate on Portugal's African colonies and other white-dominated countries in the southern part of the African continent, even at the expense of weakening its ties with the black African countries. This change of emphasis in African policy ran directly counter to the foreign minister's plans for improving relations with black Africa in order to garner greater support for Brazil and for the less-developed-countries' leadership credibility in international organizations. Deliberately timed to take the bloom off Gibson Barbosa's heralded trip to Africa, Vilar de Queiroz' announcement provoked a sharp rejoinder by Itamaraty Secretary Gen. Jorge Carvalho e Silva. (Vilar de Queiroz is currently minister counselor in Ottawa, following a tour of duty under Delfim in Paris.)

While the president decided that in the short run the Foreign Ministry's black Africa–oriented approach and the Finance Ministry's stress on the markets of the more-developed white-controlled countries were not incompatible, he took both ministers to task for not keeping their subordinates in line and for having allowed the subordinates to air, as though by proxy, policy differences in public (a shortcoming of the preceding Costa administration). Subsequently, many in the military came to resent Delfim's headline-grabbing tactics and his constant bickering with Gibson Barbosa. Furthermore, since many military men had lost money in the stock market in 1970-1971 (they had sold apartments and cars to get in on the boom, and were badly burned by the sudden crash), and others were hostile to Delfim's idea that the time was about ripe for a civilian president, the officers were disposed to turn against the high-handed finance minister. When, in the latter part of 1973, the oil crisis validated the wisdom of Gibson Barbosa's cultivation of black African governments such as Nigeria, the foreign minister's position improved substantially—albeit too late to be of much comfort to him.

The conflict between the Foreign and Finance ministries, which was intensified during the Médici government by the personal antipathy between the two ministers, has continued, in somewhat muted form, to the present. Although Silveira and Finance Minister Mário Henrique Simonsen have made sincere efforts to eliminate bickering (or at least keep it out of the public eye), the conflict remains evident. In the countervailing-duties dispute with the United States in 1974, for example, the Foreign Ministry took the harder line, while the finance minister recommended accommodation. Ultimately, the president resolved the difference on terms somewhat more favorable to Itamaraty than would have been the case in the preceding administration. At the end of 1975 Jefferson de Oliveira Lemos, a nephew of Roberto Campos, was forced to resign as head of Simonsen's *assessoria econômica* after he was so indiscreet as to remark privately that the December 4 decisions of the Economic Development Council in regard to the balance-of-payments problem represented a victory for the finance minister.[1]

Given the present institutional arrangements, however, if a stronger personality were to replace Severo Gomes as minister of industry and commerce—particularly someone with a significant degree of political clout (such as the president of Electrobrás, Antônio Carlos Magalhães)—the foreign minister might well find himself losing considerable ground to the economics-oriented ministries.

Institutional Roles in Foreign Trade

The field of foreign trade, where Itamaraty is but one of many official bodies involved, exemplifies the complexity of the Brazilian institutional structure for policymaking. Nearly twenty agencies are directly involved in formulating and executing foreign-trade policy. At the top is the National Foreign Trade Council (Concex), an interministerial body that shapes and coordinates policy and generally oversees implementation.

The minister of industry and commerce presides over Concex, and the council also includes in its membership the ministers of foreign relations, finance, agriculture, and mines and energy as well as the presidents of the Central Bank and the Bank of Brazil. Although it was largely inactive during the Médici administration, chiefly because Delfim Netto was expanding the role of the Finance Ministry, Concex has been rehabilitated by the Geisel government. Concex appears to be the agency that translates high-level decisions into guidelines for implementation and which transforms presidential objectives into coordinated operational policies. If indeed Concex was created by Kubitschek in 1960 at Itamaraty's behest, it long ago boomeranged on the Foreign Ministry's desire to use it to gain "the central role in trade promotion."[2] Indeed, as of August 1976, the president appeared disposed to transform Concex into a foreign trade secretariat directly under himself in order to upgrade its influence and authority.

If the Foreign Ministry's input into economic policy through the trade arena is not paramount, neither is it insignificant. The ministry is the negotiating arm for Brazil at the General Agreement on Trade and Tariffs, the Latin American Trade Assn., and other such multilateral forums, in addition to offering strong support in bilateral trade-expansion efforts. Itamaraty's forte is to assess the politics of the other side and to suggest corresponding strategies and tactics.

The Foreign Trade Office (Cacex) of the Bank of Brazil, a mixed-capital enterprise, carries out most of the financial transactions involved in this field in addition to administering the Export Financing Fund (Finex) and its special fund for export stimulation. The foreign exchange director of the Central Bank has monetary responsibilities in this area, as do the Economic and Trade Promotion departments of the Foreign Ministry (the latter sponsors trade fairs, expositions, etc). The Commission for the Concession of Fiscal Incentives to Special Export Programs (Befiex), itself an offshoot of the Industrial Development Council (CDI), is only one of the foreign trade arms of the Ministry of Industry and Commerce. Befiex stimulates the sale of manufactured goods abroad, while the Brazilian Coffee Institute and the Sugar and Alcohol

Institute deal in their respective commodities, whose annual sales add up to around $1 billion each. The minister of industry and commerce, thus, has substantial responsibilities in regard to Brazil's foreign trade; his support is sought by the finance, planning, and mines and energy ministers in reaching crucial decisions about Brazil's economic policies.

The Agriculture Ministry is active in foreign trade in a variety of ways. It has a monopoly on the purchase and sale of wheat, and it controls the Brazilian Institute of Forest Development (IBDF), which supervises exports of wood and other forest products; the office of the coordinator of international agricultural affairs (Cingra); and the executive commission of the Cocoa Recovery and Production Plan (Ceplac). (Until recently, Ceplac was tied to the Finance Ministry.) Like his counterparts in Industry and Commerce, the agriculture minister has a greater voice in making coffee policy under the Geisel administration than he had previously. The rising importance of soy and corn among Brazil's exports ensures that his views will continue to be heard.

The Finance Ministry retains a direct input into foreign-trade policy through the recently refurbished Coordinating Commission for Policy on Foreign Purchases, the Tariff Policy Council, and the International Taxation Study Commission. Moreover, the finance minister can call on his international advisory staff (*assesoria internacional*) for assistance in foreign-trade policy matters. Indeed, the Export Incentives Commission (Ciex) was established in August 1975 under this office, with representation from Cacex, the revenue office, and the Central Bank.

The Ministry of Mines and Energy participates through Petrobrás and its overseas operating arm, Braspetro, as well as through Nuclebrás, Electrobrás, and the Vale do Rio Doce Co. Then, too, a semiofficial trading company, Cobec (*Companhia Brasileira de Entrepostos e Comércio*), is coming to play a significant role, particularly in trade with the socialist countries and some African nations. Cobec's sales total in 1975 exceeded $300 million—up 800 percent from 1974— and was expected to double in 1976.[3]

The Coordinating Group for Trade with Socialist Countries of Eastern Europe (COLESTE) was reactivated in July 1974 after two years of disuse. Presided over by João Paulo do Rio Branco, chief of the European Department of Itamaraty, COLESTE includes the head of the Finance Ministry's international advisory staff, a representative of the Coordinating Commission for Policy on Foreign Purchases, a member of the National Security Council staff, a spokesman for the Vale do Rio Doce Co. (the government iron ore exporting firm), the head of Cacex, and the director for foreign exchange operations of the Central Bank. Also sitting in at its meetings may be representatives of Petrobrás, Electrobrás, the Merchant Marine Superintendency (SUNAMAM), and the Federal Railroad System (RFFSA). Originally established in 1962, COLESTE's activity has ebbed and flowed with the fluctuating level of Brazilian interest in trade with the Communist countries.

International Finance

The National Monetary Council (CMN) is the principal policymaking body in the area of international finance, while the Central Bank is the agency responsible for executing the CMN's decisions. Under the chairmanship of the minister of finance, but with its executive secretariat functioning almost as part of the staff of the Central Bank president, this council among other things regulates the external value of the cruzeiro and tries to bring some equilibrium to Brazil's balance of payments. The CMN's membership includes the ministers of finance, industry and commerce, agriculture, and interior; the minister-chief of the Planning Secretariat; the heads of the Central Bank, Bank of Brazil, National Economic Development Bank, National Housing Bank, and National Savings Bank; and three private-sector representatives (usually leading bankers) appointed by the president.

Under the Geisel administration the CMN has met regularly and has discussed and approved all important international financial decisions. Its vice-chairmanship has been shifted from the minister of industry and commerce to Reis

Velloso, who has far greater experience in this field as well as a broader range of concerns and responsibilities. Then, too, because the directors of the several departments of the Central Bank are no longer voting members, there no longer exists the near-automatic majority for the finance minister that had previously reduced this body to the role of a rubber stamp for Delfim Netto. All CMN members are now top-level presidential appointees; should a major dispute arise within the council, the matter would be taken to the Economic Development Council, where the president would resolve the matter. No such split seems to have occurred yet, nor is this body likely to become deeply divided so long as the finance minister and the minister-chief of the Planning Secretariat remain able to reach accommodation on matters within its purview.

On questions of international borrowing and investment, there is very close cooperation between the finance minister and the president of the Central Bank (formerly its director of foreign exchange operations). Indeed, Paulo Lira's comparatively broad policy involvement, based largely on his personal prestige, demonstrates how the importance of any given position may change with its incumbent. Lira is a presidential adviser in his own right and a trustworthy subordinate of Finance Minister Simonsen. The latter official is Brazil's governor to the International Monetary Fund and other multilateral lending institutions; Lira is his alternate, and the present finance minister has benefited from the experience that Lira gained in this field under Delfim Netto. The Central Bank has basic responsibility for overseeing day-to-day activities in the foreign-exchange market and for controlling the longer-range structure of Brazil's foreign debt, a task it has carried out with skill and growing sophistication.

The Central Bank consults increasingly with the private banking community about the flow of foreign capital into Brazil. The consultation is essentially one-sided, giving the bankers more a sense of participation than an effective voice; its real purpose is to co-opt them rather than to allow them to influence policy decisions.

Energy and Transport

Given his direct supervisory authority over Petrobrás, Nuclebrás, and the Vale do Rio Doce Co., the minister of mines and energy is now one of the leading actors in the foreign-policy arena. Indeed, he seems to have fallen heir to a substantial parcel of the influence exercised by Delfim in the two previous administrations. In view of Itamaraty's loss of centrality with respect to decisions in the nuclear field, with government expenditures on nuclear programs estimated at a present minimum of $11 billion and expected to reach more than $15 billion by 1990, the clout of the Ministry of Mines and Energy is likely to remain formidable. Indeed, plans for an eightfold increase in installed nuclear generating capacity during the 1990s (to 81 million kilowatts and sixty-three plants), at a total investment of at least $35 billion, indicate that the role of the minister of mines and energy would probably not diminish even if the present energy crisis subsides.[4] The hope that the Brazilian nuclear program will obtain sufficient foreign technology so as to achieve relative nuclear independence during the 1980s accentuates the likelihood of the minister's continuing influence. Some of Brazil's most important diplomatic negotiations may center on the enrichment and reprocessing of nuclear fuel, and Brazil will almost certainly be drawn much closer to whichever industrialized country is her major partner in this sphere, with West Germany all but certain to retain this role.

Nuclep, the subsidiary of Nuclebrás responsible for the manufacture of heavy components (the Brazilian-made proportion of components is targeted at 70 percent by 1985 and 90 percent by 1990), has been capitalized at $160 million and eventually will be 75 percent Brazilian owned—with at least 51 percent of its stock retained by the government. Nuclei, the subsidiary that will develop a demonstration uranium enrichment plant by 1981 and which subsequently will be responsible for commercial-scale production of the German jet-nozzle technique, is also to be 75 percent Brazilian owned. Nuclan, a joint company with 51 percent Nuclebrás control, will operate in the field of uranium prospecting and mining (with the Germans getting a guaranteed minimum of 20 percent of the ore). Nuclen, with an initial capital of 30 million cruzeiros, will handle the engineering work for the various installations. A fuel-fabrication subsidiary with 70 percent Brazilian ownership will be set up at a later date, and a pilot plant for reprocessing spent fuel will be built under a technical-assistance agreement between Nuclebrás and the German consortium. On its own, Nuclebrás has spun off an additional subsidiary (Nuclemon) for processing Brazil's monazite and thorium sands, which may be usable in a new type of reactor being developed in France as part of the Phoenix series of fast-breeder reactors.[5] Looking beyond 1990, Brazil signed a nuclear research cooperation treaty with France just days after the Bonn accords.

The present minister of mines and energy was a close associate of Ernesto Geisel during the years they both spent with Petrobrás (1969-1973), and the president seems to value his opinion on a fairly wide range of matters. The fact that petroleum needs are considered to be basic determinants of Brazilian foreign policy buttresses the former's position. Brazil's petroleum consumption doubled between 1967 and 1974, while domestic production of crude oil rose by slightly less than one-third. Thus the gap, less than 60 million barrels in 1968, had risen to more than 260 million barrels by 1973, and had caused a major drain on foreign-exchange earnings even before world oil prices began to skyrocket.

With 1975 sales of $7.4 billion (in U.S. dollars) and net profits of $650 million—after paying the Brazilian treasury over $1.7 billion in taxes—Petrobrás is easily Brazil's largest economic concern, public or private. Employing 44,000 workers and adding nearly $1.6 billion to Brazil's GNP, it boasts a fleet of forty-three tankers, of 2.3 million dwt (to be expanded to sixty-one ships of 4.9 million dwt by 1980). In addition to its virtual monopoly in refining and its major role in the petrochemical field, Petrobrás has expanded its distribution activities; in 1975 it surpassed Exxon and Shell to take over first place in distribution within Brazil. Its overseas exploration arm, Braspetro, currently operates in ten countries from neighboring Colombia to distant Iraq and Iran.[6] As if all this did not give Petrobrás sufficient influence in foreign affairs, it recently spun off a trading-company subsidiary, Interbrás, which is expected to do business in the hundreds of millions of dollars during its initial year of existence.[7]

Since Brazil's proven reserves of petroleum are only 125 million cubic meters (approximately 785 million barrels), and its petroleum production in 1975 was only about 10.2 million cubic meters (just under 65 million barrels), some 80 percent of Brazil's crude oil needs must still be filled by imports, a fact that constitutes a major foreign-policy constraint as well as a crucial development limitation. Indeed, in 1974 and 1975 Brazil spent $3 billion a year—nearly two-fifths of its total export earnings—to buy petroleum. With domestic production of crude oil not expected to rise significantly, and the consumption curve still shooting up from its present level of 930,000 barrels a day, Petrobrás plans to spend more than $2.3 billion during the next three years for refineries, terminals, and pipelines (much of the last for importation of equipment) in order to exploit Brazil's recently discovered offshore fields, with the effect of making oil an even more important factor in Brazil's foreign trade.[8]

In spite of the October 9, 1975, decision to award service contracts for oil exploration to foreign companies on a "risk" basis, Petrobrás will spend ever-larger sums on further exploration during each of the next several years. The fact that Silveira opposed these contracts provides another illustration of the Foreign Ministry's relative impotence in decisions that profoundly affect Brazil's international posture, position, and policy. Instead, Petrobrás (headed by a retired general) and the minister of mines and energy (a former director of financial and commercial operations for Petrobrás) are the key actors. Since as many as ten different international companies (several of them government petroleum corporations) may become directly involved in exploration for oil within Brazil, the foreign-policy role of Petrobrás and its parent ministry is likely to expand rather than diminish.[9] The Foreign

Ministry in the petroleum field will continue to provide merely the political insight and negotiating skill required to complement the technical competence of the oil exports.

Iron ore may well be destined to become Brazil's leading
export, and the steel industry is crucial to the country's
development. In this field the minister of mines and energy
oversees the Vale do Rio Doce Co. (CVRD), already the
world's largest exporter of iron ore. Vale do Rio Doce's importance to Brazil's foreign relations stems both from the
scale and range of its activities and from its joint ventures
with foreign firms, many of them state enterprises. The overseas sales of the CVRD in 1975 amounted to 50.1 million
tons of iron ore for $611 million dollars, while its total
production was 59 million tons. Employing 21,500 persons
and accounting for nearly as large a proportion of Brazil's
export trade as the coffee, sugar, or soy industry, the CVRD
is one of the most positive factors in Brazil's overall trade
balance. Indeed, in April 1976 the CVRD exported ore
worth over $100 million, breaking its previous single-month
record.[10]

The CVRD's ten fully owned subsidiaries include DOCE-
NAVE, with 1.15 million deadweight tons of its own ships
plus seventeen others totaling 1.1 million dwt currently under construction and an additional 1.33 dwt under lease; the
Paraíba Valley Mining Co. (VALEP); New York and Brussels-
based marketing companies (Rio Doce Europa and Itabira Internacional); a prospecting concern (DOCEGEO); a major fertilizer company (Valefertil); two other mining firms; a refor-
estation subsidiary; and an engineering concern. Potentially
of even greater foreign-policy impact are the CVRD's joint
ventures, such as its 41 percent share in the Rio Trombetas
bauxite project (Mineração Rio do Norte, S.A.), with Alcan
and five other foreign companies holding 49 percent and a
Brazilian private firm the remaining 10 percent. By 1985 this
project will require an investment of $700 million in order to
produce $200 million worth of bauxite annually; as early as
1979, for an investment of $280 million, it may yield 3 mil-
lion tons a year for $80 million in sales.[11] Closely related to
Trombetas is Albrás, a joint venture with the Japanese Light

Metals Smelters' Assn. CVRD and its Japanese partners will have to invest over $950 million in order to yield 320,000 tons of aluminum annually for sales in the vicinity of $300 million—just under half for export. These two ambitious projects are tied together by Alunorte, in which the CVRD, Albrás, and Alcan will invest $480 million to process bauxite into the 800,000 tons of semi-raw material needed for aluminum production. Valesul is a smaller CVRD joint venture (budgeted at $240 million) intended to produce aluminum in the Rio de Janeiro area.

Besides these large-scale international dealings, the CVRD is also engaged in a massive project to exploit the 18 billion tons of high-grade iron ore at Carajás in northern Brazil. AMZA (Amazonas Mining) will call for an investment in excess of $2.7 billion by the mid-1980s, with additional hundreds of millions needed to build a 900-kilometer railroad to the coast. Foreseen as producing 12 million tons of iron ore a year by 1979 and 50 million tons annually by 1985—thus enabling Brazil to bring up its foreign sales to 115 million tons in 1980—this project will also make possible a large steel mill at Itaqui, the port from which the Carajás ore will be shipped.[12] Originally U.S. Steel was counted on for 49 percent of the front money, but as estimates of the total required investment have continued to climb, additional foreign participants have been sought. The CVRD is also in the steel business by virtue of its 10-percent interest in the Tubarão plant (in which Kawasaki of Japan and Finsider of Italy are also partners) and its 19-percent interest in the new Açominas project—which, like Tubarão, is a $2-billion enterprise.[13] In all, the CVRD will itself invest over $10 billion during the 1976-1980 period in expansion of its activities.

Nuclebrás, Petrobrás, and the CVRD are not the only agencies under the Mines and Energy Ministry that weigh heavily in Brazil's international activities and justify Ueki's scurrying from Tokyo to Paris to Washington. Electrobrás is involved in multibillion-dollar credit negotiations for the several big hydroelectric projects planned or under way, as well as in the financing of the nuclear power generating plants. Itaipu Binacional, a concern set up with Paraguay to develop the most massive of all hydroelectric projects, is headed by former Mines and Energy Minister José Costa Cavalcanti and is subject to Ueki's coordination.[14]

The Transport Ministry, although far less significant than the Ministries of Finance or Mines and Energy, occasionally influences foreign policy. During the Costa e Silva government, the military officer who was transport minister enjoyed a close personal relationship with the president and managed to gain a major say in foreign-policy matters related to shipping. The same individual remained as minister in the Médici administration, but his lack of personal rapport with the new chief executive cost him much of his influence in foreign-policy decisions. The present transport minister, a retired four-star general about five years younger than the president, has jurisdiction over the Lloyd Brasileiro Shipping Co. and over the National Merchant Marine Superintendency (SUNAMAM), which has representatives in New York and Hamburg as well as in all major Brazilian ports.

The role and power of the transport minister is likely to become more significant in the future because Brazil is constructing at least 765 new merchant ships with a total displacement of 6 million tons during the 1975-1979 period, in addition to completing 1.3 million tons of ships under a previous contract.[15] Construction was completed of 268,000 tons in 1974 and 460,000 tons in 1975. The target for 1976 was nearly a million tons, rising gradually to some 1.23 million tons in 1980. This rate of growth would put Brazil on a par with England, France, Norway, and Spain in shipbuilding by 1980 and allow it to set its sights on joining the big three of Japan, the German Federal Republic, and Sweden during the 1980s.[16] Already the proportion of Brazil's foreign trade carried in ships under her own flag has risen from less than 38 percent in 1970 to roughly 60 percent, and as Brazilian bottoms continue to replace leased ships the foreign-exchange savings will rise significantly. Since Brazil's cumulative deficit in maritime freight from 1970 through 1975 exceeded $3 billion, this is a factor of no little importance.[17]

The $2.3 billion in shipbuilding contracts let through SUNAMAM helps tie the private firms in this field to their major customers, Petrobrás's National Petroleum Fleet (Fronape) and the Rio Doce Valley Co.'s DOCENAVE. Verolme, which has built forty-seven ships of a total displacement of more than a million dwt, has been allotted some 1.23 million additional tons under the present merchant-marine construction plan, chiefly for Petrobrás. Ishikawajima do Brasil (Ishibrás) has an even larger share, with four 277,000-ton supertankers for Petrobrás as well as a variety of tankers and freighters in the 100,000–130,000-ton range. Mauá, third in terms of steel processing and mounting capacity, is building a dozen ships a year; Emaq is close behind, and Caneco holds contracts for twenty-five ships totaling 645,000 tons by 1979 (the largest just under 40,000 dwt).[18] Along with smaller shipyards, these firms are also building over 550,000 tons of vessels for export, an area in which increased future earnings are expected.[19] Then, too, Brazil is beginning to construct warships of significant size and complexity in its own yards as a result of contracts with the United Kingdom and the German Federal Republic which called for very substantial transfer of technology and development of Brazilian capabilities in this field.[20]

From these facts concerning the importance of economic agencies and state enterprises in the foreign-policy realm, it should not be surprising that President Geisel was accompanied on his recent official visits to Paris and London, not only by his foreign minister, but also by the ministers of finance, agriculture, mines and energy, industry and commerce, and planning—as well as the presidents of the Central Bank, the Bank of Brazil, and the National Economic Development Bank. When billions in trade, investments, and credits are at stake in international diplomacy—and where the success of these negotiations has significant impact upon internal politics—the responsibilities of the economic technocrats cannot stop at the water's edge.

Notes to Chapter 5

[1] *Visão*, December 22, 1975, p. 26.

2Fontaine, in *Brazil and the United States*, p. 64, argued that this council was viewed as a vehicle for expanding Itamaraty's role, citing the *Jornal do Brasil* of November 5 and 6, 1959, as the source for this interpretation. Originally Concex was composed of the secretary general and chief of the Economic Department of the Foreign Ministry, plus representatives of the Finance and Labor Ministries, but its membership has expanded over the years with the effect of diluting Itamaraty's influence. On Concex's future see *O Estado de S. Paulo*, June 12, 22, and 23, 1976.

3*Jornal do Brasil*, April 23 and May 2, 1976; *Tendência*, July 1976, p. 82.

4*Manchete*, September 27, 1975, pp. 136-137.

5Consult *Visão*, July 7, 1975, pp. 12-22; February 9, 1976, p. 9; and March 8, 1976, p. 28, as well as *Manchete*, April 24, 1976, pp. 93-97. Although evidence of very large-scale uranium finds in the Amazon region has been raised by recent geological prospecting—with some estimates as high as 500,000 tons—Brazil's proven reserves remain a modest 16,500 tons. (See *Jornal do Brasil*, April 10, 1976.) Their distribution in Minas Gerais, Goiás, and Paraná provides reason for further hopes that exploration will sharply raise this figure. Reserves of monazite sands with a 5 percent thorium content are at least 51,000 tons, and Brazil has some 3,800 tons of thorium stored for future use. (See *Jornal do Brasil*, May 1, 1976.) All major newspapers on July 14, 1976, carried comments of future uranium self-sufficiency by the president of Nuclebrás.

6Consult *O Estado de S. Paulo*, March 5, 1976, and the Petrobrás annual report published in *Folha de S. Paulo*, March 18, 1976. The *Jornal do Brasil* of March 18, 1976, places the costs of petroleum imports for 1975 at $3.08 billion (FOB), or fairly close to $4 billion CIF. Ueki recently stated that projection of recent discovery trends would lead to a doubling of crude oil production to 17 million tons by 1980 and to 27 million tons in 1985, but that with the participation in exploration by foreign companies this could well vary between 46 million tons (about Algeria's current production) and 65 million tons (close to Libya's annual output at present). If the proportion of petroleum in Brazil's total energy consumption can be decreased from the present 46 percent to a projected 37 percent by that time—when hydroelectric power is to be up to the energy equivalent of 60 million tons of oil—this most optimistic of official scenarios could mean near-self-sufficiency at that point. See *O Estado de S. Paulo*, March 25, 1976. *Jornal do Brasil* of that date puts Brazil's total energy production at the equivalent of 94 million tons of oil in 1975, doubling by 1985.

[7]See *Jornal do Brasil*, February 20 and July 15, 1976; *Manchete*, July 24, 1976, pp. 142-143.

[8]In 1968 Brazil consumed 118 million barrels of crude oil, with domestic production providing slightly more than half (60 million barrels). By 1973 consumption had risen to 323 million barrels, while Brazil's production had grown only marginally, accounting for 19 percent of this amount. Brazil has budgeted nearly $3.5 billion in government funds for exploration during 1975-1979. In addition, the government hopes to attract at least several billion dollars in investment in exploration and recovery of oil from foreign firms, under the so-called risk contracts in areas outside of the active concern of Petrobrás, in order to reduce dependency on overseas sources of petroleum. (See Ueki's interview in *Manchete*, November 29, 1975, pp. 160-161, and *Manchete*, January 24, 1976, pp. 116-117. Also useful are *Visão*, June 9, 1975, pp. 13-14, and September 15, 1975, pp. 76-84.) Petrobrás will spend $730 million of its own resources on exploration during 1976, and may spend even larger sums on extraction of oil from petroleum-bearing schist—which is very abundant in Brazil and is located near the major centers of energy consumption. In an interview in *Manchete* on April 3, 1976, Gen. Araken de Oliveira, president of Petrobrás, announced plans to expand the pilot shale-oil plant at São Mateus do Sul, Paraná, into a commercial operation extracting some 44,600 barrels of crude a day from about 112,000 tons of rock (with significant quantities of gas and wax as by-products). This would require as much as six years of lead time and an investment of over $1 billion. *Jornal do Brasil*, June 10, 1976, reiterated that this would be done without foreign assistance or investment. A good roundup of government views can be found in Murilo Melo Filho, "O nosso Petróleo é a solução," *Manchete*, June 26, 1976, pp. 18-19. The most useful detailed treatment of the Brazilian petroleum question in historical perspective is Peter S. Smith, *Oil and Politics in Modern Brazil* (Toronto: Macmillan, 1976). *Jornal do Brasil*, May 7, 1976, reported that Petrobrás' investments in exploration and production during the first quarter of 1976 were up 82 percent over the corresponding period of 1975. Brazil's limited proven reserves of recoverable crude oil at the end of 1975 were evaluated at just under 800 million barrels, but may be sharply increased during the course of the year as production tests go forward on the offshore fields near Rio de Janeiro. *Veja*, June 23, 1976, p. 86, cited a figure of at least an additional 440 million barrels, but the issue of June 30, 1976, pp. 90-94, predicted that these fields should prove out at more than 3.5 billion barrels and perhaps as much as 10 billion.

9The first memorandum of understanding was signed on September 30, 1976 with British Petroleum according to *Veja*, October 6, 1976, pp. 104-105. A French-Italian consortium, also with government participation, was the next to follow suit, while Shell, Esso, and Texaco were continuing negotiations. Consult *Veja*, September 29, 1976, pp. 117-118 and *Visão*, May 31, 1976, pp. 61-64. *Veja*, on June 16, 1976, p. 87, and *Folha de S. Paulo*, June 10, 1976, reported a major oil strike by Braspetro in Algeria, while *Jornal do Brasil* and *O Estado de S. Paulo*, July 23, 1976, reported a similar development in Iraq. According to *O Estado de S. Paulo* of September 4, 1976 this latter field could bring Brazil as much as 200,000 barrels a day of cheap crude.

10The CVRD's annual report for 1975 was published in *O Estado de S. Paulo*, March 23, 1976. *Jornal do Brasil*, April 3, 1976, placed its revenues at $1.6 million a day during the first three months of 1976, while the same paper on April 19 projected annual sales of $2.5 billion by 1979. *Veja*, June 23, 1976, pp. 83-84, estimated an increase in CVRD's foreign sales of iron ore for the year of 34 percent to over $800 million, with Brazil's total iron ore exports for 1976 exceeding $1 billion. For the first five months of 1976 an increase of 2 percent in the volume of iron exports—to nearly 23 million tons—resulted in a rise of earning of over 27 percent. See *Jornal do Brasil*, May 22, May 29, and June 3, 1976.

11Bauxite production is programmed to reach 8 million tons a year before the end of the 1980s. The CVRD's other international activities include iron ore pelletizing plants with Spain, Japan, and Italy. The Trombetas project is discussed in *O Estado de S. Paulo*, March 4, 1976, while Brazil's aluminum needs are touched upon in *Jornal do Brasil*, April 28 and May 10, 1976.

12Consult *Visão*, July 7, 1975, p. 38; and February 23, 1976, p. 86, as well as *Manchete*, May 15, 1976, pp. 21 and vii; *O Estado de S. Paulo*, March 12, 19, 26, 31, and May 15, 1976; *Jornal do Brasil*, April 29, May 6, and May 13, 1976. Japanese investment was not obtained for Itaqui during Geisel's visit, but the contracts for ore and pelletized iron add to its feasibility. The decision to build a railroad from Carajás to Itaqui was a victory for the CVRD over the politicians of the state of of Pará, who had pushed hard for transportation of the ore to a proposed steel mill near Belém by way of the Tocantins River. Since the Ministry of Transport had favored this solution, which had the backing of its affiliate, Portobrás, the decision went to the president for the final say. For a discussion of Portobrás see *Tendência*, May 1976, pp. 66-67.

13*Jornal do Brasil*, May 13, 1976, covered the formal signing by the Italian concern, while both *O Estado de S. Paulo* and *Jornal do Brasil*, on May 25, 1976, reported the agreement with the Japanese firm. *O Estado de S. Paulo*, June 12, 1976, covered the new company.

[14]See *Jornal do Brasil*, February 25, 1976, on the projected costs of Itaipu. Electrobrás' investments in generating facilities for 1976 are budgeted at $3 billion, up from $2.6 billion in 1975. Itaparica in Bahia has received $400 million in financing by a group of French, German, and Italian banks, while a French consortium has provided $520 million toward Tucuruí (the source of power for Albrás/Alunorte). See *Veja*, October 13, 1976, p. 103.

[15]Designed to greatly enhance Brazil's capabilities in the realm of international commerce, this ambitious program will cost Cr$25 billion at 1974 prices, or close to $3.3 billion U.S. dollars. See *Jornal do Brasil*, February 22, 1976, and *Manchete*, January 22, 1976.

[16]See Presidência da República, Secretaria de Planejamento, *Programa de Construção Naval 1975/1979* (Brasília, July 1974). This constituted a sharp raising of sights from the first such plan, which covered 1971-1975 and had a target of 1.9 million dwt of new construction. The steel-processing capacity of Brazil's seven largest shipyards was to go from 65,200 tons in 1973 to nearly 272,000 tons by 1980, Indeed, by the end of 1976 they had reached close to 220,000 tons' capacity.

[17]See a series of special articles by a former head of SUNAMAM in *Jornal do Brasil*, April 24, 25, and 26, 1976. *O Estado de S. Paulo*, June 29, 1976, puts the shipping deficit for 1975 at $650 million, with that for 1976 estimated at $520 million. Brazil is also engaged in a large-scale program to enlarge and modernize its ports.

[18]A special series of articles on Brazil's shipyards can be found in *Jornal do Brasil*, March 26, April 2, April 14, April 15, April 23, April 30, May 1, May 7, May 14, May 22, and June 5, 1976. Brazil's total merchant marine should be near 10 million dwt by 1980. Other relevant articles are in *Manchete*, May 22, 1976, pp. 82-83; *O Estado de S. Paulo*, April 15, May 5, and May 8, 1976; *Folha de S. Paulo*, May 6, 1976. Also very useful is the study by Décio Mauro Rodrigues da Cunha (then chief of cabinet to the president of SUNAMAM) previously cited. *O Globo*, July 22, 1976, placed the oceangoing merchant marine of Brazil at 161 ships of a total displacement of 4.86 million tons, a figure which does not include the sizable coastal shipping fleet.

[19]Indeed, after 1980 orders from aborad are expected to keep the Brazilian shipyards busy, as they capitalize upon the ready availability of Brazilian steel.

[20]The *Jornal do Brasil*, July 23, 1976, quoted the navy minister with regard to the construction in Brazil of the last of the British-designed missle frigates and submarines and the German oceangoing minesweepers. These have by now been amply discussed in technical journals.

6
Nongovernmental
Actors

Because the executive branch of Brazil's national government enjoys an overwhelming dominance in the foreign policy field, most significant differences over international matters are essentially intramural. However, other groups are significant to some extent. Since these extragovernmental groups could reasonably be expected to play a larger role in policymaking in a more open system—to which the Geisel regime is committed, on record—they clearly merit attention. Business and financial elements will be considered first, followed by the political parties and Congress, the news media and the academic community, the church, labor, and ethnic groups, and, finally, transnational forces.

The Business Community

While commercial, industrial, and financial interests in Brazil essentially support the government's foreign policy, their role in shaping that policy is quite limited. Indeed, Brazil's pattern of state-private sector relations—which might be

substantially different in a politically competive situation—is
fundamentally asymmetrical; the government can exercise
significantly greater leverage over commerce and industry
than these groups in turn can exert upon government. The
public-sector *técnicos* may function as a mediating link, but
in the final analysis they are more responsive to the military
allies upon whom their tenure in office ultimately depends.[1]

The relationship between the state and the entrepreneurial
strata in Brazil recalls the basically corporatist structure of
Getúlio Vargas' *"Estado Nôvo"* from 1937 through 1945.[2]
Such organizations as the National Confederation of Industry
(CNI) and the National Confederation of Commerce (CNC)
were established by Vargas to be collaborative organs of the
state, rather than autonomous special-interest organizations
of the private sector. Even as these organizations functioned
during the experiment with a pluralist democratic system
after 1946, they could best be described as "semiofficial, fi-
nancially secure, sponsored organizations with indirect membership and guaranteed access" to government decision makers, and since 1964 they have become increasingly corporatist.[3] What little responsiveness to business interests is evidenced by government agencies is an important factor in the
relationship between the state and private enterprise.

Some groups representing private-sector economic interests
have long been included on government advisory and consultative bodies, especially those dealing with foreign trade and,
to a lesser extent, investment policy. During the decade prior
to 1964, these groups—the CNI, the CNC, and the commercial associations, in particular—exerted some influence over
the content of policy. Even during that period, one observer
noted that "it has been . . . Itamaraty which has been largely
responsible for the contacts that have been maintained between itself and the groups. . . . Although policy has probably been pretty well formulated by the Foreign Ministry
before the contact with the nation's business leaders, the conferences do add a legitimacy to the ministry's decisions."[4]

After 1964 these organizations became essentially symbol-
ic, and their participation in significant decisions was chiefly

ornamental. As other agencies became more prominent in economic foreign policy–making, responsibility for making contact with the business-entrepreneurial community shifted toward the technocrats of the Planning Ministry; Castelo's ministers of finance and of industry and commerce generally played a secondary role in this respect.

An important aspect of the transition from the Castelo regime to the Costa e Silva government was the increasing, if indirect, voice given to the São Paulo business community. São Paulo's influence appears to have been strengthened during the Médici administration, as Delfim Netto consolidated his influence. However, Delfim's ties with the São Paulo industrialists and bankers probably were designed more to co-opt them—and thus gain their support for his bid to become governor—than to provide real service to them in the policy realm, where he had already clearly defined his course. The role of business interests in Brazilian foreign policy is most often ad hoc, not institutionalized, and tends to be unofficial and informal. Delfim's regional headquarters in Rio de Janeiro and São Paulo, his close relationships with the Federation of Industries of the State of São Paulo (FIESP) and the commercial associations, and his Saturday-morning breakfasts with economic journalists reflected this pattern.

In providing a channel for feedback from the business community, Delfim performed a role somewhat comparable to that of congressional committees in a more representative system. He conveyed the government's concern for economic development to commercial and banking groups, and was accessible, even attentive, to the international business community. The latter function, which has significant implications for foreign policy, is one that his successor has continued to perform (although not exclusively; Reis Velloso, Ueki, and the heads of the government banks have shared in this activity). Some business leaders also attempt to influence policy through the office of the industry and commerce minister, while others try to exploit personal relationships with Civil Cabinet chief Golbery—relationships formed during his employment (from 1961 to 1964 and from 1967 through

1973) as head of Dow Chemical's Brazilian subsidiary, with offices in Rio de Janeiro and São Paulo.[5]

FIESP seems to have pushed Itamaraty to establish a commercial service within the foreign service, with the purpose of promoting exports. Itamaraty's activity in this field has been on the increase in recent years—albeit more in response to pressures from within the government than as a result of urging by the business community. In 1961 the Foreign Ministry was given authority over the trade offices Brazil had maintained in a number of the world's major cities, and four years later Brazil's embassies and consulates were made responsible for trade promotion.[6] Itamaraty's present trade promotion scheme comprises four areas: information, fairs and tourism, trade-promotion operations, and market studies and research. Activities in the information area alone during 1975 included the dissemination of 6 million copies of publications on trade opportunities; the distribution of a periodic review, *Comércio Exterior*, to Brazilian readers; and the publication of a booklet, *Brazil: Industry and Commerce*, in several foreign languages. Special courses designed for the heads of trade sections of embassies and consulates have attracted the participation of most of the diplomats in this category.

In a move designed to strengthen Brazil's limited private-sector capabilities in the trade-promotion sphere, Itamaraty has established a training cycle for foreign-trade specialists. Thirty to forty trainees can be accommodated each year in this program, which begins with six months in Brasília, followed by two years with a Brazilian mission abroad before return to the job market. The private sector has responded—or perhaps countered—with the Foundation and Center for Foreign Trade Studies, which was set up in March 1976 under former Industry and Commerce Minister Pratini de Moraes. Yet, while elements of the business community were ready to take credit for establishing this foundation, its initial funding came from the array of governmental agencies concerned with foreign trade.[7]

Bureaucratic rivalries in the trade-promotion field were intensified by the decision of the Brazilian Association of

Exporters and the Association of Trading Companies to enter into an agreement with the Bank of Brazil to provide services and facilities in the latter's expanding network of thirty-odd overseas branches. Newspaper reports that Itamaraty resented the encroachment of Cacex, Cobec, and Interbrás in an area where the Foreign Ministry had substantially stepped up its own efforts occasioned a denial from Silveira that his ministry opposed the Bank of Brazil's role expansion in export promotion.[8]

A new element in the picture is the Brazilian Association of Foreign Trade Agents, Consultants, and Technicians (Agebrás), although it is too early to predict what role it might come to play. Past experience with analogous groups in other spheres of the Brazilian economy indicates that the members of Agebrás may be more concerned with defending their professional interests than with providing effective policy input (a goal probably beyond the grasp of such a narrow and limited organization). The better-established Brazilian industrial syndicates are represented in the Latin American Free Trade Assn.'s sectoral groups, which meet every few weeks to coordinate industrial policies of the member countries; such frequent and sustained contacts not only build a transnational linkage, but also provide feedback into Brazilian policymaking through other channels. Thus, business elements concerned with exports have a more direct voice in some aspects of foreign policy than do other economic groups. Indeed, businessmen are included in almost all commodity negotiating talks, and trade organizations are consulted on specific matters related to their areas of concern. (For example, the cattle breeders' organization has a say in determining what types of cattle are to be imported.)

There is ample evidence that the government can induce the business community to support its foreign policy much more easily than business can influence foreign policy. One illustration of the asymmetry of the government-business relationship was provided by the government's decision, in late 1974, to take a more active and direct role in export promotion, thus greatly broadening the range of products with which Cobec would be involved. The Association of Brazilian Exporters responded by asking for greater support for private trading companies, but received little more than reassurances of the administration's high regard for the private sector. As a leading exporter observed at the time, Brazilian products now needed to be actively sold, not just made available for purchase, and the government had come to realize that merely offering export stimuli to producers did not always lead to effective and energetic sales efforts. Because exports ran far behind imports during 1974 and 1975, the government developed a strong interest in promoting sales of Brazilian goods. In early 1976 Interbrás was established as a foreign-trade subsidiary of Petrobrás when the government opted to play a direct role in trade with middle Eastern countries, and by mid-1976 the Geisel administration was once more actively considering the idea of establishing a foreign trade bank—an idea that had been vetoed by Delfim Netto when he was finance minister.[9] Meanwhile, the Central Bank continues to have hundreds of millions of dollars at its disposal for the purpose of stimulating exports. (These funds come from the 360-day prior deposits required to cover import authorizations.)

An emerging pattern of fairly close cooperation between business and government seems to have been facilitated by the prolonged economic boom and by a shared interest in continued growth. In the foreign-policy sphere, this cooperation rests on mutual agreement about the importance of export expansion.[10] When an export market seems threatened, as was the case when the United States announced its intention to impose countervailing duties on shoes and other Brazilian leather goods, vigorous governmental defense of private-sector interests may be interpreted by some observers as a response to pressure from the affected industry. However, although there is little doubt that in this case the shoe manufacturers were deeply concerned, Brazilian officials perceived this action by the United States primarily as a larger threat to the export expansion on which their development plan—a major factor in legitimatizing the regime—depended.

The government's vigorous protest thus stemmed from considerations largely independent of the shoe producers' special interests.

Industrial and commercial leaders in Brazil realize that they are better off under the present military-technocratic regime than they were under the regime in power before March 1964. Domestic policies, which are more important to these leaders than foreign policies, largely determine the business community's attitude toward the administration. While business leaders would of course prefer domestic policies favorable to their interests, they are generally wary of jeopardizing a system that is basically congenial—even beneficial—to their point of view. Not surprisingly, business and industrial leaders tend to favor those figures within the government who seem most sympathetic to them. Throughout the early years of the Geisel administration, Severo Gomes, minister of industry and commerce, was viewed as such a figure. However, since Finance Minister Simonsen influenced a substantially broader range of policies than did Severo Gomes, the private sector took relatively more comfort in Simonsen's belief that a "constant, frank, honest, and open dialogue" between the government and business was highly desirable. In spite of their opposition during 1976, to the state's increasingly direct role in the economy, entrepreneurial groups seem likely to support the government's basic foreign-policy stance as long as they are at least consulted on decisions that significantly affect their interests.[11] Meanwhile, they use the press—on which they have substantial influence, through advertising and a certain degree of credit control—to signal their dissatisfaction with specific policies and to ask for what they want.[12]

Major sectors of the business community and the press have become increasingly concerned about the expanding role of the government in direct economic activities. Seven of the top nine nonfinancial companies in Brazil, in terms of net profits, are state enterprises (a list headed by Petrobrás, Electrobrás, São Paulo Electric, and Vale do Rio Doce), while in the financial sector the Bank of Brazil reigns supreme with

Cr.$72 billion in deposits (third place is held by the Bank of São Paulo State, and eighth by the Bank of Guanabara State).[13] With half of all capital-goods purchases in the hands of the government by mid-1975, private entrepreneurs in this field were calling upon the regime for greater import substitution rather than soliciting orders from foreign firms.[14] Since late 1975, substantial steps have been taken toward achieving more import substitutions, essentially as a result of the government's own perception of Brazil's balance-of-payments problem.

Since mid-1975, presidential authorization has been required for the creation of new subsidiaries of state enterprises and for the takeover of private firms by the state, as well as for projects outside the normal areas of government activity. For the most part, however—because of the need to compete more effectively in international trade and to regain a high rate of economic growth—the government has continued to expand its economic activities. Indeed, such spokesmen as Severo Gomes and Sen. Jarbas Passarinho (a member of the Costa e Silva and Médici cabinets) have defended the maintenance of strong state enterprises as constituting the best defense against the potential economic threat posed by the multinational corporations. At this "historical moment when private capital is not ready," Passarinho observed, the state must "fill the empty spaces" in the Brazilian economy and take part in joint ventures in which the transnationals and foreign partners will not become dominant. Increasingly, too, the government believes that Brazil's enhanced bargaining position in bilateral international dealings can be more effectively employed if projects can be implemented by the government's own agents—thus avoiding the delay inherent in private-sector decisional processes, which often lack the sense of urgency that characterizes the regime's procedures.[15]

The enormous resources of the government's financial agencies are at the heart of its relationship with the business community and industrialists. In defense of the state's actions vis-a-vis the private sector, administration spokesmen point out that in 1975 77 percent of the Cr.$40 billion in loans authorized by the National Economic Development Bank (BNDE) were made to private firms, and that private loans will comprise 90 percent of the Cr.$200 billion to be disbursed during the 1976-1979 period.[16] When business representatives complain that these government loans do not begin to compensate for the massive resources available to such giant governmental enterprises as Petrobrás and Vale do Rio Doce, the government's response is that the mechanisms developed since 1964 for channeling savings into effective investment have been crucial to Brazil's development, and that the regime has made repeated efforts to infuse a greater degree of enterprise and vision into Brazil's private capitalism.

The statism issue has been brought to a head by the balance-of-payments crunch resulting from the energy crisis and its adverse effects upon Brazil's foreign trade. In 1974, imports of equipment, steel, and nonferrous metals cost Brazil approximately $6 billion—twice its bill for foreign oil supplies. More and more, the government came to believe that the massive investments and foreign credits necessary to provide a solution to this problem could not wait for Brazil's businessmen, but should be obtained speedily through direct action by the state. Indeed, since the legitimacy of the regime seemed in danger of being compromised by an economic recession of protracted duration, such a strategy appeared imperative. In addition to such large-scale projects as Tubarão, Carajás, Trombetas, and Açominas, the government has moved toward direct control and operation of the valuable phosphate deposits at Patos de Minas and the copper mines at Caraíbas. With fertilizer imports costing Brazil $500 million a year and threatening to go even higher, and copper imports at over 140,000 tons a year, these projects are viewed as being of the utmost urgency. Because the international credit of Brazil's major state enterprises appears better in many respects than does that of the private sector, and because these enterprises have substantial funds of their own to invest in expansion, the imperatives of the economic situation all but dictate the increased employment of the state as the vehicle for achieving expanded investment and production.[17]

In political terms, the statism issue threatens to open significant cleavages in both parties. While on the one hand Senate president Magalhães Pinto recently carried his objections to statism directly to the president, the government's leader in the lower house has stated that "Arena will defend the state's presence in all sectors of the economy fundamental to national security or necessary for the development of the country."[18] The governors of Brazil's two most populous states have come down on opposite sides of the question, and many leaders of the opposition fear that the government and its party are stealing an issue that has traditionally been one of the MDB's nationalistic trademarks.

Congress and the Parties

The role of the Brazilian Congress in foreign policy has been very limited since 1964, although there has been some personal input from members of the foreign relations committees (in particular from Raimundo Padilha, before he became governor of Rio de Janeiro state in late 1970). The president and his closest advisers realize that the absence of superministers in the government has created a need for alternative feedback channels and they believe that the national legislature can fill this need. In part because of the partial decompression of the regime and the greater hearing now accorded the MDB, which constitutes the official opposition, some potential now exists for congressional "consultation" on certain foreign-policy matters, chiefly when the regime seeks to mobilize support for its positions.

Because the Senate president, José de Magalhães Pinto, was foreign minister during the Costa e Silva government, some observers have expected that he might attempt to influence policy in this area. But any such impact seems fated to be intermittent, at best, and this former Minas Gerais governor and onetime presidential hopeful will probably continue to devote his energies to domestic politics and policy as long as he remains president of the Senate. In his efforts to enhance the position of Congress, however, Magalhães Pinto is likely to strive to maintain the illusion that the Senate participates significantly in foreign policy–making through its confirmation and ratification powers. In foreign policy–making as in related spheres, the main thrust of decompression seems to be toward raising the prestige of Congress, rather than giving it any real say in major policy decisions. (Magalhães Pinto may well, however, become head of the Senate's foreign relations committee in 1977.)

One channel through which the Chamber of Deputies may again come to exert occasional influence on foreign policy, as it did prior to 1964, is the system of congressional investigatory committees (CPIs). One highly publicized CPI during 1975, for example, studied the activities of multinational corporations in Brazil. Because a CPI must be set up at the request of one-third of the chamber, the MDB is able to demand such investigations. However, since the majority of committee members come from the government party, and since only five CPIs can function at the same time, the leadership of Congress obviously retains control.[19] While observers have speculated that some particular CPI might be used to bring businessmen disenchanted with government policies into closer alignment with the Congress, most people realize that the long list of CPIs during the 1957-1964 period (a list which also was highly publicized) had little impact on policy, even when congressional powers were much more substantial than they are at present. Moreover, a CPI on multinational corporations functioned in 1968 before it was put out of business by Institutional Act No. 5, the same act that closed down the Congress.

The political parties are not significant factors in foreign policy–making. In terms of influence, the parties range between nonexistent and marginal. Even before 1964, foreign policy was more an executive responsibility than a party concern; thus, the foreign-policy positions of the several parties have lacked coherence. At no time since their simultaneous creation in 1966 has either the government party, Arena, or the tolerated opposition, the MDB, served as an effective vehicle for formulation and execution of foreign policy. Acting through Congress, Arena has supported government

policy across the board, while MDB's attacks on government
policy during the 1974 election campaign were concentrated
chiefly on domestic issues. A substantial opening up of the
political process would perhaps serve to broaden debate over
policy. Yet, broadening the discussion of alternative goals,
orientations, and programs in the international arena would
not significantly alter policymaking mechanisms—except to
the degree that, in certain near-impass situations, the contending institutional actors on the executive side might seek
additional support from the *politicos* in order to influence
the ultimate decision maker, the president.

The Press and Academics

The role of the press in foreign policy has been, at least
until recently, indirect. A sort of double game was at work:
the Brazilian press was helpful to foreign news agencies and
reporters, and could communicate to them opinions and information that it might not print openly in Brazil. Thus, the
foreign press could say openly what some Brazilians would
have liked to say. And, once a certain image of Brazil had
been projected abroad (i.e., printed elsewhere), the Brazilian
press could safely pick it up and reprint it—ostensibly, the
words and views were not its own. Indeed, given the nature
of press censorship from the end of 1968 until early 1975,
this strategy was perhaps the media's only effective way of
influencing foreign policy—although a few journalists had
some small say, based on personal ties rather than on institutional attachments.

While there generally is substantial congruence between
Brazilian foreign policy and the international views of the
Jornal do Brasil, the country's leading daily, the *JB* does not
influence policy to a substantial degree; rather, the *JB* serves
as a vehicle to mobilize support for the government's international stance and actions. This paper's sharp turn against
the policies of Foreign Minister Silveira during 1976 caused
no discernible change in the course of Brazil's international
relations.[20] Some independent analysis, at times critical, can
be found in the pages of *O Estado de S. Paulo*, a São Paulo

daily that boasts a circulation of 200,000, as compared to 185,000 for the *Jornal do Brasil*. Mass-circulation newspapers do not receive serious attention from the foreign-policy elites, with the possible exception of Rio's conservative *O Globo*. A mirroring of official policy similar to that formerly found in *JB* appears in the mass-circulation weekly magazines—particularly in *Manchete*, whose political and international commentator is closely attuned to the regime's policies, periodically turning out best-selling books that stress Brazil's progress and greatness under such titles as *The Brazilian Miracle*, *The Brazilian Challenge*, and *The Brazilian Model*.[21] *Manchete*, a slick pictorial weekly put out by Bloch Editores, has a circulation of 190,000, as compared with 120,000 for the newsweekly *Veja* and 240,000 for *Realidade*, the latter's monthly running mate. Editôra Abril, the publishing house that puts out these last two magazines, also publishes *Comércio Exterior* ("foreign commerce"), while *Tendência* ("trends"), a magazine directed to businessmen and managers (roughly a counterpart of *Business Week* or *Fortune*), is a product of the Bloch firm. The fortnightly *Visão*, with a circulation of 125,000, has roughly the same relationship to *Veja* that *Newsweek* or *U.S. News and World Report* has to *Time*.

The foreign press determines certain parameters of foreign policy to the extent that it influences the international climate within which Brazil must operate. Foreign input into the Brazilian mass media, although significantly reduced during the past decade, still is substantial. The impact of the foreign press on policymakers is relatively small, however, and in any event, public opinion is not a major factor in determining Brazilian foreign policy.

Although Brazilian foreign-policy decisions are not subject to the influence of research "think tanks" or other systematic academic inputs, as are such decisions in the United States, each administration has included a few professors with good connections to Itamaraty or to the Higher War College who have had some impact on the views of certain policymakers. The lack of academic influence on foreign policy is not simply a result of the authoritarian approach that has characterized the system since 1964. One veteran observer, after describing in detail the foreign-policy views of a variety of Brazilian intellectuals and prominent schools of thought during the Kubitschek-Quadros-Goulart period, concluded: "There are many factors hindering the effectiveness of Brazilian intellectuals in influencing foreign policy. They simply have not concerned themselves with foreign policy long enough to be taken seriously by the actual foreign policy-makers."[22]

Although several universities, including the University of Brasília, have finally established courses in international politics, the subject is studied only by a small number of social-science majors, and does not seem to interest a significant proportion of the student population. While in the public-administration field there has been an enormous outpouring of translations of U.S. and European texts, as well as the beginning of a Brazilian literature in this field, a parallel trend has not yet begun with regard to international relations. Journals such as the *Revista da Política Internacional* are read only by foreign-policy professionals and by a handful of international lawyers and professors; these journals emphasize speeches, documents, and treaties rather than policy-oriented articles.

The Church and Labor

Since 1964 the Catholic church has had little influence on Brazilian foreign policy. What little force it has brought to bear generally has been exerted by means of playback from abroad rather than directly; the government, in turn, has responded defensively rather than positively. Indeed, the church's lack of significant impact on Brazil's international policy exemplifies the difference between merely gaining some attention and really being listened to. The church has been, on occasion, a source of problems affecting international relations; however, such problems have been minimized by the substantial rapprochement between the Catholic church hierarchy and the government which Golbery engineered as an important element of the partial "decompression" of the political situation sought by the Geisel administration.

The labor movement has even less influence on foreign policy than the church has—although, to a limited degree, U.S. and international labor leaders play a role in conditioning the attitudes of other countries toward Brazil. And, whereas the Brazilian church (the largest in the world) is of very great importance to the Vatican, with several of its representatives occupying high-level positions within the international Roman Catholic hierarchy, the Brazilian labor movement has no significant voice within international labor circles. (Indeed, it is not a leading factor even within hemisphere labor organizations.) So long as organized labor in Brazil has little success in affecting domestic policies of immediate concern to it—and only recently, some twelve years after the 1964 revolution, has it been able to reduce the proportion of unions subject to government intervention—it will not be a factor of any real weight in foreign-policy considerations.

Ethnic Groups

Intellectuals, the press, the church, labor—all these are conditioning factors, rather than central actors, and are peripheral to most decision making. Other groups are either too peripheral or too narrow in their interests even to be considered actors. For example, the significant Jewish representation in the communications field (as well as in certain other kinds of business) has not had a noticeable effect on Mideast policy. While it might be argued that the Jewish presence was canceled out by that of the sizable Lebanese community, in reality neither group made a concerted effort to influence policy on this issue, because each understood that petroleum was the key factor. Indeed, despite the Middle East crisis, relations between the 160,000 Brazilian Jews and the estimated 2 million nationals of Arab descent are quite good. This sanguine state of affairs may be due in part to the fact that only about 80,000 of the Arabs are Moslems; the most influential persons in this community are of Lebanese origin. (Jordanians, Egyptians, and Syrians are far less significant.) Economic cooperation between Jewish and Arab entrepreneurs is quite common in Brazil. Moreover, in spite of the relatively small number of Jews in the Armed Forces, three Jewish army officers have attained four-star rank in recent years (Isaac Nahon, Idálio Sardenberg, and Waldemar Levy Cardoso).[23]

The other ethnic groups with possible foreign-policy relevance—in addition to members of the U.S. community, most of whom are employed by multinational firms—are the Portuguese and Japanese. The former group is deeply divided between supporters and critics of the present Lisbon regime. Indeed, both the prime minister of the precoup government and General Spinola, leader of the center-right faction within the original "revolutionary" military movement which subsequently split with the left-leaning administration, came to live in Brazil. The Portuguese community in Brazil also includes many who emigrated earlier to escape the Salazar regime as well as thousands of recent arrivals from Angola.[24] Their presence in Brazil contributes to a generalized and often vague conception of Brazil's "special ties" to the former mother of Portuguese Africa. A shift from close alignment with Portugal toward support of independence for its African territories began before the end of 1971, motivated by the government's perception that such a shift would benefit Brazil economically and politically in Angola, Mozambique, and Guinea-Bissau, once those territories became independent, in addition to improving Brazil's standing with the less-developed-countries of the Afro-Asian world.

Similarly, the 700,000 Brazilians of Japanese descent, who constitute a significant economic-political community in São Paulo, have little impact on Brazilian foreign policy. What has mattered in Brazil's relations with Japan is that Japan is a major source of investment capital and advanced technology and provides a market for Brazilian iron ore. Indeed, trade with other countries seems to be the dominant concern of all ethnic blocs in Brazilian society. Unlike the situation in the late 1930s—when German and Italian immigrant groups retained a strong sense of identification with their mother countries, contributing to Brazil's ambiguity toward the

European conflict—foreign national groups now have limited policy relevance. Mass immigrations such as those that occurred from 1870 to 1940 are phenomena of the past, and communities of non-Brazilian origin have largely been absorbed into a society that often has functioned as a melting pot even more effectively than the United States.

Transnational Forces

External factors still constitute important restraints on Brazil's policy choices, albeit significantly less so than was the case a generation or even a decade ago. Significant cosmopolitan linkages (including multinational corporations and even U.S. government representatives) can affect the policymaking process, but transnational forces are not central to basic policy decisions. Indeed, in contrast to the situation that exists in other Latin American countries, there is relatively little sensitivity to these factors in Brazil. Then, too, these linkage factors are sometimes countervailing. For example, foreign investments in Brazil come, not predominantly from a single country, but rather from sources that are to some degree competitive. The United States leads the way with investments valued at nearly $2.4 billion at the end of 1975 (of a total of roughly $7 billion), but West German investment has been rising much more rapidly in recent years to over $870 million and will expand significantly as a result of the nuclear agreements. Registered Japanese holdings had shot up to nearly $840 million by December 1975, with hundreds of millions in the pipeline. Indeed, real Japanese investment was reported to have exceeded $1 billion at the end of 1975.[25] Switzerland is not far behind as a source of investment dollars, with over $890 million, and the United Kingdom narrowly leads Canada for fifth place ($430 million and $411 million, respectively).

While U.S. holdings in Brazil nearly tripled from 1969 through 1975, Japanese investments were multiplied by better than sixteen, Swiss holdings saw nearly a ninefold increase, those of the German Federal Republic increased by some 400 percent, British investments quadrupled, and

French investment spurted from a paltry $34 million to $300 million.[26] Since total West European investments substantially exceed those of the United States and are growing at a significantly faster rate, while Japan is fast closing the gap, the external center for decisions that vitally affect Brazil is not necessarily Washington; and while the U.S. Chamber of Commerce in Brazil can still gain the ears of national decision makers, it certainly cannot begin to dictate policy. The hearings accorded to foreign investors may at times result in reinforcing already-existing pressures, but the influences generated are effective largely to the degree that they correspond to the interests of substantial internal actors.

Brazilian agencies in the international policy field tend to respond to specific external linkage pressures according to the nature of the personal relationships established between the key Brazilian officials and the foreign actors involved; personal style and rapport are crucial factors. With few exceptions, pride in a special relationship with the United States is essentially a residual factor, and one that often involves significant ambivalence. Individual sensitivities are important; some elements on the Brazilian side—as is often the case elsewhere as well—may have an exaggerated view of their importance. Others attempt to exploit foreign negotiations in their own interagency power struggles. None of these ploys is exclusively Brazilian, but Brazilian negotiators are often especially adept at the personal and political side games of the bargaining process.

Notes to Chapter 6

[1]Speaking on "The Influence of the ESG in the Political and Social Thought of Brazilian Elites," Armed Forces chief of staff Corrêa pointed out that there were almost 1,300 civilian and more than 1,600 military graduates of the Higher War College in the present regime, along with 25,000 individuals who had been through extension courses offered by its alumni association. He recommended a further course on national mobilization as a way of increasing the proportion of civilian policy-

making elites processed in the intensive experience of the ESG itself. See *O Estado de S. Paulo*, March 9, 10, and 11, 1976.

[2]That the roots of this relationship go back much further into Brazil's historical experience is the theme of Raymundo Faoro's provocative *Os Donos do Poder: Formação do Patronato Político Brasileiro*, rev. ed. (Porto Alegre: Editôra Globo, 1975), particularly of vol. 2.

[3]Philippe Schmitter, *Interest Conflict and Political Change in Brazil* (Palo Alto, Calif.: Stanford University Press, 1971), p. 180.

[4]Fontaine, "Foreign Policy-making Process in Brazil," p. 148.

[5]In 1974 Paulo Egydio Martins, Castelo's last minister of industry and commerce, was chosen by the Geisel government to be governor of São Paulo despite Delfim's claim to that key office. Martins' possible role as a link between the business interests and the federal executive has been hampered by his problems in governing with a legislature firmly controlled by the opposition party, yet the potential cannot be ignored. See the discussion of his relationship with the president by David Nasser in *Manchete*, July 10, 1976, pp. 26-27.

[6]See Paulo Tarso Flexa de Lima, "Diplomacia e Comércio: Teoria e Práctica," *Revista Brasileira de Estudos Políticos* 42 (January 1976): 157-173.

[7]See *O Estado de S. Paulo*, March 28, 1976. The foundation's initial $1.4 million budget came from the Bank of Brazil and the Central Bank (Cr.$3 million each), followed in descending order of generosity by Petrobrás, Itamaraty's Rio Branco Institute, the Vale do Rio Doce Co., Furnas Hydroelectric Center, the Bank of São Paulo State, Lloyd Brasileira Shipping, the Sugar and Alcohol Institute, Cobec, the Bank of the Northeast, the Bank of Guanabara State, and the National Economic Development Bank. (Consult also *O Estado de S. Paulo*, March 16, 1976.) The first group of economists and administrators trained in the Itamaraty internship program was discussed in *Comércio Exterior*, March–April 1976, pp. 40-41.

[8]Ibid., March 16, 28, and 30, 1976.

[9]*Tendência*, April 1976, pp. 52-55; *Jornal do Brasil*, April 3, 1976.

[10]The government also devotes significant effort to affecting the outlook of the business community. *Comércio Exterior* is published for Itamaraty by the major publishing firm Editôra Abril on a bimonthly basis with a circulation of 38,000. All top officials meet with exporters in regional and national gatherings. See, for example, the coverage of the Third National Meeting of Exporters in *Veja*, June 23, 1976, pp. 83-84.

[11]Witness the dismay of many businessmen when the Industrial Development Council was reorganized without their prior consultation. *Jornal do Brasil*, April 25, 1976.

[12]The private-sector's use of the press is particularly evident in the controversy over "statism." *Visão* has been engaged in a sustained campaign against "statization" of the economy since early 1975, and it has been joined by *O Estado de S. Paulo* and, to a less intense degree, *Jornal do Brasil*. See, for example, "Brasil: Capitalismo de Estado?," *Visão*, May 26, 1975, pp. 43-94, and the entire edition of April 19, 1976, as well as a series of feature articles by Oswaldo Martins in *O Estado de S. Paulo*, March 4, 5, 6, and 7, 1976, followed on March 9 by an editorial, "Statism, Instrument of Totalitarianism."

[13]Of Brazil's 200 largest nonfinancial firms in terms of liquid assets, 78 are state enterprises, including nine of the first ten and 20 of the first 22. The six largest have assets of over $11 billion, and the public sector's assets are 72 percent of the total. (See *Visão*, "Quem é Quem na Economia Brasileira," August 31, 1976.) In employment terms, the Federal Railroad Network (RFFSA) has nearly 112,000 persons on its payroll, followed by the telephone holding company with 69,000. For an all-out attack upon government bureaucracy, see the cover article, "A Burocracia e seu Ritual," in *Veja*, June 2, 1976, pp. 52-61.

[14]*Visão*, June 23, 1975, pp. 51-60, contains the Basic Industries Assn.'s complaints in this regard.

[15]*Visão*, January 12, 1976, pp. 21-23, carried the interview with Senator Passarinho. See *O Estado de S. Paulo*, March 7, 1976, for a discussion of the June 1975 CDE decision on disciplining the proliferation of state-enterprise subsidiaries.

[16]See *Visão*, April 5, 1976, pp. 48-50, and the interview with Bank of Brazil president Ángelo Calmon de Sá in *Veja*, March 27, 1976, pp. 120-121. An annual report for 1975 on the BNDE was carried in *Folha de S. Paulo*, April 29, 1976. *Jornal do Brasil* of the same date is useful, along with *O Estado de S. Paulo*, May 8, 1976. *Jornal do Brasil*, April 8, 1976, states that the National Housing Bank (BHN) planned to loan Cr.$220 billion in 1976 for over a million housing starts—a major boon to the private sector. The Federal Savings Bank (Caixa Econômica Federal), with deposits of $3.5 billion at the end of 1975, has taken on the added function of financial agent for the cabinet-level Social Development Council, as discused in *Manchete*, March 6, 1976, pp. 114-115.

[17]See *Jornal do Brasil*, May 13 and 20, 1976; *Folha de S. Paulo*, May

20, 1976; and *Manchete*, May 29, 1976, p. 139.

18"Até Onde Vai O Estado?," *Veja*, May 19, 1976, pp. 20-25. The quotation is from p. 20.

19See *Visão*, November 24, 1975, pp. 24-29.

20Searing editorials were published in *Jornal do Brasil*, July 19 and July 22, 1976. On Brazil's newspapers consult *Visão*, August 8, 1976, pp. 36-49.

21Murilo Melo Filho, *O Desafio Brasileiro* (Rio de Janeiro: Bloch Editores, 1970); *O Milagre Brasileiro* (Rio de Janeiro: Bloch Editores, 1972); and *O Modelo Brasileiro* (Rio de Janeiro: Bloch Editores, 1974).

22Fontaine, "Foreign Policy–making Process in Brazil," p. 116. See also his *Brazil and the United States*, pp. 20-53. Unfortunately, both are heavily weighted toward views and authors from the pre-1964 period.

23As of 1970 there were roughly 65,000 Jews in São Paulo, some 50,000 in Rio de Janeiro, perhaps 12,000 in Porto Alegre, and a scattering in the other cities.

24Approximately 7,500 Portuguese immigrants, the vast majority of them from Angola, arrived in Brazil between January and August 1975, and they were continuing to arrive at a monthly rate higher than the annual average for the 1970-1974 period. See *Visão*, November 11, 1975, pp. 17-22.

25*Veja*, November 5, 1975, p. 95. Japanese investment in Brazil may reach $9 or $10 billion by 1985, according to *Tendência*, May 1976, p. 12. *Manchete*, July 31, 1976, p. 23, said that $6 million in investment was expected to follow President Geisel's September state visit to Japan; and *O Estado de S. Paulo*, July 8, 1976, quoted Japan's foreign trade minister as saying that Brazil could expect some $20 billion in Japanese investment during the next ten years.

26The following table can be constructed from data in *Veja*, November 5, 1975; *O Estado de S. Paulo*, May 11, 1976; and *Jornal do Brasil*, July 22, 1976:

Country	1969	1971	1973	1975	percent in 1975
U.S.	815	1096	1759	2395	32.1
Germany	177	331	521	871	11.7
Japan	55	124	319	841	11.3
Switz.	104	191	358	890	11.9
U.K.	109	273	324	430	5.8
Canada	167	294	360	411	5.5
France	34	129	205	300	4.0

Between December 1971 and the end of 1975, investment from the Benelux countries rose from $72 million to over $430 million, putting Western European investment in Brazil a full one-third above that of the United States.

7
Overview
of the
Foreign-Affairs Community

The array of institutional actors and the roles these actors play in Brazilian foreign policy–making provides a backdrop against which the basic general features governing Brazil's foreign policy can be easily distinguished. In order to identify important continuing trends operating in the context of this basic structure, it is necessary to analyze the most significant institutional characteristics of the foreign-affairs community. Once this is done, an effort will be made to isolate the arenas in which Brazil's several foreign-policy instruments operate and to draw some conclusions about the roles of the several central actors at different levels of decision making.

Institutional Characteristics

The Brazilian foreign-affairs community remains relatively small despite its rapid expansion during the 1960s and 1970s. Chiefly concentrated in the executive branch of the national government, it is largely restricted to high-level officials. Within the Armed Forces, for example, the decision-making community does not extend far beyond the service ministers'

149

cabinets and the general staffs, except for officers assigned to intelligence services—and even these are concerned chiefly with internal security.

While small in comparison with the overall size of the policy-relevant groups in Brazil and even with the federal bureaucracy, the foreign-policy community is sufficiently large to have become fairly specialized. Unlike the Foreign Ministry, with its broad range of responsibilities in the international sphere, those components of other ministries and agencies which are directly involved with foreign policy tend to be quite differentiated (e.g., the finance minister's international advisory staff, or Braspetro and Nuclebrás under Mines and Energy).

All elements of the foreign-affairs community are essentially elitist, notwithstanding the middle-class origins (in many cases all but forgotten) of many of the military men and of a fairly large proportion of the economic technocrats. The foreign service has traditionally been an upper-class and upper-middle-class career, and the other foreign-policy elites demand a university education as a minimum entrance qualification. Even before 1964 there were few significant foreign-affairs-conscious groups below the upper socioeconomic levels, and this situation has become more pronounced under the essentially authoritarian system that has been in effect since that time.

Brazil's foreign-affairs community has remained highly adaptive and relatively unified. Important foreign-policy shifts have occurred several times since 1930; the present generation has seen a shift away from close cooperation with the United States after Vargas' return to power in 1951, a reapproximation with the United States after his death in 1954, an experiment with an "independent" foreign-policy stance in the early 1960s which approached open hostility toward the United States, a sharp reversal of this trend when the military came to power in April 1964, and a steady move toward more autonomous foreign-policy positions beginning in 1969. Yet, throughout this period, a substantial consensus was maintained and fundamental agreement on foreign-policy

objectives was only rarely shaken by divisive debates. Moreover, influential policymakers have tended to accept modifications required by evolving world events and by changes in
Brazil's international priorities as a result of the country's
concern with internal development. The determination to
pursue Brazil's national interests within the limitations imposed by contemporary international and internal problems
was discernible in the 1930s, continued to be apparent in the
1950s, and is still obvious in the 1970s.

The major components of the foreign-affairs community
tend to be quite new—and hence relatively inexperienced actors in the policy arena—with the exception of the Foreign
Ministry. Even Itamaraty has been subjected to a fundamental recharging, however; over the years its emphasis has
shifted from diplomatic representation to economic and technical negotiations. Except for their existence in very primi-
tive forms, the other basic components of the foreign policymaking process—presidential staff agencies, the SNI, the
Armed Forces General Staff, Petrobrás, Nuclebrás, etc.—date
from the 1950s or later; some are only a few years old. In
many cases, their foreign-policy roles are even newer. For example, Petrobrás was set up in 1953, but it did not take on
any significant international policy responsibilities until the
late 1960s; while the EMFA was not important in the foreign-policy area until after 1964, and the Ministry of Mines
and Energy gained prominence in this field only with the
energy crisis and Brazil's subsequent balance-of-payments
problems.

The autonomy of the foreign-affairs community as a whole
is substantial, largely because public opinion counts for so
little in Brazilian policymaking. Brazil's international policy
organs are not prisoners of tradition nor bound by related
myths that might dictate policy decisions inappropriate to
the present situation. National Security Doctrine remains
flexible and subject to continuous revision; hence it has not
become a straitjacket on policy, as some ideologies have. The
"Itamaraty ethos" is itself subject to modification because
the Foreign Ministry must operate in conjunction with (and

often subordinate to) other governmental components that have greater authority to set fundamental orientations and priorities.

Despite all these considerations, the Brazilian foreign-affairs community is not monolithic in its attitudes and outlook. Although a substantial diversity of interests is represented within it, divisions most often arise in regard to second-rank issues and implementation of policy, particularly in the complex and uncertain economic sphere. Different conceptions of the world in which Brazil exists, as well as different ideas about the basic nature of Brazil's place within that world, do not keep natural adversaries from working together to formulate policies and, at times, even to set priorities, if not goals.

Arenas of Operations

Brazil makes use of all conventional instruments for the conduct of foreign policy: diplomacy, political strategy, economic leverage, armament, and propaganda. The agencies involved in administering these instruments are, as we have seen, numerous, and the relationships among them are complex. Now it is appropriate to sort out these agents and instruments according to arenas of foreign-policy operations. This will be done first in terms of types of decisions, and then according to the functions of various agencies and their geographical areas of activity.

Types of Decisions

The term "strategic decisions" refers to irrevocable policy actions that intensely affect a relatively large number of environmental components, decision makers, and decisional institutions for a substantial period of time.[1] These decisions are usually made by the president himself and his closest advisers, with the concurrence of other senior spokesmen in the Armed Forces (through both institutional channels and informal consultation). Prior to the Geisel administration, the decisional process almost certainly would have included formal consultation of the National Security Council; at present, however, the Economic Development Council and, to a lesser degree, the Armed Forces High Command are likely to be the crucial top-level bodies involved in such decisions, while a cabinet meeting would subsequently serve to inform other ministers. Nonmilitary ramifications in the political arena would have been considered by the Political Development Council.

Certainly the option during 1974-1975 for development of a complete nuclear cycle was a strategic decision in the full sense of this term. Brazil's shift toward the pro-Arab side on Middle East issues at the end of 1973, and its assertion of a 200-mile territorial sea limit during the 1970-1972 period, also qualify, albeit with lesser impact and much narrower ramifications upon many of Brazil's foreign-policy decision-making institutions. Strategic decisions in the Brazilian context generally follow the perception of some fundamental change in the international situation or the emergence of some urgent and compelling internal problem whose resolution requires action in the international sphere. Presently, the latter case exists in regard to the slowdown of economic growth in conjunction with a serious balance-of-payments deficit, a two-headed problem which has caused Brazil to engage in major efforts to seek additional credits and investments from Washington, Paris, Tokyo, and London, as well as to launch a coordinated campaign, via both bilateral negotiations and multilateral forums, to obtain improved access to the markets of the industrialized nations for Brazilian exports.

Tactical decisions are of lesser scope and duration of impact, and either precede or follow strategic decisions. Most tactical decisions also involve the president, particularly those that are rooted in fairly recent strategic decisions. Thus, the decision to recognize the MPLA regime in Angola followed the more basic decision to seek credibility with Afro-Asian governments, even at the cost of losing some traditional allies and sources of capital and credit. On the other hand, the establishment of diplomatic relations with the People's Republic of China and the decision to attain nuclear independence exemplify strategic decisions that were preceded by tactical decisions which pointed the way. In the first of these cases, the according of official status to Brazil's commercial mission to Peking was the key tactical decision; in the latter, Brazil's decision to remain outside the nuclear nonproliferation treaty and the creation of Nuclebrás had similar import.

In the making of tactical decisions, conflict and competition between major components of the foreign-affairs community are prevalent, particularly since a policy line implicit in one strategic decision may not be totally compatible with that implicit in another. This lack of compatibility, as well as the issue of role expansion versus the preservation of established spheres of responsibility, has been at the root of such Itamaraty–Finance Ministry conflicts as the dispute over policy toward Africa during the Médici government, and is also central to the growing rivalry between the Foreign Ministry and the Ministry of Mines and Energy.

While there still is significant room for interagency disagreements and even conflicts in the area of implementary decisions—the continuous flow of day-to-day foreign-policy actions that execute strategic and tactical decisions—the roles of the various policy actors are becoming increasingly distinct. Jurisdictional disputes are no longer allowed to get out of hand, and coordination mechanisms have been strengthened. The major source of controversy may lie at the place where the attempts to implement one policy impinge on the efforts to carry out another. (Such conflict is likely to occur wherever a complex set of policies directed at multiple national objectives is pursued through a variety of foreign-policy instrumentalities, not just in Brazil.) Further complications arise from the "blurring of the traditional distinctions between national and international policy" remarked on by a vice-chief of Brazil's Armed Forces General Staff.[2] For, in the view of Brazil's top policymakers—most of whom, both military and civilian, have passed through the Higher War College—national security is, in the final analysis, dependent on development (just as it is also a crucial precondition for development). In terms of foreign-policy considerations, "security is obtained through a combination of measures taken to guarantee the execution of national policy and to oppose adverse factors."[3] Clearly there will be many differences of opinion even as to the compatibility of various policies aimed at implementing the discrete facets of this formulation.

Furthermore, some components of the foreign-affairs decision-making community—notably the presidential staff agencies (among the most influential), the Congress, and the political parties (much less significant)—are not operation entities; or at least, they do not operate abroad. Other institutions—most prominently the Foreign Ministry, but also the military establishment, the Bank of Brazil, Petrobrás and the SNI—do have agencies, branches, representatives, or agents outside Brazil's borders. This situation leads to potentially significant differences of outlook and impact, since some of the participants in policymaking have direct roles in carrying out policies beyond Brazil's borders, while others in the decision-making process are not called on to implement policy in foreign countries.

Interinstitutional and even personal bargaining among policymakers continues to be important in the evolution of Brazilian foreign policy. This kind of informal negotiating is possible largely because of the autonomy of the foreign-affairs community, and autonomy that is the result of the relatively weak influence of public opinion, historical memories, and national myths, as well as of the limited influence of the media and intellectuals, the parties and Congress, the church and labor movement—exactly those institutions that might be expected to stimulate and keep alive public opinion, tradition, and myths. In view of the fact that all elements of the foreign-policy community, with the exception of the Foreign Ministry, are primarily concerned with internal factors and policies, this autonomy requires that a close eye be kept on bureaucratic interests and trade-off bargaining in policy arenas apparently far removed from foreign relations.

Functional/Regional Concentration

The presidency not only is involved in all major decisions

across the board, but also has a heavy responsibility for the ceremonial side of foreign affairs, a side that includes state visits (which are becoming increasingly frequent as Brazil continues its greater international activity and upward mobility), border meetings with neighboring heads of state and governors of key Brazilian states, and personal conferences with Brazil's diplomatic representatives to certain foreign countries and to key international bodies.[4] It seems safe to assume that the president also pays close personal attention to whatever covert activity Brazil may engage in regarding its neighboring countries, especially Bolivia, Uruguay, and Guyana (and possibly Paraguay, Peru, Chile, and Argentina). The chief of the SNI reports to him at least once a day, and—having served as both military head of the March 31, 1964, movement and commander-in-chief of the Armed Forces—the Brazilian president is not likely to let the military's dealings abroad slip from his own purview.

The Armed Forces' specific sphere of foreign-policy responsibility—in addition to any covert intelligence activities it may undertake—includes the normal representational and reporting activities of military attachés, negotiation of arms purchases from Western industrialized powers and of limited sales to Brazil's smaller neighbors, and exchanges of personnel for training purposes. Similarly, the Finance Ministry and other economic agencies are central to the administration of Brazil's complicated and varied international financial and commercial transactions—in itself no small matter for a fast-developing country whose foreign trade has exceeded $20 billion (U.S. dollars) in each of the past three years and whose foreign indebtedness more than matches that figure.

The Brazilian Foreign Ministry performs a particularly important role in the conduct of bilateral relations in which basic directions have been established and the general tone is not subject to abrupt changes. This is the case with respect to most of Latin America and many European countries, but less so in relations with Africa and Asia.[5] Itamaraty's professional diplomats bring to the day-to-day conduct of affairs considerable expertise, useful language skills, and, in many instances, good personal relationships with the policymakers of other countries. These strengths carry over to the traditional multilateral intergovernmental organizations such as the United Nations and the Organization of American States, where the high quality of Brazilian diplomatic representation is generally recognized.[6]

The Foreign Ministry is less central to multilateral affairs of a primarily economic nature, and even less to major bilateral negotiations on matters of trade and finance with the industrial powers. Brazil's professional diplomats are also likely to be upstaged by ranking technocrats on issues that have significant technical components (such as those related to energy) or which require Brazil to deal with countries where Itamaraty's familiarity with cultural idiosyncrasies and political nuances is limited (as may be the case in the Middle East and much of Africa). Highly specialized matters that require scientific expertise, such as nuclear energy, also tend to slip out of the Foreign Ministry's hands. (Although Ambassador Paulo Nogueira Baptista's presence as head of Nuclebrás helps cushion the impact of this tendency.)

The Foreign Ministry is, however, the one major agency concerned exclusively and continuously with foreign affairs, and it strives energetically to maximize Brazil's policy capabilities on multiple fronts. Itamaraty's long and generally fruitful experience with political ends and means, together with its increasing familiarity with basic economic factors, afford it a generally flexible and effective policy mix. Its policymaking influence at any particular time is substantially affected by the relationship of the foreign minister to the president, since it lacks any real constituency of its own.

If Brazil's interests in the rest of Latin America are primarily political and strategic, its instruments for advancing those interests are often economic. Bilateral trade and aid is not Brazil's primary concern in the cases of Bolivia, Paraguay, and Uruguay. Given these countries' small economies, limited foreign commerce, and relatively unfavorable international financial standing, however, economic considerations loom much larger on their side of the table—thus giving Brazil substantial leverage. While a credit of $50 million extended to Uruguay has little intrinsic importance to Brazil, to Uruguay its magnitude may be sufficiently crucial to incline that small and troubled republic toward Brazil in the diplomatic tug-of-war that has long existed between Brazil and Argentina.[7] The joint construction of the vast Itaipu hydroelectric complex will tie Paraguay much closer to Brazil, since the latter's purchase of most of the former's share of the electricity generated may well become the major source of the Asunción government's revenues.[8]

Bolivia presents a somewhat different balance of opportunities and costs, since in that country Brazil is not as directly involved in an influence contest with Argentina as it is in Uruguay and Paraguay. In the latter two countries, Brazilian strategists seem to want to preserve some aspects of the historical buffer function while strengthening economic and political ties to Brazil. With respect to Bolivia, where Brazilian influence is already paramount, Brazilian policymakers may not—at this time, at least—wish to open themselves to responding to economic demands from La Paz disproportionate to the tangible benefits that might thereby accrue to Brazil. It could be disadvantageous to both Brazil and the Banzer government if the latter were perceived, either at home or abroad, as a Brazilian client. Since Brazil sees Bolivia as a potential window into the Andean Pact, close relations between the two countries should be built on a solid foundation that succeeding regimes are likely to accept and preserve; it is not in Brazil's interest to form excessively close ties to the present Bolivian government (which faces a multiplicity of internal problems that dependence on Brazil would not solve). Meanwhile, cooperation between the Brazilian Armed Forces and the Bolivian military is being fostered through training, exchange of visits, and arms transfers (up to the level of jet fighter/trainers and armored personnel carriers).[9]

Brazil does not, of course, seek to dominate Argentina; rather, it hopes to check and contain its longtime rival for South American leadership. One facet of this strategy is the enhancement of Brazil's influence—at Argentina's expense—

on their three common neighbors. In addition, the Brazilian government has striven to extract maximum advantage from the marked contrast between its own political stability and Argentina's virtually chronic state of political crisis. While blunting Buenos Aires' initiatives within the La Plata Basin Commission, Brasília has sought to build mutually advantageous bilateral relations on the basis of trade and the two countries' shared interests—particularly in respect to naval and maritime matters—in South Atlantic security. The replacement of María Estela ("Isabelita") Martínez de Perón by a military regime in March 1976 gave rise to renewed efforts to improve Brazilian-Argentine relations. One such effort was the naming of Oscar Camilión, known to be an advocate of cooperation between his country and Brazil in opposition to alleged centers of imperialism, as the new Argentine ambassador in Brasília.[10]

Brazil's relations with Peru, Colombia, and Venezuela involve primarily Amazon-basin considerations and emphasize efforts to prevent the Andean Pact from becoming an instrument for containment of Brazilian influence. With Venezuela there are additional factors, including the political-strategic issue of that country's territorial claims against Guyana and mutual concern about the sharp turn to the left evinced by the Burnham government during 1975-1976. Brazilian state enterprises have entered the bidding for construction of a major railroad in Venezuela, and speculation about possible bilateral exchanges of petroleum for soy and other foodstuffs has been rekindled by Brazil's acceptance of the Caracas góvernment's proposals for a Latin American economic system. With regard to Colombia, Brazil's major interest is in its potential as a source of coal, while relations with Ecuador and Chile—the only two South American countries not territorially contiguous with Brazil—center upon essentially political-strategic concerns. In the case of Chile, Brazil's policy is complicated by its commitment to support Bolivia's quest for some form of outlet to the Pacific.

If, in Latin America, Brazil uses largely economic means to further political ends, a case can be made that Brazil uses political means to further its economic interests vis-a-vis the United States and Western Europe.[11] The critical nature of dealings with the industrial powers and the massive scale of the stakes involved not only demand the involvement of the entire Brazilian foreign-affairs community but also help it to arrive at a greater degree of consensus than it otherwise might achieve.

Brazil's interest in the Middle East is essentially economic—the imperative need for oil—but negotiations with Middle Eastern countries involve a significant political dimension, since the chief objective of the Arab governments is to oblige Brazil to favor the Arab position in multilateral forums. It appears that Brazil's vote at the United Nations on the question of Israel is more highly prized by the Arabs than, for example, its stance at meetings that wrestle with the shape of the international economic system. Thus, Brazil was one of only four Latin American countries to vote for the Arab resolution in the U.N. General Assembly on October 17, 1975, condemning Zionism as racist. Trade relations have increased markedly with Algeria, Iran and in particular Iraq, and should continue to flourish for at least the next few years.[12]

As regards Brazil's African policy, varied political and diplomatic means are employed to promote economic goals that are not confined to Africa. African support is important to Brazil in international economic and financial agencies and conferences. Since the beginning of the world energy crisis, friendly African nations have also been valued in their role as intermediaries with their Arab allies in softening the adverse impact of petroleum politics on Brazil.[13]

Showing the Flag

Outside Brazil, apart from flying visits by top policymakers, the most visible Brazilian presence is found in its diplomatic posts. The relative importance of these posts depends on their location; for example, to Brazilians their embassy in La Paz may not mean much, while it may be seen as important by Bolivians. Some Brazilian third-world representation may not seem important to either Brazil or the host country.

The most rapidly speading Brazilian agency abroad is the Bank of Brazil, which is steadily expanding its branches on all continents (from eleven overseas agencies in 1970 to thirty by early 1976). In major commercial and financial centers trade offices may exist separate from the Brazilian embassy or consulate, while in a few cities Braspetro, Lloyd Brasileiro, or the Brazilian Coffee Institute may be visible.

The Brazilian flag is shown by the private sector more prominently by Varig, its international airline, than by other concerns, most of which are buried in rather anonymous offices in financial and shipping districts. In many North African and Middle Eastern countries, however, the thousands of Brazilian technicians working on large construction projects—airports, highways, and housing—are the most conspicuous symbols of Brazil's presence.[14] In the world's major centers Brazilian journalists can be found; fairly sizable bureaus are maintained in New York and Paris by the chief magazine-publishing concerns, such as Editôra Abril and Bloch Editores, as well as by newspapers such as *Jornal do Brasil* and *O Estado de S. Paulo*. Brazilian artists, musicians, and writers are prominent in a number of cultural centers, and it is increasingly possible to find Brazilian restaurants in major cities. As a result of the recent economic boom, Brazilian tourists are increasingly numerous in the United States and Western Europe. Finally, when one speaks of the Brazilian presence abroad, there is the incomparable Pelé, his impact multiplied enormously by television and films, along with a host of other stars of the *futebol* world who have been imported to hype the gate as well as improve the quality of the game from Madrid to Milan and from Seattle to Santiago.[15]

Notes to Chapter 7

[1]Michael Brecher distinguishes among strategic, tactical, and implementing decisions in "Formulation of High Policy Decisions: Israel," in Frank B. Horton III, Anthony C. Rogerson, and Edward L. Warner III

(eds.), *Comparative Defense Policy* (Baltimore, Md.: Johns Hopkins University Press, 1974), pp. 169-170.

[2]Meira Mattos, "Uma Geopolítica," p. 1.

[3]Lavanère-Wanderley, *Estratégia Militar e Desarmamento* (Rio de Janeiro: Biblioteca de Exército, 1971), p. 34.

[4]Geisel visited Paraguay late in 1975, and France and the United Kingdom in April and May 1976. He travelled to Japan in September 1976 and was scheduled to make other state visits during 1977.

[5]As measured by the quality of diplomatic personnel assigned there, Buenos Aires is clearly a top-priority post. Not only did Silveira serve as ambassador to Argentina before assuming the position of foreign minister, his predecessor there was Pio Corrêa (a former secretary general), and Gibson Barbosa had been chargé in Buenos Aires in the late 1950s. Recently João Pinheiro was moved from Buenos Aires to Washington following the death of Araújo Castro. Other high-priority embassies in South America appear to have been Peru (where Araújo Castro and George Álvares Maciel represented Brazil in the late 1960s), Uruguay (where the present secretary general was chargé at about the same time), and Paraguay (with Gibson Barbosa as chargé in 1966-1967).

[6]By far the best treatment of Brazil's role in multilateral forums and intergovernmental organizations is Wayne Selcher's 1976 external research paper, "Brazil's Multilateral Diplomacy."

[7]Following the mid-1975 meetings between Geisel and Uruguayan President Bordaberry, Itamaraty spokesmen were quoted as saying that Uruguay's "pendulum" policy of leaning first toward one of its neighbors and then toward the other might be a thing of the past, in light of the hold on the pendulum Brazil had gained by virtue of extending credit, agreeing to the joint development of the hydroelectric and navigational potential of the large lake on the two nations' common border, and bailing out Uruguay through purchase of its otherwise unmarketable beef surplus. See *Veja*, June 18, 1975, pp. 19-20. Argentine reaction to Brazil's increasingly strong ties with Uruguay, as reported in *Folha de S. Paulo*, June 24, 1976, tends to bear out this prediction.

[8]At the time of Geisel's trip to Asunción, Brazil made a $3.5 billion loan to Itaipu Internacional. Paraguay is to repay its part over 30 years beginning in 1983, and will in effect be paying in electricity. See *Veja*, December 10, 1975, pp. 22-23. *Manchete*, November 22, 1975, pp. 74-81, includes discussion of this vast project's impact on Paraguay.

Relevant documents are in *Resenha de política exterior do brasil 2*, no. 7 (October, November, and December 1975): 5-22.

9*Veja*, May 5, 1976, p. 28, stated that there are some 40,000 Brazilians living on the Bolivian side of their common border. *Correio do Povo* of Porto Alegre, May 11, 1976, discussed Brazilian plans to utilize Bolivian natural-gas supplies in order to reduce ore from the large new reserves at Urucúm in Matto Grosso State. Previous agreements with Bolivia have provided for railroad construction and assistance in the establishment of a steel industry in Bolivia by Brazil in return for long-term guarantees of natural-gas supplies.

10*Veja*, May 26, 1976, p. 25. Total Brazil-Argentine trade in 1975 was $651 million and was rising moderately during 1976. See *O Estado de S. Paulo*, October 17, 1976.

11The limitations of such a distinction are underscored by the director of the graduate economics program of the Getúlio Vargas Foundation, University of Chicago Ph.D. Carlos Geraldo Langoni, when he cautions that "at present the economic problem is much closer to the political area," to which a Brazilian news magazine added, "It ceases to be technical—like inflation and investments—and becomes political, discussing the economic system itself." See *Veja*, June 11, 1975, p. 79, and Langoni's widely read *A Economia da Transformação* (Rio de Janiero: José Olympio Editôra, 1975).

12According to *Veja*, April 21, 1976, pp. 107-108, Brazil's trade with Algeria in 1975 exceeded $330 million, with a surplus of over $100 million in Brazil's favor. *O Estado de S. Paulo*, May 19, 1976, put the surplus at $300 million in Brazil's favor on goods and services of some $400 million. Construction of universities, hospitals, railroads, and airports, along with development of port facilities, are major items. The commodity sold by Brazil in greatest amounts is sugar. *Visão*, November 24, 1975, pp. 43-46, discusses other Middle East business activities of Brazil.

13For Itamaraty's attention to Africa, see *Veja*, July 14, 1976, pp. 22-23.

14In Mauritania the Mendes Júnior construction company is building a 600-kilometer desert road under a nearly-$1-billion contract, with 300 Brazilian workers employed. See *Veja*, December 31, 1975, p. 62, and *Visão*, January 26, 1976, p. 61.

15Several starters from Brazil's 1974 World Cup soccer team have been playing for teams in Spain and France, while Italian soccer's high salaries have long attracted big-name players from Brazil. Then, too, Emerson Fittipaldi, world-champion Grand Prix racing driver in 1972 and 1974, is piloting a Brazilian-made car for a Brazilian sponsor during the 1976 circuit. Another Brazilian, Carlos Pace, has entered the select company of the recognized contenders for the Formula I championship. Brazil has also made a concerted effort to upgrade its representation in all Olympic sports, in view of the size of the international television audience that watched the Montreal games.

8
Critical
Continuing
Questions

Brazilian progress toward major-power status is almost certain to continue through the rest of the 1970s and into the 1980s. The fundamental question in the short run is one of rate, while in the longer run the question centers on the extent of this upward international mobility. Although developments in the external environment will continue to be important—probably more as constraints than as facilitating factors—Brazil's movement toward joining the select circle of global powers will depend most heavily on greater internal development and its ability to achieve a preeminent position among the nations of Latin America. This does not mean that Brazil must establish paramountcy over its South American neighbors, but rather that its economic growth, political stability, and range of international activity must increasingly set it apart from the other significant countries of Latin America (notably Mexico and Argentina). There are substantial indications that the German Federal Republic, Japan, the USSR, and China already view Brazil as a leading candidate for inclusion in the ranks of the world's major powers; in their eyes, Brazil's vast potential for further development outweighs its present economic weaknesses and possible sociopolitical shortcomings. Great Britain and France—particularly with Ambassadors Roberto Campos in London and Antônio Delfim Netto in Paris striving to outdo each other in projecting the image of a dynamic and confident Brazil—seem likely to follow suit, as they throw off the blinders of their historically stronger ties to Argentina and Mexico. Certainly the state visits to the latter countries by President Geisel in April–May 1976 marked a significant step forward in this regard.[1]

Since, to a great extent, a country becomes a major power when other major powers recognize it as such, the general prospects for Brazil's acceptance into the global power club during the present generation look promising. Although the attitude of the United States may still affect the timing of Brazil's arrival, it can no longer determine the eventual outcome of this process. This realization appears to have been at the root of Secretary of State Kissinger's actions and statements during his February 1976 visit to Brazil.[2] The U.S. secretary of state was doing little more than recognizing a new fact of international life, albeit with considerable diplomatic flourish, when he termed Brazil "a nation of greatness, a people taking their place in the front rank of nations . . . a nation now playing a role in the world commensurate with its great history and its even greater promise." In viewing Brazil as both an industrial country and part of the developing world, and in stressing its "vastness, diversity, and potential," Kissinger was touching upon themes that were soon to be echoed in Paris and London in acknowledgement of Brazil's arrival on the world scene.

Although Brazil's candidacy for major-power status has met with substantial receptivity on the part of those countries already at the top of the international stratification system, a number of factors could well brake the pace of that nation's arrival. First among these would be a halt to Brazil's progress toward becoming an industrialized country, as a result of either a breakdown of the political order or a decision to reverse the fundamental direction of policy. A second factor could be failure of the regime, even though remaining in power, to cope with the economic problems and challenges facing the country, precipitating a loss of international standing and influence as Brazil became mired in stagnation. Either of these developments is possible, but neither is part of the most likely course of events.

This chapter focuses upon three crucial sets of basic factors conditioning Brazil's international role and capabilities: (1) the probable limits of change with respect to Brazil's foreign-policy elites, (2) the obstacles in the road toward an opening of the political system, and (3) some of the continuing economic problems affecting Brazil's forward movement, particularly the present balance-of-payments situations.

Continuity/Limits of Change

In the mid-term future, it seems likely that the Brazilian economic and political systems will be increasingly consolidated, even institutionalized. This is perhaps more probable with regard to foreign policy–relevant facets than to other aspects of the policymaking processes. While continuity of foreign-policy elites does not guarantee continuity of policy, it does make such continuity more likely. In the Brazilian case, the marked continuity of foreign-policy elites since 1964 probably will extend through the rest of this decade and perhaps well beyond. These groups in Brazil have shown that they can learn from experience and adapt to changing circumstances. Perceived failures in the foreign-policy sphere or setbacks resulting from changed international circumstances would probably lead first to a reassessment of policies and only later, after this had proved inadequate, to a reevaluation of fundamental objectives.

Given the strength of the regime and the manifest weaknesses of the Brazilian left, the possibility that a revolution might radically alter the political system and thus overturn the present foreign-policy elites appears remote. Indeed, ouster of the military from power appears further away than it did at the beginning of the decade.[3] Translation of widespread disaffection into effective mass action has been a slow process throughout Brazilian history, and the regime's ability to co-opt important elements of the students and workers shows few signs of diminishing at present.

While new elite groups linked to the processes of change accompanying Brazil's development may well emerge in time, these processes are not taking place at a rate sufficient to have more than a gradual influence on policymaking before the mid-1980s. In the absence of either revolution or the emergence of new elites through the dynamics of moderniza- tion, rifts within the officer corps or between the military and their diplomatic and technocratic allies would be the most likely source of major policy change in the foreseeable future. Intramilitary conflicts are likely to be absorbed with- in the political processes of the Brazilian Armed Forces, while the probability of the latter development is minimized by the careerist orientation of very large segments of these civilian groups and by the relative fragmentation of these groups, in comparison with the hierarchical structure of the military establishment. Serious divisions among civilian for- eign-policy elites would probably be reflected in military cir- cles, or the Armed Forces might support that faction with whose views they substantively agreed. Taking these consider- ations into account, it is likely that any changes resulting from internal adjustments in the regime during the next dec- ade would create only modifications of emphases and priori- ties, not basic alterations in goals or orientation.

Given the consistent career patterns among the Brazilian officers corps, it seems unlikely that the orientation of the upper ranks of the military establishment will undergo drastic changes during the next decade. There will, however, con- tinue to be a steady turnover of personnel at all ranks, in con- formance with the inflexible provisions of the up-and-out promotion system in all three services. Dissidents may well survive for a time, up to the ranks of major or lieutenant colonel; but the rigorous schooling of the Staff and Com- mand College and of the Higher War College, reinforced by the keen competition for the limited promotions to general-officer rank, will ensure a substantial degree of consensus at the higher military levels on Brazil's place in the world and on the military's role in the political process.

Promotion patterns in the military have been impressively stable since 1964. Only a fraction of those officers promoted to full colonel by Costa e Silva (1967-1969) are likely to be major generals even by 1980. (The others will be retired along the way as the pyramid narrows sharply at each rank.) Similarly, only a few of those promoted to colonel under the Médici administration (1970-1973) will reach major-general rank during the early to mid-1980s. Put another way, almost all the candidates for advancement to four-star rank during the remainder of the Geisel government were full colonels before the 1964 revolution; the lieutenant colonels of 1964 are either in retirement or have recently achieved promotion to brigadier general. Turnover is steady, if gradual, with twelve years the maximum total time in the three general-officer ranks. Thus, none of the four-star officers who last participated in the selection of a new president will still be on active duty the next time succession comes up; their places will be taken by individuals who were their immediate subordinates on the previous occasion, and who were probably brigadier generals the time before that. In other words, less than half the officers who were brigadier generals at the time of Médici's selection in 1969 were still on active duty, as major generals, during the choice of Geisel in late 1973. A substantially smaller proportion of these officers will have avoided compulsory retirement and will be at the peak of the Brazilian army command structure when the time comes to choose Geisel's successor in 1978. The same holds for corresponding ranks in the navy and air force.

That substantial continuity will be maintained into the 1980s appears likely from the following projections:

● No one is likely to be a full general by 1980 who was not already a brigadier general by 1971 or 1972.

● The divisional generals of 1980 will come from among

those who had reached the rank of colonel by the end of the Costa e Silva government or the very beginning of Médici's administration.

● Only those who were lieutenant colonels during Costa's presidency have any significant chance of becoming brigadier generals by 1980.

● Officers promoted to lieutenant colonel during the early 1970s will generally not be up for promotion to brigadier general before the mid-1980s. The cream of this group might become full generals during the early 1990s.[4] (The four-star generals promoted during 1976 had taken from twenty-one to twenty-four years to reach this point since promotion to lieutenant colonel.)

These facts reinforce other strong indications that any changes in foreign policy resulting from shifts in the composition of the military elite are likely to be gradual and incremental, albeit in the direction of some variant of greater nationalism.

Career patterns in the Brazilian foreign service parallel those in the military.[5] Today's first secretaries (average age roughly forty with fifteen years of service) include most of those individuals who are likely to be ministers second class in the mid-1980s and ministers first class during the 1990s. Many of today's ministers first class are apt to be on active service at the ambassadorial level at least through the mid-1980s, and perhaps as many as half of the present ministers second class will be the senior Brazilian diplomats of the 1990s.

On the basis of these projections about the stability of the system and the continuity of career patterns, current elite views regarding Brazil's place in the world and basic foreign-policy objectives are not likely to change substantially during the remainder of this decade as a result of either (1) replacement of the present foreign-policy elites by other groups and individuals with different views (considered quite unlikely in the short run, and possible, though not probable, within fifteen years), or (2) major shifts in the views of the present elites through alterations in their internal composition (demonstrated to be an essentially gradual and continuous process, likely to be incremental in the short run and not necessarily cumulative over the longer haul). Indeed, increased socialization of the current student generation in accordance with the present brand of National Security Doctrine could conceivably introduce an element of ideological inertia. Combined with stable and adequate recruitment patterns, such inertia could extend the present set of values and goals well into the future.[6]

The relative strength of the factors making for continuity does not mean that elite views on foreign policy are certain to remain static, but rather that they are most likely to be modified as a concomitant of continued directed change from above, both in response to and in anticipation of political circumstances that might otherwise lead to a decline in the regime's viability which could either contribute to its demise or require that it resort to intolerable repression in order to remain in power. Thus, it is necessary to examine the variables in the current political situation.

Political Issues/The Future of Decompression

The Geisel government very early came to understand that its range of choice might be unacceptably narrowed if steps were not taken to accommodate the social mobilization and desire for participation unleased by such side effects of the economic-development process as increased urbanization, expanded education, and improved communications. Well aware of the backlash within the military establishment which had been generated by Castelo's and Costa's efforts at political normalization, Geisel attempted to achieve decompression by creating escape valves and an improved strategy for the co-optation of moderate opposition elements as well as measures for institutionalization and for the building of legitimacy. The end of the "economic miracle" and of the atmosphere of confidence which had accompanied it during most of the Médici government contributed to Geisel's difficulties in implementing plans in the political-development sphere during 1975 and 1976. Future trends and controversies in this arena will have a heavy impact on both decision making and the content of Brazilian national policy. While this impact will be most pronounced in domestic matters, foreign-affairs ramifications will also be significant, so a close examination of the current impasse is in order.

Progress toward decompression peaked with Geisel's March 1, 1975, message to the new Congress, and with the hopes expressed elsewhere that incoming governors in states where the MDB had a majority in legislative assemblies would be able to work out viable relationships with the opposition legislators.[7] Golbery, chief architect and advocate of decompression—who, in the course of his duties, would ordinarily see the president at least two or three times a day—was unable to work during all of May because of a detached retina. After having been back on the job for only eleven days, he then had to take extended leave to go to Spain for an eye operation. Uncertainty over whether Golbery would be able to reassume his key office worked to the advantage of the opponents of his enlightened political policy.[8] (Indeed, many observers doubt that he ever regained the influence he had exerted on the president prior to this enforced absence.)

In early May the president invoked the extraordinary powers of the fifth Institutional Act after years of disuse, a move possibly designed as much to remind the MDB of the need to be prudent as to satisfy the military hard-liners. When a group of discontented young *durista* officers expressed the view that, in light of the results of the November 1974 elections, the revolution was defeated and more than ten years of effort by the Armed Forces was in danger of going down the drain, Army Minister Sílvio Coelho da Frota responded with an order of the day reiterating that Institutional Act No. 5 and Decree Law 477 (which placed severe restrictions on the political activity of students) were "indispensable to assure the climate of peace, order, security, and stability in which Brazil lives, a climate so different from that of the international arena."[9] After the Senate voted to drop charges of corruption against one of its members, the president used his exceptional powers to remove the legislator from office, thus underscoring that the fifth Institutional Act was a deterrent to corruption within the regime as well as a safeguard against subversion by its opponents. At the beginning of August, on the eve of the reopening of Congress after its winter recess, Geisel stressed that decompression was as much economic and social as political, and that, moreover, decompression must be gradual if it was to be long-lasting.[10] Political development was increasingly substituted for decompression in the government's policy statements, with the clear implication that this was a long-term process.

By the last quarter of 1975 decompression was clearly at a standstill, if not permanently sidetracked. Hard-line elements, particularly in São Paulo, were heating up the issue of communism and subversion in answer to the opposition's efforts to focus attention upon the questions of torture and the violation of civil liberties. The October 25 death of young journalist Vladimir Herzog while undergoing interrogation at second army headquarters brought matters to a head: In spite of the authorities' verdict of suicide, much of public opinion considered him a victim of torture.

In the midst of substantial unrest over this incident and rumors of military-centered conspiracies against him (supported by businessmen opposed to the burgeoning economic role of the state), Geisel visited São Paulo and managed to turn the situation to his decided advantage. Temporarily, at least, many wavering officers reacted against the hard-liners' excesses and rallied to the president's vigorous leadership initiatives. Near the end of the year, the army minister organized a luncheon in honor of the president which was attended by no fewer than 117 general officers. Pledging full confidence in Geisel's leadership, Frota ruled out intrigues within the army.[11] Yet military outrage over criticism by an MDB senator stemming from the Herzog incident was contained only by means of a retraction hastily engineered by leaders of both parties who were interested in avoiding a repetition of the events that had led to the fifth Institutional Act just seven years earlier.[12] And when two young São Paulo MDB state deputies refused to retract statements that evidence of Communist support for them in the 1974 elections had been obtained from their constituents by the use of threats and possibly torture, Geisel acquiesced in stripping them of office and of their political rights on January 5, 1976.[13]

At this juncture, the president resisted hard-line pressures to use the Institutional Act against a much larger number of opposition figures. Then, when a worker accused of distributing Communist party propaganda died while in the custody of a second army security unit, Geisel relieved Gen. Ednardo D'Avila Mello of his command, replacing him with a close personal friend as well as a professional associate, Gen. Dilermando Gomes Monteiro, at that point the most junior of Brazil's four-star generals and a known advocate of dialogue and Christian precepts.[14] Thus, prospects for a significant improvement in the political atmosphere of São Paulo seemed brighter than had been the case for several years.

Decompression was soon to encounter additional difficulties. With campaigning for the municipal elections (scheduled for November 15, 1976) under way, two Rio Grande do Sul MDB congressmen either were carried away by the enthusiasm of a party rally in the interior of that state—perhaps underestimating the care with which the SNI was monitoring campaign statements—or went too far in consciously testing the limits of the regime's toleration of criticism.[15] Once again there were right-wing pressures for heavy application of the Institutional Act. In view of the fact that this crisis coincided with preparations for the late March general-officer promotions and with celebrations of the twelfth anniversary of the 1964 revolution, the government had some difficulty devising a formula that did not involve purges on a scale that would place the November elections under a cloud, if not in jeopardy. In the end, only the two relatively junior deputies and one excessively vociferous defender from among the leadership ranks of the MDB lost their seats. Divisions within the opposition party were, if anything, accentuated by debate over how to respond. Following the issuance of a firm, but not inflammatory, manifesto, the moderate leadership of the

MDB seized upon the imminence of the president's visits to France and England as a respectable justification for attempting to bury the incident.[16]

In this delicate political environment, the late March army promotions followed seniority quite closely. The five oldest of the ranking divisional generals were retired, and the first three in terms of time in grade of those remaining were elevated to four-star rank. Both Ayrton Pereira Tourinho (sixty-one, an engineer) and Ariel Pacca da Fonseca (sixty, artillery) worked with Geisel at earlier stages of their careers—the latter quite closely, as coordinator of the secretariat of the National Security Council at the beginning of the Castelo Branco government. Fernando Belfort Bethlem (sixty-two, originally a cavalry officer) is somewhat more identified with the nationalist wing of the army, but was cabinet chief under Geisel's first army minister.[17] On balance, then, these promotions probably represented a step forward for Geisel in reshaping the High Command more in his own image. The same can be said for the promotions, in late July, of Tácito Theóphilo Gaspar de Oliveira (sixty-two) and Argus Lima (sixty-three) to full generals. The former had served under Geisel in Castelo's Military Cabinet, while the latter had been a cavalry officer, the branch that all three retiring four-star generals represented.[18]

As of October 1976, decompression appeared to be stalled rather than abandoned or moving forward. Over a dozen years after the military seized power, the Brazilian Armed Forces remains divided over the fundamental nature of the political system it wishes to see come into being. Critics of decompression cite the U.S. defeat in Southeast Asia; events in Portugal, Greece, India, and Italy; the situation in Angola; and the continuing Middle East crisis to argue that, with the world in such a mess and Brazil increasingly required to care for its own defense and security, this is not the time to weaken the regime by introducing the divisiveness of political competition or by permitting congressional restraint of the executive. Still smarting over the outcome of the 1974 elections, the hard-liners argue that there is not enough time before 1978 to adequately strengthen the government party and that, with the bloom off the "economic miracle," all electoral advantages are on the side of the opposition. Moreover, in their view, decompression unleashes distributive pressures that jeopardize continued development and thus undermine security.

Military liberals draw very different conclusions from the domestic and foreign panorama. They feel that after a long period of authoritarian rule, a political boiling point is eventually reached at which a radical turn to the left (so evident in post-Salazar Portugal) becomes a possibility. Then, too, the liberals say, the economic pie has grown sufficiently to make some distributive measures desirable—at least in order to counterbalance the pronounced concentration of income evident since 1960—particularly to the degree that such measures might broaden the internal market. Furthermore, they point out, the political situation is the only negative factor in Brazil's improved international image, tending to cloud the country's potential for leadership. Supporters of Arena argue that it is too early to say that the party could not make a go of decompression. Rather than viewing an opposition victory in 1978 as nearly inevitable, Arena president Francelino Pereira and secretary general Nélson Marchezan believe that their party has not begun to exploit effectively those issues that could carry it to victory in the municipal elections of November 1976 as well as in the state and congressional balloting in 1978. They point to Geisel's increasing prestige and popularity, the nationalist appeal of the 1975 nuclear agreement with Germany, the potentially rich petroleum discoveries, and such independent foreign-policy moves as the insistence on a 200-mile territorial waters limit.[19] Many military figures agree with this assessment, to which President Geisel subscribes fully.

Brazil's history indicates (as do the author's own soundings in this regard) that a majority of the officer corps is aligned neither with the hard-liners (*ultras, extremados, inconformados,* or *radicais*) nor with the moderates (*conciliadores, compreensivos, normalizadores,* or *liberais*). Most probably harbor ambivalent attitudes, based upon their perception of the situation as ambiguous. Under such conditions, leadership will continue to be a critical element in determining the future course of military politics and hence of national affairs. In this regard, it should be remembered that turnover in the upper reaches of the military hierarchy is continuing apace, with another wave of retirements and promotions due after the November elections and more to follow in March 1977.[20]

Thus, while either a significantly greater opening of the political system or a turn toward tighter restrictions and lessened competition remains possible—each with discrete implications for Brazil's future foreign policy—the more likely course of events appears to be a continuation of the situation of limited but real competition which has prevailed during the Médici and Geisel governments, with variations and short-term fluctuations depending upon specific events. Whether this prediction of fundamental continuity is as accurate for the economic realm as for the political arena is a question that must be explored next.

Economic Issues

Economic considerations will continue to weigh heavily on Brazilian policy and policymaking. Developmental successes, particularly those related to economic growth, constitute major components of Brazil's foreign-affairs capacity, while the country's remaining economic vulnerabilities impose important restraints on international policy. Of greatest immediate importance is continuation of the "economic miracle," or a reasonable facsimile thereof. Real GNP growth dropped in 1975 to just over 4 percent, and export earnings at $8.7 billion fell far short of the $10 billion target. Necessary for continuation of growth even at this reduced level (basically comparable to that of 1967, the transition year between the Castelo Branco and Costa e Silva administrations), much less for any substantial recovery, are such measures as those adopted in early 1976, providing broadened and even more energetic programs for export stimulation; further incentives for import substitution, through increased government purchases of Brazilian-made equipment rather than of foreign products; and reinvigoration of internal demand, through instituting salary increases greater than the rate of inflation. During the first half of 1976, the government was faced with resurgent inflation accompanying a strong GNP growth rate keyed by the industrial sector.[21] During July, policies were adopted to curb the rise in the cost of living, even at the expense of slowing the economy's rate of growth.[22]

From the perspective of the final quarter of 1976, the Brazilian economy shows both present and future strengths as well as a number of serious weaknesses. Clearly Brazil's policymakers are no longer complacent; as they did in 1966 and 1967, they are searching for measures that will facilitate a return to higher growth rates in the near future. Leading officials on the economic side of the Geisel government remained consistent throughout the first two-thirds of 1976 in estimating a trade deficit of only $1 to $1.5 billion on exports of at least $9.5 billion and imports of around $11 billion, along with a balance-of-payments deficit comparable to those of the past two years ($1 to $1.2 billion). The achievement of these figures would require holding the services deficit near the 1975 level in order to make possible a current-account deficit substantially smaller than those of the past two years. With interest and amortization on Brazil's mounting foreign debt up significantly since 1975, the resulting picture calls for very substantial amounts of new foreign financing and investment—more than would normally be forthcoming either with or without a general upturn in the world economy.[23] These considerations were very much on President Geisel's mind as he set out on the active personal diplomacy mission that brought him and his key ministers in direct contact with government and private-sector bankers and entrepreneurs in Paris, London, and Tokyo.

Brazil's trade performance can be assessed meaningfully only against the background of global trends. The total value of world exports rose 20 percent in 1972, 37 percent during 1973, and 47 percent in 1974. (The last figure was swollen by the quadrupling of crude-oil prices.) During 1975, however, world trade contracted, while Brazil's exports rose 8.9 percent in nominal value. Thus, although disappointing to the Brazilian government, this performance was relatively quite creditable. Given the generally unfavorable international economic situation still prevailing in 1976, foreign sales of $9.5 billion by Brazil might well be considered a reasonably strong performance, while exports of $10 billion would be excellent. The prospects are good for Brazil reaching the first of these goals, and the latter goal is not completely out of reach.

Primary commodities should bring in at least $5 billion in 1976, up from $4.4 billion in 1975. Soy should lead the way on estimated sales of $1.8 to $2 billion (most from soybeans, the rest from bran, meal, and oil), presenting a favorable comparison with the soy export total of under $1.3 billion during 1975—a figure already matched by midyear.[24] Coffee may well challenge soy if prices remain on the rise and if sales of 12 million sacks bring in from $1.7 to $1.8 billion ($932 million was realized from a substantially greater sales volume in 1975); sales for the first nine months of 1976 hit $1.29 billion. Sugar sales, predicted at $400 million—down sharply from the 1975 total of $1.05 billion for 1.73 tons—represent the one dark spot on the agricultural scene, but cocoa exports (of perhaps $400 million) and corn sales (more than doubling to $350 million) bid fair to help offset this decline. Iron-ore exports are running ahead of the 1975 pace and should exceed $1 billion, perhaps by a significant margin (up from $909 million).[25] Industrialized products, including manufactured items, would have to reach the target of $4 billion if Brazil is to meet with substantial success on the export side of the ledger.

Curbing of imports is fully as important to success in narrowing the trade deficit as is expansion of exports. If, as seems likely, consumer goods can be reduced $200 million or more from the 1975 total, and if steel imports can be cut back to $600–$700 million while capital-goods purchases are curtailed some 12 percent for a savings of $400 million, then total expenditures on imports may be held to about $12 to $12.5 billion (even with a moderate rise in petroleum

imports).[26] In the short run, little can be done about reduc-
ing the imports of such major items as fertilizers, nonferrous
metals, wheat, and coal—not to mention petroleum.[27]

After a very slow start, Brazil's foreign trade performance
improved steadily during the first half of 1976. January saw a
trade deficit of $490 million on imports of $994 million and
exports of only $504 million, but in February the deficit was
reduced to $237 million, with $864 million expended on imports against $627 million earned by exports.[28] While Jan-
uary 1976 exports had been down $218 million from the ini-
tial month of 1975, those for February were up some $54
million. March export sales of $725 million were slightly
above those for the corresponding month in 1975, and imports were held to $940 million for a deficit of only $215
million. Overall, first-quarter export proceeds of $1.86 billion
were down $158 million from January–March 1975, but the
cumulative trade deficits were nearly equal.[29] In April, exports rose marginally to $735 million (the same as in 1975),
so at the end of four months the trade deficit stood at just
over $1.3 billion, with exports down 6 percent from the cor-
responding period of 1975 and imports reduced a full one-
sixth as the effects of the restrictions enacted the previous
December began to be felt. May witnessed a significant up-
surge in soy sales to bring exports to $789 million as imports
stayed at about $980 million, and, on the strength of a record
$300 million in coffee sales, exports in June reached $1 billion—up nearly $300 million over the corresponding month
of 1975.[30] Moreover, for the first time in 1976 export earnings equalled imports, bringing the semester's balance-of-
trade deficit to $1.53 billion. Since exports rose in value
every month of the first semester—with those in June fully
double January's level—the prospects for a reasonably strong
second semester appeared promising. Third quarter exports
of $2.75 billion compared to $3.23 billion in imports brought
the trade deficit to $2 billion (on exports of $7.16 billion).

The trade deficit, although an important factor, is only
one of the major elements in Brazil's very tight balance-of-
payments situation. Even if the latter is kept to $2.3–$2.5

billion (compared to $4.7 billion in 1974 and $3.5 billion in 1975), interest payments of at least $2.1 billion on the accumulated foreign debt make it no simple task to hold the services deficit down to about $3.7 billion and bring the current-account deficit down to around $6 billion (which would be a marked improvement over the preceding two years, when the latter deficits reached $7.1 and $6.9 billion). In spite of government efforts, the shipping and tourism deficits remain important drains in this respect.[31] The predicted financial gap (the current-account deficit plus debt amortization) for 1976 of roughly $8 billion would be significantly smaller than 1974's $9.1 billion or the $9 billion total for 1975, but a massive inflow of loans, credits, and new investment will be required if the payments deficit is to be kept near the target of $1 to $1.2 billion. While failure to attract investment money would cause a heavy drain on Brazil's foreign-exchange reserves, success in this respect would add to Brazil's mounting foreign debt.[32]

Fundamental economic policy issues impinging upon foreign policy go well beyond the international trade balance-of-payments/foreign-debt equations. The basic legitimacy of the regime has rested to a considerable extent upon economic performance, measured essentially in terms of GNP growth. After averaging some 10 percent a year from the late 1960s through 1974, real GNP growth fell to 4 percent in 1975. The technical complexities of a debt-led export model of development are beyond the grasp of noneconomists in Brazil, both military and civilian, whose fundamental criterion for evaluating the success or failure of government policy is their perception of significant improvement in the development realm.

The GNP growth rates predicted for the United States and other industrial powers in 1976 may well be higher—in some cases, at least—than Brazil will achieve, but to make such a comparison would be, in a basic sense, misleading. Because the GNP of the United States decreased in both 1974 and 1975, growth of 7 to 8 percent in 1976 would leave the economy only up about 4 percent from 1973 (stagnant, in per-capita terms). Similarly, West German economic growth of 5 to 6 percent in 1976 would bring that country's GNP to less than 3 percent above its 1973 level.[33] Even a 5 percent rise in the Brazilian GNP for 1976 would mean a cumulative growth of nearly 20 percent in the economy over the past three years—three times that of Japan, and in marked contrast to Great Britain's complete stagnation during that period. Whether the Brazilian government can effectively present 1976's economic performance to the policy-relevant sectors of society in this relatively favorable light remains to be seen; certainly the heavy media coverage of the situation in France, Great Britain, and Japan before the president's visits to these industrialized powers helped prepare the way. Then, too, by predicting at the beginning of the year an economic expansion only slightly exceeding population growth—less than 3 percent—the Geisel administration established a frame of reference in which anything over 1975's 4-percent rate could be pointed to as a positive accomplishment, rather than compared apologetically to the 10-percent standard that all but became an accepted norm during the Médici years.[34]

Although the outcome of the several interrelated economic policy problems remains in doubt, certain factors point to their eventual resolution. First, Brazil now has many complex and quite sophisticated financial and developmental agencies and instruments that did not exist during the early and mid-1960s. Government intervention will almost certainly be carried as far as is necessary to attain results commensurate with the regime's needs for performance sufficient to keep an adequate base of support. Second, Brazil is in a much stronger international position than was the case before the 1968-1975 period. It has considerable bargaining leverage with the industrialized countries and can be expected to use this leverage to the fullest. Third, the balance-of-payments crunch, as it persists, is likely to cause the Brazilian government to make increasingly heavy demands for export production upon multinational corporations operating in Brazil. Finally, the Brazilian government will continue to seek to take advantage of the relative diversification of the country's economy and to exploit its potential to move toward self-sufficiency in important areas in which it is still an importer (steel, nonferrous metals, capital goods, wheat, and fertilizers).[35]

Indeed, the personal sales pitch of President Geisel on his state visits, Ueki's vigorous negotiating in Japan at the end of January and in the United States in May, and the administration's pushing forward with bidding on service contracts with risk clauses in the petroleum field—all these testify to a determination to storm ahead reminiscent of Kubitschek's "damn the torpedoes" reaction to the obstacles placed in the way of his forced-draft development program (by the United States and the International Monetary Fund) in 1959.

Trade with the United States remains a major sore spot. The cumulative deficit over the 1973-1975 period reached $4.0 billion, as the proportion of Brazil's exports taken by the United States continued to drop significantly. Whereas in 1967 and 1968 one-third of Brazil's export sales were to the United States and trade was relatively balanced, during the 1969-1972 period this proportion dropped to about one-fourth and the annual deficit mounted from $75 million to $408 million.[36] During 1973-1974 the U.S. share of Brazilian exports dropped to one-fifth as the trade deficit doubled and redoubled ($882 million and $1.5 billion). Then, as both sides of the bilateral trade decreased in value in 1975, the deficit grew slightly—a most unsatisfactory situation from the Brazilian point of view. Moreover, during the first five months of 1976 the Brazil–U.S. trade deficit reached nearly $645 million, up nearly $13 million from the corresponding period in the "bad" year of 1975.[37] The fact that for several years running the trade deficit with the United States, to which a substantial proportion of debt service is also destined, has been substantially larger than Brazil's global balance-of-payments deficit has had a significant impact upon public opinion, not just on the thinking of policymakers. In contrast, Brazil's trade deficit with the European Common Market countries for January-May 1976 was less than $60 million on exports of $995 million and imports of $1.054 billion. (As recently as 1974 Brazil's deficit with the EEC was $460 million.)

Notes to Chapter 8

[1]The Brazilian daily press and news magazines covered these trips in great detail during the last week of April and the first week of May, including the texts of speeches and communiques.

[2]Kissinger's statements are reprinted in the *Department of State Bulletin* 74, no. 1916 (March 15, 1976); 322-326. See also *Resenha de politica exterior do brasil*, 3, no. 8 (January, February, and March 1976): 35-49 for the toasts and communique.

[3]For the perspective of the left before the eradication of the urban guerrilla bands and the bankruptcy of the kidnapping tactic see João Quartim, *Dictatorship and Armed Struggle in Brazil* (New York: Monthly Review press, 1971); Miguel Arraes, *Brazil: The People and the Power* (London: Penguin Books, 1972); and Márcio Moreira Alves, *A Grain of Mustard Seed* (Garden City, N.Y.: Anchor Books, 1973). Also relevant is John W. F. Dulles, "The Brazilian Left: Efforts at Recovery, 1964-1970," *Texas Quarterly*, Spring 1972, pp. 134-185; and Neale J. Pearson, "Guerrilla Warfare in Brazil," prepared for the October 1972 meeting of the Midwest Assn. of Latin American Studies.

[4]Biographic data and information on career patterns are drawn from the annual *Almanaque do Exército*. Even for the fortunate minority, the average is nearly seven years as lieutenant colonel, six years as colonel, more than four years as brigadier general, and over four years as divisional general before reaching the top rank. Thus, an officer making lieutenant colonel in 1976 could hope to become a colonel in 1983, a brigadier general in 1989, a divisional general in 1993 or 1994, and— with a good bit of luck as well as ability—a full general between 1997 and 1999. Changes in the promotion procedure now under consideration might open this up somewhat, but even if adopted would not be likely to reduce the time necessary to rise to the top by more than a few years.

[5]One can roughly think of third secretaries as lieutenants, second secretaries as captains, first secretaries as majors and lieutenant colonels, counselors as colonels, ministers second class as brigadier generals, and ministers first class near the level of divisional generals, with the very top ambassadors bearing some relation to the rank of full general.

[6]A limited amount of somewhat dated attitudinal information on the technocratic stratum is contained in Carlos Estevam Martins, *Technocracia e Capitalismo* (São Paulo: Editora Brasiliense, 1974), pp. 132-214.

7See Ernesto Giesel, *Mensagem ao Congresso Nacional 1975* (Brasîla, 1975.

8Golbery's eyesight was a major topic of Brazilian political journalism for more than three months. *Manchete*, July 12, 1975, pp. 126-129, carried an optimistic article on his operation in Barcelona. Back on the job by early August, Golbery had a great deal of lost ground to recover.

9Quoted in *Manchete*, May 24, 1975, pp. 22-23.

10See Murilo Melo Filho, "O Fechamento da Abertura," *Manchete*, August 16, 1975, pp. 12-13, for this story.

11*Veja*, December 31, 1975, p. 21; *Manchete*, January 10, 1976, p. 26.

12See Schneider, *Political System of Brazil*, pp. 266-278.

13Murilo Melo Filho, "O Fantasma do AI-5," *Manchete*, January 24, 1976, pp. 12-13; *Veja*, January 14, 1976, pp. 21-26.

14On General Dilermando see *Jornal do Brasil*, January 22, 1976, and *Veja*, January 28, 1976, pp. 20-23. *Folha de S. Paulo*, January 22, 1976, discusses the inquiry into the "suicide" of Manual Fiel Filho and the release of other suspected Communists following his death.

15Murilo Melo Filho, "Dias de Tensão, Dias de Distensão," *Manchete*, April 17, 1976, pp. 20-22.

16Murilo Melo Filho, "Pacificação ou Nova Luta," *Manchete*, April 24, 1976, pp. 24-25.

17*Veja*, April 7, 1976, p. 28. See also *Visão*, February 9, 1976, pp. 21-22, for an article, "The Military: Consolidation of the 'Geisel Doctrine.'" There is some biographic information on the new generals in *O Estado de S. Paulo*, April 1, 1976.

18See *Veja*, August, 1976, pp. 22-23, and *Jornal do Brasil*, August 1, 1976. Also of interest are *Manchete*, July 24, 1976, pp. 26-26A, and July 31, 1976, p. 23.

19One of the best discussions of this division is in Murilo Melo Filho, "O Dilema do Sistema: Radical ou Liberal," *Manchete*, July 26, 1975, pp. 24-25.

20Useful articles on the promotion system include Murilo Melo Filho, "Cada General Cumpriu Seu Papel," *Manchete*, February 7, 1976, pp. 18-20; "Assim Marcha O Exército," *Manchete*, February 28, 1976; *Veja*, January 7, 1976, p. 24; and *Manchete*, December 27, 1975, p. 14. None of these sources explains the full workings of Brazil's rigorous system of up-or-out. Compulsory retirement for army generals (Brazil's

four-star rank) is linked to three basic factors—age, time in grade, and
date of original promotion to flag rank—with whichever of these has the
earliest effect on any specific case requiring transfer to the reserves. The
maximum age for active-duty service at this level is sixty-six years, but
retirement at a younger age is occasioned by four years of service at
that highest of ranks or twelve years since promotion to *general de bri-
gada.* Divisional generals (three stars) can serve only to age sixty-four,
while the ceiling for a two-star general is sixty-two. In addition, if one-
fourth of the positions at each level have not opened up during a calen-
dar year, then a sufficient number of individuals are retired in order of
age until this quota is met. (This extraordinary provision is termed *ex-
pulsoria* to distinguish it from the routine *compulsoria.*) These vacancies would then be filled the following March, with the other dates for
general-officer promotions falling in July and November. Since promotion panels require time to complete their work, vacancies resulting
from retirements or deaths coming less than thirty days before one of
these dates would not be filled until another trimester has passed.

21For before-the-fact estimates of the 1976 economic outlook, see
Veja, December 10, 1975, pp. 86-89; December 17, 1975, pp. 100-102;
December 24, 1975, pp. 69-70; December 31, 1976, pp. 52-56; and
January 7, 1976, pp. 57-58. *Tendência,* April 1976, pp. 13 and 48, is
useful on early 1976 trends, as is *Veja,* June 16, 1976, pp. 86-87.

22"Um adjuste contra a inflação," *Veja,* July 28, 1976, pp. 120-123.

23According to the *Jornal do Brasil* of April 2, 1976, Finance Minister
Simonsen estimated that Brazil's imports could be held to $10 billion
by cutting capital goods to $3 billion (from nearly $4 billion in 1975),
holding petroleum imports at $3 billion, reducing steel imports to $700
million, cutting expenditures for wheat to $400 million, and keeping
fertilizer imports at $500 million. *O Estado de S. Paulo,* April 15, 1976,
quoted Planning Minister Velloso as predicting exports of $9.5 to $9.7
billion, led by industrialized products at $4 billion. Bank of Brazil presi-
dent Calmon de Sá was cited by the same paper on April 7, 1976, as
projecting Brazil's 1976 exports at $9.6 billion and imports at a low
$10.6 billion. *O Estado de S. Paulo,* July 19, 1976, quoted Simonsen
on $9.5 and $10.8 billion for a trade deficit of $1.3 billion and a current-
account deficit of under $5 billion. These figures are consistent with
those cited in an interview in *Manchete,* July 3, 1976, pp. 22-23.

24*Manchete,* June 5, 1976, pp. 136-137, reviews the prospects for these
exports. *O Estado de S. Paulo,* May 5, 1976, placed coffee exports for
the first four months at over $400 million on sales of approximately

3.7 million sacks. *O Estado de S. Paulo,* June 29, 1976, cited June sales of $300 million, and on the same paper on July 6 gave a total for coffee of $805 million for the semester. *Jornal do Brasil,* May 7, 1976, said that the Brazilian Coffee Institute was selling its reserve stocks to exporters and might have only 4 to 5 million sacks left at the beginning of the 1977-1978 harvest. *O Estado de S. Paulo,* September 24, 1976, estimated the 1976-1977 harvest at under 6.4 million sacks, down from 22.2 million for the 1975-1976 growing season. The basic situation of the Brazilian coffee industry is analyzed in *Visão,* June 9, 1975, p. 42, and August 18, 1975, pp. 54-61. The Brazilian Coffee Institute bought some 5 million sacks on the eve of the killing frost that set off the international price rise. Their sale at present high prices affords the government an opportunity to finance rebuilding of the coffee industry without resorting to tax revenues. *Jornal do Brasil,* October 28, 1976, is the source for the soy sales estimates.

[25] *Visão,* July 21, 1975, pp. 60-70, reviews the emergence of Brazil as a major sugar exporter. Final 1975 figures are from *Jornal do Brasil,* April 11, 1976. According to *Veja,* April 14, 1976, p. 84, the 1976-1977 sugar harvest of some 130 million sacks would be up sharply over the 1975-1976 yield of only 98 million sacks. The problems of this industry are discussed in *Visão,* October 11, 1976, pp. 91-93. *Jornal do Brasil,* May 12, 1976, placed iron-ore exports up to that point at just under 20 million tons by the CVRD alone, up 5 percent from the same period in 1975.

[26] *Jornal do Brasil,* June 5, 1976, listed minerals (including petroleum) and capital goods as responsible for $6.55 billion of Brazil's 1975 import bill, with chemicals ($1.44 billion) and iron and stell ($1.26 billion) as other major components. *Manchete,* June 26, 1976, pp. 182-183, put primary materials imports for 1976 at $4 billion, down from $5.7 billion in 1974.

[27] *Folha de S. Paulo,* April 1, 1976, placed coal imports at over $300 million in 1975, but said that a new government requirement that 30 percent of Brazilian coal must go to steel production would drop the bill for 1976 to about $200 million. See *Veja,* June 23, 1976, p. 86.

[28] *O Estado de S. Paulo,* March 25, 26, and 30, 1976.

[29] See both *Jornal do Brasil* and *Folha de S. Paulo* of May 6, 1976. *Jornal do Brasil,* May 25, 1976, and *O Estado de S. Paulo,* May 21, 1976, surveyed trade through April, while *O Estado de S. Paulo,* June 3, 1976, included estimates for May, maintaining that the trade deficit might be held to $1 billion on exports of $9.5 billion and imports of

only $10.5 billion. *Jornal do Brasil*, June 1, 1976, pointed out that in May 1975 exports were only $716 million and imports an inflated $1.2 billion, so that the performance in May 1976 marked a sharp improvement, putting Brazil ahead of the past year's pace in exports and cutting imports by over $1 billion. *O Estado de S. Paulo*, June 25, 1976, gave a total of $1.3 billion for the January-May trade deficit. See also *Jornal do Brasil*, June 4, 1976, and *O Estado de S. Paulo*, June 16 and July 14, 1976.

[30]See *Veja*, September 8, 1976, p. 102 and September 29, 1976, pp. 115-116; *Jornal do Brasil*, October 7, 1976; and *Folha de S. Paulo*, October 28, 1976.

[31]In 1975, interest on the external debt reached nearly $1.9 billion and amortization exceeded $2 billion. *Jornal do Brasil*, May 20, 1976, estimated amortization for the current year at $2.4 billion, while *Folha de S. Paulo* of the same date put it at $2.8 billion. Most informed sources agree on an intermediate figure of $2.6 billion. The shipping deficit in 1975 was $648 million—down from $901 million in 1974, but still a major expense. (See *Tendência*, May 1976, pp. 55-56 and 69.) This deficit was expected to continue to go down gradually as the Brazilian merchant marine grows, and a 20 percent reduction was thought to be possible in 1976. The tourism deficit was estimated at $500 million in 1975, although Central Bank accounts show only $341 million. The Planning Secretariat arrived at a figure of $580 million by taking into account unregistered purchases of dollars by tourists seeking to get around the limits imposed by the government. (See *Tendência*, April 1976, pp. 14-16.) *Manchete*, June 26, 1976, p. 14, placed the figure still higher, as did *Veja*, June 16, 1976, pp. 78-84. According to *Veja*, September 29, 1976, pp. 115-116 the services deficit for the first semester was $1.949 billion and the current account deficit $3.479 billion. The balance-of-payments deficit came to $1.136 billion. *Veja*, August 8, 1976, p. 102 put money loans during the same period as totalling $2.38 billion, financial credits at $1.20 billion, and direct investments at $500 million. An added strain on the balance-of-payments has come from augmented petroleum imports designed to build up Brazil's stocks before the expected rise in crude prices at the beginning of 1977. See *Folha de S. Paulo*, September 9, 1976.

[32]Brazil's foreign-exchange reserves reached a low point of $3.69 billion in October 1975, as compared with a peak of $6.54 billion in February 1974, but they rose significantly in December to finish the year

above $4 billion. By the end of May 1976 they had dropped to nearly
$3.4 billion. (See *O Estado de S. Paulo*, March 13, 1976; *Folha de S.
Paulo*, May 20, 1976; *Jornal do Brasil*, October 14, 1976; and *O Estado
de S. Paulo*, July 8, 1976.) By midyear, reserves had risen to $3.8 billion
(chiefly in convertible currencies). In 1975 Brazil had a balance-of-payments deficit of $1.5 billion for the first half of the year, but rang up a
surplus of $300 million in the second semester; whereas in 1974 the
bulk of the deficit (some $827 million) was incurred during the final
six months. (See *O Estado de S. Paulo*, March 2, 1976.) Brazil could
draw almost at will some $650 million from the IMF, and obtain an ad-
ditional $254 million without signficant conditions if it encountered
serious balance-of-payments difficulties. Some $738 million more could
become available with the imposition of an approved austerity program.
(See *O Estado de S. Paulo*, March 24, 1976.) It is quite unlikely that
Brazil will need to have recourse to such measures.

33See the table in the *New York Times*, May 30, 1976, section 3, p.11.

34The inflationary aspects of policies designed to restore growth continue to pose difficult policy choices. A good first-quarter growth rate,
with GNP up 10 percent over January–March 1975, accompanied by a
sustained sharp rise in the cost of living, was followed by only a slight
moderation of these trends during the second quarter. Beginning in
June and July, the government placed relatively greater emphasis upon
containment of inflation, but prices seemed certain to rise at least 45
percent for the year even if tougher antiinflation measures were taken
after the November elections.

35Steel production in the first nine months of 1976 was up 10.5 percent over the same period in 1975, at 6.8 million tons making 9.5 million tons for the year possible. (See *O Estado de S. Paulo*, October 12,
1976.) In May iron-ore exports were up 27 percent by value over 1975
and were expected to run even higher during the rest of the year. (See
Jornal do Brasil, June 3, 1976, and *O Estado de S. Paulo*, May 22,
1976.) *O Estado*, June 18, 1976, placed iron-ore sales at $400 million
by the end of May and $500 million at midyear. Most of this increase
over 1975 was due to higher prices rather than markedly greater volume. (See *O Estado de S. Paulo*, July 16, 1976.)

36*Veja*, May 12, 1976, p. 85; *Jornal do Brasil*, May 6, 1976; *O Estado
de S. Paulo*, May 9, 1976.

37*Jornal do Brasil*, July 27, 1976, estimated U.S. sales totals from January through April at $438 million and purchases by Brazil at $1.01

billion. *Visão*, May 31, 1976, pp. 56-58, provided the following data on
U.S.–Brazil trade and balance of payments (in millions of dollars):

	1968	*1969*	*1970*	*1971*	*1972*	*1973*	*1974*	*1975*
Trade	14	-3	-148	-195	-281	-685	-1359	-1500
Services	-304	-298	-390	-423	-630	-510	-510	-1184
Current Account	-257	-264	-493	-599	-833	-1169	-1862	-2691
Capital Movement	297	330	501	624	742	699	1558	1969
Balance of Payments	40	66	8	25	-146	-470	-304	-922

The figures on the deficit for the first months of 1976 are put together
from data in *O Estado de S. Paulo, Jornal do Brasil,* and *Folha de S.
Paulo,* August 19, 1976. *Jornal do Brasil,* October 21, 1976 says that
the 1975 deficit of $1.756 billion was virtually half of Brazil's total
trade deficit, although trade with the United States amounted to under
one-fifth of Brazil's foreign commerce.

9
Outlook and Prospects
for
Brazilian Foreign Policy

Now that the major factors conditioning, if not determining, Brazil's international role and position have been examined, some further projections, forecasts, and predictions can be made—specifically for 1980, more generally for 1985. The first section of this chapter considers Brazil's relations with certain key countries and regions; the subsequent section is devoted to exploration of future trends in policymaking; the final section considers possible variations in the basic course of events during the next few years.

Bilateral Relations

Given the uncertainties of the international economic situation and Brazil's great development appetites, export expansion and diversification of markets will almost certainly remain a major goal of Brazilian policy. Although recent trends are likely to suggest future trends—quite strongly for the rest of the 1970s and less directly beyond 1980—straight-line projections could be significantly off the mark, particularly in situations where important policy options are possible on both sides, as in the case of Brazil's relations with the United States. Perhaps the clearest example of a relationship that will not continue to develop along the lines of past years is that between Brazil and the German Federal Republic. Here the 1975 nuclear agreements call for as much as $8 billion in payments from Brazil to the GFR over the next fifteen years (perhaps up to $5 billion, at 1975 prices, for the generating plants, and a sum that could well exceed $1 billion for the enrichment and reprocessing facilities and related technology). This fact alone will vastly alter the situation that existed in 1974, when Brazilian exports to the GFR were just under $800 million, with imports at $1.5 billion. Brazilian sales to Germany, particularly of iron ore and uranium, will almost certainly have to be boosted substantially to keep the trade imbalance from becoming unacceptably cumulative.[1] West German investment in Brazil is also apt to rise significantly, probably surpassing by the early 1980s the current level of U.S. investment.

President Geisel's 1976 trips to Paris and London, where Ambassadors Delfim Netto and Roberto Campos were assiduously cultivating the financial communities, resulted in the prospects of a sharp upturn in trade and investments. Geisel's visit to France yielded large-scale agreements on financing for hydroelectric projects in the Northeast as well as for sugar shipping facilities in Santos. By the end of May 1976, Electrobrás president Antônio Carlos Magalhães had confirmed arrangements for at least $900 million in financing, and Ministers Ueki and Reis Velloso, who had accompanied the president, were considering a number of major proposals. Taking into account the interest aroused on the part of several important European business groups, by mid-1976 the $2.4 billion in new credits mentioned during the trip seemed likely to materialize.[2] Long-term purchases of Brazilian iron ore and joint research efforts in the nuclear and solar energy fields are very apt to move forward. Thus, France should at least hold its position as Brazil's ninth or tenth most important trading partner, while it could move up a notch to sixth place as a source of investment by 1980.

Geisel's stay in England—during which he was accompanied by the presidents of the Bank of Brazil, the Central Bank, and the National Economic Development Bank, as well as by Finance Minister Simonsen—resulted in agreements for at least $1.64 billion in new financing. The largest portion of the package (just over $1 billion) was for Açominas, a major new steel mill in Minas Gerais programmed to produce 6 million tons annually by the end of 1979 and 10 million tons a year eventually.[3] Other agreements involved $400 million for construction of a railroad between Belo Horizonte and Volta Redonda (home of the National Steel Co.), $200 million in credits to Siderbrás (the government's holding company in the steel field), and a $40 million line of credit to the National Economic Development Bank for equipment imports by Brazilian enterprises. Other projects totaling at least $425 million remained under active consideration in the wake of the presidential visit, with cooperation in the petroleum field having a high priority. Indeed, it was viewed as a near-certainty that British Petroleum would be one of the successful bidders for an oil exploration concession under the "risk contracts," and that some form of joint venture would be established for the manufacture in Brazil, with British know-how, of equipment for offshore drilling. Yet continued growth in British trade and investment are not apt to improve the United Kingdom's relative position; for, although magnitudes should be up sharply by 1980, the United States, Japan, and Germany will continue to lead the way as Brazil's customers and suppliers.

With regard to Brazil's future relations with Japan, growth will mark the next decade—growth ranging between substantial and spectacular. Total trade with Japan grew from less than $650 million in 1972 to $1.06 billion in 1973, and doubled to $2.05 million in 1974. While Brazil's purchases from Japan declined in 1975 from well over $1.3 billion to $927 million, sales to Japan expanded by 35 percent to $883 million.[4] Japanese investment in Brazil has been on the rise—from $319 million in 1973, to $598 million at the end of 1974, to $739 million by mid-1975 and over $1 billion by that year's end. Investments programmed in the fields of iron ore, bauxite, and aluminum will keep this figure moving sharply upward through the rest of the 1970s and well into the 1980s. Indeed, recent estimates have foreseen Japanese investment of the magnitude of $9 to $10 billion by 1985, an amount which would almost certainly allow Japan to replace the United States as the leading source of foreign investment for Brazil. The results of President Geisel's state visit to Japan in September 1976 provide a good indication of the rate at which this may occur.[5]

Although the extent of Brazil's economic ties with major industrialized powers can be predicted with considerable assurance, trends in bilateral relations with countries of the Middle East, with the Soviet Union and Eastern European nations, and with the Chinese People's Republic depend on less-certain economic factors and are subject to greater influence by political considerations. In general terms, it is likely that Brazil's continued need for petroleum imports will lead to increased commerce with Arab oil-producing countries and to more investment by these countries in Brazil. The magnitude of Brazil's purchases from these nations will dictate increasing efforts to boost sales in order to keep trade from becoming even more imbalanced. Thus, an entire recent issue of *Comércio Exterior* was devoted to trade opportunities in the Middle East, and Itamaraty has instituted Arabic language training for its diplomats.[6] Saudi Arabia may move into the top ten of Brazil's trading partners on the strength of oil sales, while Brazilian activity with respect to Iraq and Iran will increase. Algeria perhaps best exemplifies the countries with which long-term balanced trade may be possible.[7]

The future of trade between Brazil and the USSR is very difficult to forecast since it depends very heavily on Soviet decisions to purchase from Brazil rather than from alternative suppliers, deliberations into which a variety of unpredictable factors may enter. It is likely that, bearing in mind Brazil's increasing international importance, Moscow will perceive some advantage in keeping trade with Brazil from slipping back into the doldrums of the late 1960s and early

1970s.[8] Trade with Eastern Europe is likely to increase, particularly that with Poland—where there is already a multiyear agreement to augment and diversify trade centering on Brazilian iron ore and Polish coal—and possibly with Rumania, which has issued an invitaion to President Geisel for a state visit.[9] Dramatic change in Brazil's relations with China is not probable, although the Brasília regime is likely to respond positively to Chinese initiatives for increased trade (since this was the primary motivation in the decision to establish diplomatic relations). With increased production of soy, wheat, corn, and rice, Brazil's commerce with the socialist bloc may come to involve substantially larger amounts of basic foodstuffs by the 1980s.[10]

Significant modification, but probably not root change, is likely to occur in Brazil's relationships with the African countries over the course of the next decade. While its economic interests may eventually diverge from those of the third-world nations, Brazil will, for some years yet, continue to seek major modifications of the international economic system which would benefit developing countries. Silveira sought to launch a successful Brazilian initiative at the seventh special session of the U.N. General Assembly. His carefully prepared opening speech on September 1, 1975, calling for new rules for North-South trade and the structuring of a political and legal framework for specific negotiations on market access and prices, fell between two stools.[11] Instead of providing a bridge between the position of the less-developed countries—whose spokesmen arrived already fired up by the Lima Conference of Nonaligned Countries—and that of the industrialized nations, Silveira's proposals were too tame for the former, while his call for a new general trade agreement was still unwelcome to the latter. After this rebuff, the Brazilian Foreign Ministry seemed disposed to drop back for some time to a lower profile, avoiding isolation by supporting third-world demands in a generally nonpolemical and constructive manner. (Indeed, as of late 1976 this had been Brazil's basic comportment within the Conference on International Economic Cooperation, as it ground on in Paris.)

Brazil's imperative as an "intermediate" country is to build credibility and strengthen ties with the developing countries while its basis for international influence matures during the rest of this decade. Between now and 1985 Brazil will certainly attempt to increase its trade with such African countries as Nigeria, Senegal, and Gabon, while it strives to build cultural, if not political, links to the former Portuguese colonies—particularly Angola.[12] Brazilian policymakers will continue to assess the costs and benefits involved in siding one way or another in third-world clashes with industrialized powers, and when the opportunity is there Brazil may well try its hand as conciliator and voice of moderation. Not until the late 1980s or the 1990s, if even then, is Brazil likely to have developed economically to the point at which its community of interests with Western industrialized nations generally overrides its shared concerns with the less-developed countries. In the meantime, by finding opportunities as well as dilemmas in its perhaps increasingly ambivalent position between the have and have-not countries, Brazil may eventually carve out a viable and accepted role that does not involve competing for leadership of any contending bloc.

Brazilian relations with the rest of Latin America, particularly its South American neighbors, may well come closest to continuing the trends observable in the recent past. Paraguay, Uruguay, and Bolivia are likely to be drawn increasingly close to Brazil. Efforts probably will be made to neutralize Venezuela's suspicions that Brazil has pretensions toward continental hegemony, but much will depend upon developments centering on Guyana—a situation that could either bring Brazil and Venezuela into substantial agreement and cooperation or lead them toward confrontation.[13] It seems likely that the relationship between Brazil and Peru will become closer, but this probability could change as the result of either internal political developments in Peru or tensions between that country and Bolivia and Chile. Argentine-Brazilian relations could improve on the basis of the affinity of interests between the two military regimes, but there is a strong probability that the present Argentine government or its successor might resort to exploiting popular fears of Brazilian "imperialism" as a way of rallying nationalist sentiment and diverting attention away from internal crises.[14]

Trade will continue to be primarily of political importance to Brazil, but of greater concern economically to the Spanish American countries; in almost every case of bilateral trade within the South American continent, such trade is substantially more important to the economy of the other trading partner than to that of Brazil. In 1974, Brazilian trade with Latin American Free Trade Association (LAFTA) countries amounted to 10 percent of Brazil's total foreign commerce, some 12 percent on the export side and 7.5 percent with respect to imports.[15] Only in the case of Argentina did such trade reach significant dimensions—with sales of $302 million and purchases of $360 million—and these totals represented a much more important fraction of Argentina's international commerce than it did of Brazil's. Total trade of $164 million with Uruguay loomed very large in that small country's trade picture, as did more than $132 million in trade with Paraguay (plus substantial contraband). In Chile's extremely tight economic pinch, Brazilian trade of nearly $230 million—with a favorable balance of $46 million—was of more than marginal importance to the Santiago regime, while for Brazil this figure represented only 1 percent of total foreign trade.[16]

Brazil will surely strive to increase these trade figures substantially in the years ahead, but political/strategic considerations may often loom larger in this endeavor than will simple economic motives. Trade will almost certainly be an instrument of political and military policy in dealings with Argentina as well as in negotiations with Brazil's smaller neighbors. Manufactured goods are likely to show a significant rise among Brazilian exports to neighboring countries by the end of this decade. Brazil's policymakers will continue to monitor Latin American responses and reactions to their initiatives very closely, and shifts in relationships between other South American countries will influence Brazilian decision making, as will internal political changes in those countries. Peruvian-Chilean relations and probable succession problems in Argentina and Bolivia are cases in point.

Perhaps the most serious questions exist with respect to

Brazil's future relationship with the United States. In spite of rhetoric to the contrary on appropriate ceremonial occasions, the old U.S.-Brazil partnership is a thing of the past. The era of Osvaldo Aranha and Getúlio Vargas on the one hand and FDR and Sumner Welles on the other is a historical memory only a little less remote than that of the Baron of Rio Branco and the "unwritten alliance" prior to World War I. Few veterans of the Brazilian Expeditionary Force are still on active duty, and they will soon be retired. Among those presently in power in Brazil there is little sentimentality for "the good old days"; what they want is a new relationship of equality, no more confining for Brazil than for the United States. Times have changed, and the United States is becoming relatively less important to Brazil as the latter country worries less about the traditional need to counterbalance its hemisphere rivals by forming close ties to the United States. Indeed, Brazil seems likely to become so diversified in its international interests and relationships that no one country, not even the United States, can become uniquely important to its foreign policy. The United States is no longer the dominant trading partner, the preponderant source of capital and financing, or the exclusive arms supplier. Realistically, this situation has existed for most of the twentieth century; for, in fact, the interwar period saw Great Britain, France, and Germany heavily involved in the Brazilian economy, and prior to World War II foreign military training for Brazilian forces was conducted by the latter two of these countries, not by the United States.

Brazilian perceptions of the United States and its relationship to Brazil's interests are far from static. Influenced during the 1973-1975 period by the dual U.S. trauma of Vietnam and Watergate, these perceptions contain a large element of uncertainty. Among foreign-policy elites, there are very real fears that the gains in bilateral relations stemming from the Kissinger visit and from that of Treasury Secretary Simon in April 1976 may be jeopardized by the change of administrations in the United States. These fears about the "reliability" of the United States were intensified during the first half of

1976 by Brazilian interpretations of statements about the Geisel regime made by the major Democratic presidential contenders, and—after the national Democratic convention—by the thrust of Democratic nominee Jimmy Carter's foreign-policy statements. After the election Brazilian officials became understandably concerned about Kissinger's successor.[17]

Achieving a closer and better relationship with the United States is a basic long-range objective of Brazilian policy, since the U.S. remains one of the world's superpowers and is still the leading single trading partner of Brazil. Brazil's acute sensitivity to its trade deficit with the United States is due in part to the realization that, in the short run, there is relatively little that can be done about the massive drain caused by petroleum imports from the Middle East. Brazilian policymakers, remain, on the whole, very much aware that the United States exerts considerable influence over international financial agencies. These policymakers clearly intend to give the United States time—probably until near the end of the Geisel administration, at least—to demonstrate, via concrete actions, a desire for strengthened ties. To this end, Brazil has deliberately stayed out of raw-materials producers' cartels, and has generally avoided taking confrontational positions in international trade forums and intergovernmental organizations.

The Simon visit and Ueki's follow-up trip to the United States in May 1976 helped remove some of the immediate obstacles to improved relations. Brazil agreed to reduce and to eventually remove fiscal incentives to certain exports which were considered by the United States to constitute subsidies that would bring into play countervailing duties under the trade act.[18] The United States, in return, agreed to reduce tariffs on Brazilian shoes and to urge investment in priority areas of Brazil's development plan, not only to U.S. investors, but also to the oil-producing countries. Mines and Energy Minister Ueki returned from the United States with agreements for $500 million in new financial credits, including $200 million for the BNDE from a consortium of San Francisco banks and several World Bank loans in the electric power field.[19] Deliberately timed to follow on the heels of the

Paris and London presidential visits, Ueki's active bilateral economic diplomacy exemplifies Brasília's view of relations with the United States as existing within a broader arena of dealings with all the Western industrialized powers.

Over the long haul, all these relationships will be affected by Brazil's changing economic role in the global system. There is little doubt that by 1980 Brazil will have become a major factor in world trade. Iron-ore exports will have nearly doubled to between 120 and 130 million tons, giving Brazil first place in that important category. While Brazil will also remain the world's leader in coffee exports, its soy production of around 15 million tons will cement its position as second only to the United States in international sales of that commodity. Production of 10 to 11 million tons of sugar will enable Brazil to export from 3.5 to 4 million tons, a very significant proportion of global commerce in sugar. By 1980 Brazil will also have become a major exporter of corn, while ceasing to import wheat, and may have added rice to its agricultural exports. Then, too, substantial exports of bauxite—perhaps over 3 million tons—will add to Brazil's export diversification. Imports of steel will have decreased significantly, along with those of nonferrous metals (particularly copper and aluminum), and purchases of phosphate-based fertilizers will have been cut sharply. Brazil will still be importing petroleum in large amounts, along with capital goods, but its exports of manufactured items will have risen.[20]

By 1985 the picture will have changed for the better, at least in regard to exports of iron ore (by then expected to have reached 165 million tons a year) and bauxite (possibly as much as 8 million tons annually). The energy situation may have shown the most dramatic improvement by this time, with installed electrical-generating capacity having risen from 20 million kilowatts in 1976 to 33 million by 1980 and to over 50 million in 1985.[21] By that time Brazil will have doubled its total energy production—from the equivalent of 94 million tons of oil in 1975 to about 190 million tons—and, with luck, will have increased its crude-oil production to somewhere between 40 and 65 million tons.[22] Unless the latter figure is reached, however, petroleum will still be the single leading import.[23] Coal needs will have doubled by 1980, and perhaps increased another 150 percent between that date and 1985. On the other hand, self-sufficiency in steel—with production of over 40 million tons in 1985, compared with 8.3 million in 1975 and 22 million in 1980—and in aluminum should have been achieved, and indeed Brazil is likely to have become an exporter in these fields.[24] These gains will not have been achieved without sacrifice, however, as the country will have invested between $2.4 and $3.2 billion a year in expansion of its steel industry, with at least $4.6 billion by 1984 having gone for importation of capital goods needed for steel plants. Investments in attaining self-sufficiency in nonferrous metals will have cost the country roughly $5 billion more.[25] The pursuit of goals such as these will markedly affect Brazil's bilateral relations with the industrialized powers, including the United States, as well as decision making in Brasília during the course of the next decade.

Policy Processes

The adjectives used previously in this book to describe the Brazilian foreign-affairs community—small, specialized, elitist, adaptive, unified, and autonomous—are likely to remain appropriate through the remainder of the 1970s and into the next decade. The first three characteristics are subject to very slow and inherently evolutionary change; adaptivity and unity, on the other hand, are features that can be lost in a relatively short period of time. Yet, the most likely course of events in Brazil—essentially, a further unfolding of tendencies visible during the past twelve years of military rule—should not place these latter qualities in serious jeopardy. And, while autonomy is in large part a function of a political model marked by severely restricted competition, even a substantial opening-up of the political system would do no more than alter the degree of autonomy of the foreign-policy elites. Effective public opinion, operative historical memories, and widespread expertise in the international field—all these are lacking in Brazil, and, by their very nature, would tend to develop slowly.

Clearly, the impact of the energy crisis—with the consequent slowing down of Brazil's economic growth and accentuation of its balance-of-payments problem—has caused economic and political decisions, as well as internal and international factors, to become even more interrelated than was the case before. This complexity is likely to characterize policy-making throughout the coming decade. On the institutional side, the foreign policy–making process in Brazil is likely to experience further differentiation as expansion of the country's international activities and involvement continues. While new agencies in this field, such as a ministry of foreign trade or at least a foreign trade bank, may be established by future governments, most of the necessary elements and instruments for deciding on and implementing a sophisticated international policy already exist.[26] Hence, the overhauling and reorganization of present institutions is more likely than their replacement by new agencies. Moreover, gradual and incremental reapportionment of authority and responsibilities is more apt to occur than a large-scale revamping of Brazil's foreign-affairs establishment. Presidential style may vary more than the scope of the office itself. Succeeding presidents may become more personally concerned with foreign policy or somewhat more detached, but variations are apt to be within the range established by the past four administrations. Conditions are such that no Brazilian chief executive in the foreseeable future will be able to assume direct control of foreign affairs—to do so would take too much time away from supervision of developmental programs and from political responsibilities—or, on the other hand, to detach himself from international policy considerations. Variations will be matters of degree, based on personal preference and on the prominence of foreign-policy questions at any particular time.[27]

The roles and impacts of presidential staff agencies are likely to remain significant, although the importance of one or another component of the executive office may fluctuate if it does not change permanently. The *Gabinete Civil* has been more influential on a wider range of policy matters than the *Gabinete Militar* in all post–World War II governments except two: that of Costa e Silva—during which Civil Cabinet chief Rondon Pacheco, subsequently more at home as governor of Minas Gerais, fell short on the dynamic and creative side (being viewed by many observers as a "plumber" rather than as an "architect")—and the unusual situation in 1954-1955 following Vargas' death, when Gen. Juarez Távora was the dominant figure in the caretaker government of Vice-President Café Filho.[28] The foreign-policy role of the SNI is still far from institutionalized, and there is a real potential for its influence and activity to expand under an aggressive head and a permissive president. By way of contrast, the Planning Secretariat is not likely in the future to have any greater say in foreign policy than it presently enjoys under Reis Velloso.

The influence of the Armed Forces on foreign-policy matters could increase or decrease, largely as a result of internal political considerations. Brazil has known two brief periods of junta government—in April 1964 and again in September-October 1969—and a future succession crisis could bring the Armed Forces back into such direct rule. On the other hand—possibly after 1978, but more likely not until the mid-1980s—Brazil might turn to a more civilian-dominated government, wherein the military's effective voice on foreign affairs might be restricted to defense-related questions or at least circumscribed by a more limited definition of security than now exists.[29]

Among the ministries, it is quite unlikely that Itamaraty will reestablish primacy in foreign policy–making, at least in regard to major strategic decisions and the fundamental setting of priorities. With effective leadership (such as might be provided by someone like Roberto Campos, with his background as the dominant cabinet minister in the Castelo government and the experience in intergovernmental infighting which he acquired during the Goulart, Quadros, and Kubitschek administrations) the Foreign Ministry could regain the upper hand, at least temporarily. Even then, however, its

influence would depend heavily on astute bargaining and bureaucratic alliances. More likely is a nondramatic recupera-
tion toward a position of *primus inter pares* based on improved technical capabilities, particularly in the economic
and energy fields. Even this is far from certain, since failure
to modernize training and broaden recruitment could further
erode the Foreign Ministry's role while other ministries continue to enhance their own international expertise.

The Finance Ministry will probably not again achieve the
predominant position in international policy it briefly occupied under Delfim Netto during the Médici government. As
was the overarching influence of the Planning Ministry during
the Castelo years, this temporary situation was largely the
product of a single dominating priority. But the chances are
at least equally remote that Finance will cease to have a major voice on foreign-policy questions. Other economic agencies are apt to see their influence ebb and flow according to
the relative salience of energy questions and pressures for
reform of the international financial system. The future of all
the finance-related agencies, however, is likely to be heavily
conditioned by the outcome of the present debate over the
appropriate economic role of the state.

The controversy over statism has substantial implications
for the future character and conduct of Brazil's foreign affairs. In recent years, public-sector enterprises have played an
increasingly prominent role, not only in Brazil's purchases of
foreign goods and sales of Brazilian products, but also in direct international links, through Petrobrás' risk contracts, the
Vale do Rio Doce Co.'s joint ventures, and Nuclebrás' cooperative undertakings. The creation of Imbel, an enterprise in
the field of armaments and military equipment manufacture
headed by a recently retired three-star general, may now project the military directly into this line of activity.[30] Moreover, the growing role of government trading companies
(Interbrás and Cobec) in dealings with East European and
Middle Eastern countries has been justified on the ground
that such governments are more comfortable doing business
with state entities than with private companies—a postulation
that is likely to have continuing operational validity.[31]

Whether the final outcome is some reduction of the government's direct involvement in the economy or (as seems more likely in light of the imperatives accompanying rapid development in a centralized system) continued role expansion by government agencies and enterprises, statism will remain an issue with significant foreign-policy implications for at least the next several years.[32] By 1977 and 1978 it should be much clearer whether state enterprises are better equipped than the private sector to withstand inflation and economic contraction. Evidence should also be available to support a more reasoned judgment as to the relative abilities of the two sectors to drive effective bargains with other countries and to serve as a barrier to increased penetration of the economy by transnational companies. Yet it is probable that statism will remain a recurring, if not continuous, issue through the presidential succession and into the next government.[33]

The foreign-policy weight of the Industry and Commerce Ministry is closely related to that of the business community; its influence will increase or decrease depending on the outcome of the statism controversy. While a more dynamic minister, or one personally closer to the president, would have some effect, a major voice for Industry and Commerce in foreign policy-making would require backing by the private-sector entrepreneurial stratum—who, if they possessed sufficient clout, would be more likely to seek to reach the president directly. A partial political opening-up based on the regime's efforts to secure its more active and effective backing in the 1978 elections, could enhance the business and financial community's access to the policymaking process, yet the latter's influence would be felt much more in the realm of domestic policy than in foreign affairs.

The role of Congress, the parties, labor, the church, intellectuals, and the mass media depends fundamentally on future internal political developments—particularly on whether the government chooses to pursue the policy of decompression or opts for a further tightening down of the system in the opposite direction. Essentially, the impact of such groups on foreign policy is largely a function of their broader public policy influence, which would be enhanced significantly only in a more open political system. Currently, prospects for achieving a more open system, at least by 1980, seem very much in doubt. In this respect, the most important political event during the rest of the 1970s is likely to be the 1978 elections, which will determine the successor to Geisel as head of the revolutionary movement of March 31, 1964, and as president of Brazil. If state governors are chosen by direct election, such an event will have occurred for the first time since 1965 (and in that year governors were elected directly only in half the states). In any case, the relationship of the presidential succession to the elections in 1978 will be significantly different from that which pertained in 1974. In that year Geisel, who had been chosen by the Armed Forces and ratified by Arena during the latter part of 1973, was "elected" in January, was inaugurated in March, and presided over the congressional balloting held in November. Thus, local elections were held only after the new national government was firmly established in power. Moreover, the new president effectively chose the governors-to-be, who were installed in office a year after his inauguration.

The sequence of events will be more complicated in 1978-1979. First, Geisel's successor will be selected by the military and presented to the government party for confirmation almost simultaneously with the election of the state governors, two-thirds of the Senate, all of the Chamber of Deputies, and the state legislatures. Indeed, the countrywide electoral campaigns will be in full swing during the period corresponding to that when Médici finally agreed to Geisel as his successor and Arena endorsed the choice. Then, too, the results of the elections in 1978 could create a climate of unrest during the formal presidential succession process, since the electoral college provided for under present law is essentially the Congress elected in 1974 (except for senators elected in 1970 and some representatives of lame-duck state legislatures). Should the opposition have emerged victorious in the November balloting, it might well be uncomfortable at the prospect of the incumbent—but repudiated—government having the full say as to who would be the new president.

While it is not possible to predict with any certainty who will constitute the military High Command during the critical period of the state and congressional elections and presidential succession (November 1978 through March 1979), considerable flesh can be added to the skeleton provided in chapter 8. In essence, neither any of the individuals serving as four-star generals as of mid-1976 nor anyone who didn't already hold three-star rank at that point will be among the "Cardinals of the Brazilian military church" the next time they decide on a president for the country. Instead the *Alto Comando* will be composed of officers promoted to full general by Ernesto Geisel between July 1976 and November 1978.

During his first nine months in office in 1974, Geisel promoted six of his near-contemporaries within the army to four-star rank. Because 1975 was barren of such promotions, Ramiro Tavares Gonçalves and José de Azevedo Silva (as the oldest at this level) were tabbed for early retirement.[34] Walter Menezes Paes fell victim to the four-year maximum in this highest rank, and Ednardo D'Avila Mello opted to get out early after falling into political disgrace. Following the ensuing promotions of Ayrton Pereira Tourinho, Ariel Pacca da Fonseca, and Fernando Belfort Bethlem in March 1976, the four-year rule forced the transfer to the reserves of Army Minister Frota, Armed Forces chief of staff Corrêa, and third army commander Oscar Luis da Silva. Thus, only Reynaldo Mello de Almeida remained of those promoted to full general before Geisel's inauguration, and he was due out by November (at age sixty-two, occasioned by the limit of twelve years as a general officer).

Hence, almost two years before presidential succession time the High Command was already composed entirely of individuals promoted by President Geisel. Yet the steady turnover would continue. First, the twelve-year maximum would catch Euler Bentes Monteiro in March 1977 (just after his sixtieth birthday), despite his being younger than almost all the three-star generals. Moacyr Potyguara, elevated in August 1976 to chief of the Armed Forces General Staff, would reach age sixty-six in September 1977, and army chief of staff Fritz de Azevedo could last only two months longer before the dozen-year limit would apply to him. Venitius Nazareth Notare would fall afoul of four years in grade in March 1978, and Dilermando Gomes Monteiro would be retired for the same reason by November. At that time he would be joined by all three of the full generals promoted as recently as March 1976, as well as one of those advanced to four-star rank in July 1976 (since their initial promotions to flag rank had come in November 1966).

As of late 1976 the candidates most likely to join the select group of full generals during the remainder of Geisel's administration included Carlos Alberto Cabral Ribeiro, José Pinto de Araújo Rabello, César Montagna de Souza, Edmundo da Costa Neves, Carlos de Meira Mattos, Hugo de Abreu (Geisel's chief of the *Gabinete Militar*), Walter Pires de Albuquerque, Ernani Ayrosa da Silva, and perhaps SNI chief João Baptista de Oliveira Figueiredo. (It also seemed possible—depending upon circumstances—for Geisel to promote two or three others to four-star rank by March 1979, if not by November 1978. Early in the period, candidates for such promotions could include Arnaldo Calderari and José Fragomeni; later, Antônio Bandeira and Antônio Carlos de Andrada Serpa would be the most likely beneficiaries.) There seems little reason to believe that as a group these officers differ in any significant way from the 1976 High Command in basic political or international outlook. Their subsequent attitudes and positions on foreign-policy questions in the late 1970s would seem to depend most heavily upon the intervening course of events and their perceptions about the successes and failures of existing policies.

The municipal elections of November 1976, although a step forward on the road to possible decompression, promised to cast relatively little light on what might be expected in 1978. In the first place, since mayors are not elected in state capitals and in certain other "national security" municipalities, over 25 percent of the registered electorate would have no direct way of expressing their preferences. As these

areas include most of those where MDB candidates ran particularly well in 1974, overall election results would certainly
favor the government. Moreover, local elections involve issues
and rivalries far removed from the national issues that were
so salient in 1974 and that are likely to be of importance in
1978. Then, too, the 1972 municipal elections were held under circumstances that resulted in a landslide victory for the
government: 3,349 mayors for Arena, 436 mayors for the
MDB, and 167 mayors appointed.[35] In terms of municipal
councilmen, the government party went into the 1976 election with 29,331 incumbents, as compared to only 5,936 for
the opposition party. With the MDB lacking organization in
nearly one-third of Brazil's municipalities, a statistical victory
for the government in 1976 seemed a foregone conclusion; a
more meaningful criterion was whether Arena would receive
more votes than the sum of the MDB ballots and those cast
blank or nullified, as occurred in the November 15 election.

Much greater attention has been given in this study to the
relative influence of different factors and institutions upon
Brazil's foreign policy than to the evaluation of the latter's
effectiveness. Little has been said about responsibility for the
successes of Brazilian policy, and no explicit effort has been
made to allocate overall credit. Critics of Brazilian policy
might argue that Brazil's upward mobility in the international
arena has been fundamentally a result of factors outside its
control, or even that Brazil's successes were achieved in spite
of unwise policies. In addition, the regime is presently faced
with the need to sustain growth under markedly less advantageous conditions of price and international demand than
those that prevailed during the Médici years and the "economic miracle." Hence, some assessment of the quality of
decision making is essential for an accurate forecasting of
future developments.

Observation of Brazil's internal politics and international
behavior for some two decades leads to the conclusion that
the country's increasing capability to deal with foreign-policy
challenges and opportunities will persist into the future, re-
gardless of political developments. Brazil has, on balance,

been both rational and effective in managing its foreign-policy liabilities and in exploiting its assets in the international arena. Of course, opportunities have been missed and mistakes made, but these have been relatively few. It is hard to build a strong case—even with the benefit of hindsight—that errors of omission or commission have been many or particularly serious. To say, as some have said, that Brazil disguises its weakness by trumpeting its potential greatness is not a telling criticism. Indeed, if such a strategy works, as it seems to have done, then it seems a most efficient way of achieving the desired end with a minimum expenditure of resources.

One question remains unanswered and essentially unanswerable: Has the restricted role of Congress and the virtual absence of widespread public debate in Brazil facilitated that country's adoption of rational policies and their effective implementation? Or has the lack of significant input from Congress and from the public permitted premature, misguided, or even erroneous decisions? Whatever the answer might be with respect to domestic policies, when one takes into account the low level and quality of input from such representative organs during the pre-1964 period, one must doubt that Brazilian foreign policy has suffered from the autonomy of the policymaking elites. A definitive judgment would be possible only after some substantial change in the openness of the Brazilian political system. Until then, the prospect seems to be for continued headway toward attainment of major-power status and toward fulfillment of Brazil's developmental potential under the present system of decision making, albeit not without much effort and sacrifice.

Other Possible Variations

The analysis in this study and the ensuing projections about Brazil's foreign-policy prospects have dealt with the most probable course of events. Given the uncertain nature of some of the contingencies involved, a brief look at a wider range of possibilities may also be in order. The most basic possible variations include:

- Substantial success in both the political and economic dimensions.
- Increased friction over political strategy or even the abandonment of decompression, accompanied by continued satisfactory performance in the economic realm.
- Progress with decompression, but a deepening economic recession.
- Significant reverses on both political and economic fronts.

Each of these courses would have a different impact upon foreign policy, in all cases less profound and direct than the effects in the domestic policy arena.

In the first of these alternative futures, Brazil's foreign-policy community would continue to benefit from essentially supportive internal developments. The combination of continued good economic prospects with an authoritarian political situation, or even with deepened political cleavages (the second scenario), would not necessarily affect foreign policy significantly during the rest of the Geisel administration or even for the duration of its successor. The foreign-policy community would, to a substantial degree, be able to remain above the storm and perhaps carry on with somewhat increased autonomy. For it is not on foreign policy, but rather on internal political questions, that the hard-liners diverge sharply from the military moderates, and the struggle for dominance between these contending factions has been present since 1964 without any clear reflection in foreign-policy shifts. The abandonment of decompression would, however, have an important impact on Brazil's emergence toward major-power status, to the degree that Western industrial democracies found the regime's greater repressive features abhorrent or that signs of instability led them to doubt its staying power.

A breakdown of the present consensus on foreign policy would be more likely under a combination of successful political decompression and sustained economic decline. Under these circumstances, elements presently without much say on policy matters—particularly Congress, the parties, the press, churchmen, and even labor—would realize substantially enhanced opportunities to influence foreign-policy decisions. Moreover, the economic imperatives of recovery efforts would be likely to take precedence over all other considerations in shaping Brazil's international initiatives. The statism issue might well become the center, not only of political debate, but of significant political realignments as well. The result could be policymaking inconsistency and disharmony within the foreign-affairs community to an extent well beyond that manifest during the declining period of the Costa e Silva government.

The basic cleavage during the first stages of a protracted economic crisis would very likely occur between proponents of policies designed to increase access to international capital markets and advocates of more nationalistic policies. The former, espousing views fundamentally identified with Finance Minister Simonsen and his associates, would seek to avoid confrontation with Brazil's chief suppliers of capital and credit. They would work to assure that multinational corporations would continue to invest in Brazil by making the country attractive to them as a platform for exports. Deeply concerned with the monetary requirements and the financial imperatives of a debt-led growth model, they would stress sound fiscal policies in order to curb inflation and would strive to keep balance-of-payments difficulties from retarding economic expansion. The Simonsen group would give priority to achieving closer relations with the United States as a means of attaining the type of market access necessary to preserve the present development model. In multilateral economic forums, such as the Conference on International Economic Cooperation and the General Agreement on Trade and Tariffs (GATT), they would seek approval of a formula that would permit fiscal incentives for exports and propose other measures designed to give freer play to Brazil's relatively sophisticated measures in the economic sphere. In brief, this group would advocate intensified reliance on some of the basic measures of Brazil's present policy mix and would recognize the realities of the existing international economic order, rather than experimenting with new departures.[36]

Those elements within the regime which felt that significant changes in policy were needed to cope with the persistence of the economic crisis would also find the roots for their program in Brazil's current political economy. Suspicious of the major transnational companies and favorably inclined toward state control of economic activity, the latter group would view the policies of their intramural rivals as lacking foresight and as being little better than an effort to make dependency work more effectively. In their view, the balance-of-payments constriction, instead of being allowed to dictate Brazil's policies, should be accepted as an opportunity to alter the regime's economic model. Sensitive to the possibilities inherent in Brazil's latent nationalistic tendencies (which had been subdued during the successful run of the Campos, Delfim Netto, and Simonsen policies), this group would find a point of departure in the import-substitution and statism policies invoked by the 1975-1976 government in response to Brazil's economic difficulties. They would increase public-sector investment even further to compensate for the belt-tightening effects of fiscal policies, and would try to increase exports of Brazilian firms instead of providing further incentives to multinationals or focusing the administration's efforts on making the environment more attractive to outside investment. Barter arrangements and specific investment projects, often government-to-government and involving bilateral joint ventures with new partners, would be given priority by this group over efforts to enlist the United States as an intermediary in attempts to obtain traditional sources of capital and financing.

The Foreign Ministry under Silveira would probably be at the core of this latter faction, most likely in alliance with Industry and Commerce Minister Severo Gomes (as was the case in their joint opposition to petroleum risk contracts). Although Ueki and Reis Velloso have been more inclined toward the other policy line (or at least toward alignment with Simonsen within the Economic Development Council),

Ueki has substantial institutional interests in moving toward a "statist" direction, while Reis Velloso could well swing in the "nationalist" direction if the more traditional approach failed to yield satisfactory results. More important, the president himself probably would lean increasingly toward the nationalist side if this last condition prevailed, rather than see the legitimacy of his government compromised by inadequate performance.

The greatest potential for change, beyond the bounds of the incremental and generally continuous adjustments foreseen in the body of this study, lies in a compounding of negative political and economic factors. Simultaneous failures on both these fronts would certainly undercut the government much more than would a situation in which reverses on one front would be offset by accomplishments on the other. Gains as a result of decompression might even persuade present opposition elements to support the regime's policies, in the international sphere as well as in the domestic arena. Indeed, a political realignment in which the moderate elements of the MDB might join the centrist bulk of Arena to form a new dominant party cannot be ruled out, even during the 1976-1978 period. Dashed political hopes combined with economic disappointments on a major scale would, in sharp contrast, cause present supporters of the regime to join an opposition that is itself moving toward a more intransigent position. Perceived mismangement of the economy would have the further effect of sharpening divisions within the Armed Forces and of deepening cleavages between the military and civilian sectors in a manner that could affect foreign policy.

All these alternative futures are based on variations of the present situation, and all have a relatively limited time frame, since even the most pessimistic of these scenarios—that of perceived failures in both political and economic areas—would most likely play itself out through the escape valve of the 1979 presidential succession. In order to project beyond that point into the 1980s, it is necessary to move to a more hypothetical plane. The single assumption that needs to be made is the presence in power of some form of military-technocratic regime, either one that basically represents a continuation of the Geisel administration or one that has pledged itself to a sweeping modification of policies followed since 1964.

Should this new government successfully engineer a reasonably satisfactory rate of economic growth and come fairly close to meeting the expectations it had aroused, it would be in a position roughly analogous to that of the Geisel administration in 1974-1975; in that case, the basic assertions of this study, in terms of Brazil's international behavior, would probably hold true. Although some shifts of emphasis and style would result if either of the two major schools of economic policy should emerge as dominant, it is more likely that the new government will—in its basic policies at least— effectively approximate a synthesis of the Geisel and Médici regimes.

In this context, a sharp economic downturn would almost surely lead to increased criticism of government policies and to a broadened discussion of alternatives. Should such a downturn coincide with the latter stage of a presidential term (as would be the case in 1982-1983), it might in large part be absorbed into the succession debate, probably weakening the hand of the incumbent. The succeeding administration would then have the option of trying a new economic game plan under the direction of a changed group of economic technicians. But in a recession coinciding with the early years of a presidential term—say, 1979 or 1980—criticism of the administration would likely focus on the changes the new government made in the economic ministries, with one faction within the military calling for the return of the faces and policies of the old governmental team. If, on the other hand, the new president had carried over the economic policies and technocrats of the former government, the first round of demands would be for the replacement of the old team by fresh leadership. Only if a recession continued or deepened into a real depression would more fundamental questions concerning the basic nature of the political economy come to the fore.

The time of a recession would affect its political ramifications in yet another way, since the regime would almost certainly point to the revolution's overall economic record in answering critics of a short-term recession. Thus, a worsening of the economic situation would be met by government assertions that a consolidation phase naturally occurs following a period of sustained rapid growth. Indeed, such notes were struck following the decline in the growth rate in 1975, and the explanation seems to have been accepted by many segments of the population.

Under most eventualities, a recession of up to two or three years' duration coinciding with a generalized international economic decline could be managed politically through modification in priorities and changes in responsible policymaking personnel, combined with promises that the recession was only the prelude to a renewed spurt of accelerated development—much as the 1964-1966 period paved the way for the recovery of 1967 and the subsequent sustained boom. Such a strategy would be particularly effective if the 1975-1976 slowdown had resulted in a new boom by 1978 or 1979. A protracted recession that phased into economic stagnation might well give rise to serious cleavages within the governing elites, and could even lead some elements within the military establishment to advocate disengagement from direct control and responsibility for governing the nation. Indeed, a long and deep depression might be the only development likely to bring about very substantial and even abrupt changes in the evolving political system. The Geisel regime has been able to use rapid economic growth (much as Vargas and Kubitschek used growth plus inflation) to satisfy conflicting demands for public goods by distributing relatively constant shares of an expanding pie. Without such growth, difficult and politically costly choices would have to be made, and public discontent would rise, probably even more than it rose during the austerity period under Castelo. For, under present circumstances, blame would have to fall upon the present holders of power instead of being heaped upon the shoulders of a discredited regime that had already been overthrown and punished severely, as was the case in 1964-1965.

Faced with rising popular dissatisfaction, sharp criticism

from aspiring elites, and policy disagreements among its own technocratic allies, the military, in such a situation of protracted economic crisis, would confront a choice between a policy of increasing repression and one of disengagement from responsibility for economic decisions. The first alternative would be extremely distasteful to the populist/modernizing elements in the officer corps, while the second would be very difficult to achieve without withdrawing from political control as well. The Armed Forces might seek a way out of this dilemma through forging an alliance with moderate opposition leaders, a course that would almost certainly involve opening up the system to a substantial degree of competition. In a period of economic retrenchment, the distributive and social policy requirements of such a strategy could well lead to an increased degree of economic nationalism (as was the case in 1953-1954 with Vargas and a decade later under Goulart, when growth rates fell off sharply). This strategy would also create a polarization of the regime greatly exceeding the 1975-1976 divisions over decompression.

In a very tight squeeze, such as that hypothesized above, many of the military might decide at a fairly early state that resorting to a strongly nationalistic stance might be opportune. With many of the younger officers convinced by that time that the economic model had reached its developmental ceiling in an international environment in which interdependency seemed to mean continued dependence for the developing countries, leaders looking for a means of retaining or regaining support might be able to bring about a shift to a radically nationalist stance on issues such as the multinational companies, perhaps even rather quickly.[37]

Even under the most clouded of these prospects—whether it came to pass in 1977-1978 or during a subsequent administration—the most likely foreign-policy turn would be toward accentuated nationalism, the basic direction in which Brazil already is steadily moving under present circumstances; thus, there would be no fundamental reversal of policy trends. This hypothesis provides yet another reason to believe that the underlying strategy of Brazilian foreign policy is likely to remain fairly constant, although tactics and intensity will vary with changing internal and external conditions. Brazilian nationalism may be confident and relatively nonabrasive or it may take on a greater stridency, depending on the shifting fortunes of the national quest for development and security. While a world economic crisis on the scale of the 1930s would certainly set Brazil back, such a crisis would have a more devastating impact on less-well-endowed countries lacking Brazil's potential for an autarkic road to development (a potential that will appear much greater after 1980 than it does today, and which will represent a more realistic policy option after 1985).

In the light of all these considerations, it seems reasonable to forecast continued upward international movement for Brazil. Short of total collapse of the international economic system, it is hard to conceive of adverse circumstances that could hit this emerging South American giant any harder than the global energy crisis has. Yet Brazil has withstood this adversity better than most other countries, including many of the Western industrialized powers. On the internal side, a drop in coffee production of the magnitude resulting from 1975's killing frost would have been little short of disastrous even as late as 1970. In fact, although the coffee crisis worked a hardship on a still-important sector of Brazilian society, in essence it accentuated the decline of this once-crucial export more than it threatened the foundations of Brazil's economy—in spite of the fact that it coincided with a sharp drop in sugar exports.[38] In the short run, although the confidence of significant elements of the public may have been shaken by the 1975 economic downturn, their gloom seemed likely to be dispelled in the near future by recovery, by vast development projects, by major petroleum discoveries, and by other reminders of Brazil's potential and capabilities. Even some of the more skeptical Brazilians suspect that it just may be true that "God is Brazilian," or at least that "nothing can hold back Brazil."[39] If Horace Greeley were living today, he might well suggest, "Look South, young man," for Brazil today is a country strongly reminiscent of the United States at the turn of the last century, on the eve of its breakthrough to a place as a major world power.

Notes to Chapter 9

[1]"Brasil entra na corrida mundial da força nuclear," *Tendência*, July 1975, pp. 44-47, contains a detailed discussion of the complex arrangements for establishing a number of joint Brazilian-German enterprises to carry out different aspects of the accords. The initial figure was put at Cr.$34 billion, but the total eventual funding of all facets, including the development and commercial application of the jet nozzle centrifuge method for separation of isotopes, may reach three or four times that magnitude. (See also "Brasil Atômico," *Manchete*, July 19, 1975, pp. 16-17, and the interview with Paulo Nogueira Baptista in *Manchete*, August 14, 1976, pp. 152-153.) In late July 1976, credit agreements were signed with German banks for nearly $2 billion in financing for the Angra II and III generating plants. (See *O Estado de S. Paulo*, July 13, 14, 22, 23, and 24, 1976; *Jornal do Brasil*, July 14, 22, and 24, 1976; *O Globo*, July 9 and 24, 1976; and *Folha de S. Paulo*, July 14, 1976.)

[2]See *Tendência*, April 1976, pp. 59-67; Murilo Melo Filho, "As duas viagens de Geisel à Europa," *Tendência*, May 1976, p. 7; *Veja*, April 28, 1976, pp. 21-24; *Manchete*, May 8, 1976, pp. 4-9; *Veja*, May 5, 1976, pp. 16-24; *Manchete*, May 15, 1976, pp. 100-106; *Visão*, May 3, 1976, pp. 42-54; *O Estado de S. Paulo*, April 16, 1976; *Folha de S. Paulo*, May 6, 1976; *Jornal do Brasil*, May 13 and 27, 1976.

[3]See *Veja*, May 12, 1976, pp. 16-23; *Visão*, May 17, 1976, pp. 42-48; *Manchete*, May 22, 1976, pp. 4-17 and 128-129; *Manchete*, June 5, 1976, p. 31; *Jornal* do Brasil, April 25, 1976; *Folha de S. Paulo*, April 29, 1976; *Jornal do Brasil*, May 5, 1976; *O Estado de S. Paulo*, May 7, 1976.

[4]These figures are apparently FOB for Japan's exports and CIF for Japanese imports. (See *Tendência*, May 1976, pp. 10-15.) Coming from Japanese sources and including estimates for 1975, they differ from those cited in footnote 18 of Chapter 4, which were FOB across the board and Brazilian in origin. These latter figures do not show any significant drop in purchases from Japan in 1975. Both sets of figures indicate that Brazil's sales to Japan rose by 20 percent in 1975. See *Veja*, September

22, 1976, pp. 14-23; *O Estado de S. Paulo,* September 11 and 15, 1976; *O Globo,* July 9, 1976; *Jornal do Brazil,* September 16, 1976.

[5]See the coverage in *O Estado de S. Paulo,* July 8, 1976, in which the Japanese minister of foreign trade is quoted as predicting $20 billion dollars in Japanese investment in Brazil in 1986. See also *Veja,* July 14, 1976, pp. 106-108, and *Folha de S. Paulo,* July 29, 1976.

[6]"Os Mercados do Oriente Médio," *Comércio Exterior,* March–April, 1976.

[7]The Algerian case illustrates that Brazilian services, particularly in the construction and engineering fields as well as in shipping, may be of considerable importance in balancing the bilateral payments flow with these countries. The 1975 trade was $169.5 million in Brazilian sales and only $77.6 in purchases. (See *Jornal do Brasil,* August 5, 1976, and *O Estado de S. Paulo,* May 19, 1976.) Simonsen went to Iran in June 1976 to discuss substantial bilateral trade and investment possibilities, and Iraq has agreed to purchase a significant amount of Brazilian iron ore. (See *O Estado de S. Paulo,* May 25, and July 14, 1976, and *Jornal do Brasil,* June 2 and July 14, 1976.)

[8]Consult *Veja,* April 14, 1976, p. 27. Brazilian exports to the Soviet Union were $403 million with imports of only $123 million, for a substantial surplus in Brazil's favor.

[9]A recent agreement with Poland calls for $3.2 billion in trade during the 1976-1980 period. See *Veja,* March 3, 1976, p. 57, and July 21, 1976, p. 21.

[10]Several Brazilian sales of soy to China have been reported, and Brazil is looking for future opportunities to sell grain to the Soviet Union.

[11]The texts of seven speeches by Silveira at the United Nations are reprinted in *Resenha de política exterior do brasil* 2, no. 6 (July, August, and September, 1975): 29-46.

[12]Consult Wayne Selcher, "Brazil's Relations with Portuguese Africa in the Context of the Elusive 'Luso-Brazilian Community,'" *Journal of Inter-American Studies and World Affairs* 18, no. 1 (February 1976): 25-58.

[13]See *Folha de S. Paulo,* June 3, 1976, in which the words of the departing Argentine ambassador and the writings of his successor are interpreted as indicating that Argentina would try to reopen the Itaipu case, at least for internal consumption. See also *O Estado de S. Paulo,* May 19, July 3, and July 15, 1976; *Jornal do Brasil,* May 22, July 9, and July 15, 1976; *O Globo,* July 25, 1976.

[14]Argentine fears related to Brazil's rise have been fanned repeatedly during the 1970s by a variety of spokesmen and publications.

[15]Consult the January 1976 external research paper by Gertrude Heare, "Brazil: Changing Patterns of Foreign Trade," pp. 24-26, 36-39, and 42-45.

[16]Trade with Brazil was of relatively little importance to Venezuela, with its swollen oil revenues, or to Peru and Colombia. Brazil's influence with these countries is likely to remain relatively low until economic ties are bolstered significantly. Establishment of a Brazilian-Colombian joint venture to provide Brazil with as much as 2 million tons of coking coal a year by 1980 and perhaps as much as 10 million tons annually after 1985 was discussed in *Visão*, July 26, 1976, pp. 86-88; *Jornal do Brasil*, June 1 and 7, 1976; *O Estado de S. Paulo*, May 28, June 1, and June 2, 1976. Serious economic initiatives with regard to Venezuela were covered in *Jornal do Brasil*, May 17, June 2, and July 27, 1976. Brazil's troubled relations with Guyana are discussed in *O Estado de S. Paulo*, July 10, 14, 15, 16, and 17, 1976; *Jornal do Brasil*, July 14 and 15, 1976; *Folha de S. Paulo*, July 14, 1976. *Jornal do Brasil*, August 5, 1976, reported the possible formation of a binational company to exploit copper and other minerals in the upper Amazon region of Peru, accessible only to Brazil in terms of transportation to markets.

[17]This judgment is based on many conversations with Brazilian officials, journalists, scholars, and politicians in Rio de Janeiro and Brasília during July 1976.

[18]Consult *Veja*, May 19, 1976, pp. 86-89; *Manchete*, May 29, 1976, pp. 136-137; *O Estado de S. Paulo*, May 15, 1976; *Folha de S. Paulo*, May 20, 1976.

[19]*O Estado de S. Paulo*, May 18, 1976. To the United States, as to other industrialized nations, particularly Great Britain, the total picture of liquid capital movement is as important—if not more so—than is the trade balance. *Tendência*, May 1976, pp. 65-66, explains in some detail how this has worked in the case of Brazil and France.

[20]These are, of course, estimates that can be affected by international economic considerations to some degree, as well as by construction schedules for new plants, facilities, and even infrastructural projects. Whether or not these exact figures are reached in 1980, a year sooner, or one or two years later is of little consequence for the basic argument of this section. What is important, for example, is not that Brazil be exporting $2 billion worth of cellulose in 1980, but that it is on the way

to become a significant exporter of this product in the foreseeable future. See *Manchete,* June 26, 1976, p. 183, on this particular case.

[21]See *Jornal do Brasil,* May 29, 1976, and *O Estado de S. Paulo,* October 10, 1976, which puts the price tag at $37 billion.

[22]Brazil's second and third nuclear generating plants are scheduled to come on line at the end of 1982 and mid-1984, by which time five others should be under construction. Brazil plans on being able to manufacture three nuclear generators a year beginning in 1985. By the year 2000, some sixty nuclear plants are to be producing 70,000 megawatts of electrical generating capacity, roughly three-and-a-half times the installed hydroelectric capacity in 1976. (See *Jornal do Brasil,* May 16, 1976.) With regard to petroleum, during the period 1965-1975 Brazil went from importing 10.9 million tons to imports of 29.9 million tons yearly. Consumption in the first of these years was 15.6 million tons, rising to 38.5 million tons in 1975. The most optimistic hypothesis on production to 1985, based upon marked success with the risk contracts, is for domestic production to rise to 23.3 million tons in 1980 and to 65.7 million tons in 1985—complete self-sufficiency. Projections based on the last few years of offshore drilling would yield a prediction of 46.4 million tons production in 1985, requiring over 19 million tons in imports. A less optimistic estimate, based on straight projection of recent production trends, would put domestic production at only 27 million tons, with imports at nearly 39 million tons in 1985. (See *Jornal do Brasil,* June 6, 1976.) "Petróleo, aqui e agora," *Manchete,* August 14, 1976, pp. 40-41, forecasts domestic production of 800,000 barrels a day in 1980—roughly two-thirds of expected consumption. Ueki reportedly reaffirmed at the Higher War College that self-sufficiency would be reached in 1985. (See *Jornal do Brasil,* July 9, 1976.)

[23]"A urgéncia de ter petróleo," *Manchete,* June 5, 1976, pp. 14-15. Brazil's coal situation was analyzed in *Veja,* May 26, 1976, pp. 84-86; *Jornal do Brasil,* March 31 and April 14, 1976; *O Estado de S. Paulo,* June 1, 1976. This last source put Brazil's reserves at over 20 billion tons, not counting the lignite deposits of the Amazon basin. *O Estado de S. Paulo,* June 22, 1976, said that energy investments between 1975 and 1979 will total $30 billion.

[24]On steel see *O Estado de S. Paulo,* March 26, April 1, 2, 7, and 15, and July 17, 1976; *Tendência,* June 1976, pp. 36-40; *Visão,* September 29, 1975, pp. 43-47; *Jornal do Brasil,* April 15, 1976. By 1987 not only is the Carajás project to provide 50 million tons a year of iron ore, but the related Itaqui steel mill should be producing 17 million tons—twice Brazil's total production in 1975 and the equivalent of the country's

estimated demand in 1979. (This is well covered in *O Estado de S. Paulo*, May 15, 1976.) The CVRD is seeking $10 billion in external financing to raise its sales by 1980 to $4 billion a year, more than four times the total income from iron-ore sales realized by Brazil in 1975. (See *Jornal do Brasil*, May 22, 1976.)

[25] See *Jornal do Brasil*, April 9, 1976, which put the price tag for investment in aluminum alone at $3.8 billion. *O Estado de S. Paulo*, April 11, 1976, estimated capital-goods imports for mining by 1984 at $1.3 billion, with the petrochemical industry needing $2.1 billion and merchant marine expansion some $4.9 billion. Add in capital goods imports of $3 billion for the petroleum industry, and the total mounts up to at least $20 billion in less than a decade just for essential capital goods. The science and technology plan approved by the CDE at the end of March 1976 (covering the 1975-1977 period) involves expenditure of nearly Cr.$23 billion, in 1975 prices, or roughly $2.5 billion. This is nearly double the annual funding level of the First Basic Plan of Scientific and Technological Development, which was its immediate predecessor. (See *O Estado de S. Paulo*, April 1, 1976, as well as the *Jornal do Brasil* and *Folha de S. Paulo* of the same date.) Development of the 100 million tons of copper ore at Caraíba, which would require an investment of at least $446 million by 1979 to produce half of Brazil's needs, could eventually save Brazil as much as $250 million a year on its import bill in the early 1980s. (See *Veja*, July 28, 1976, p. 127, and *Jornal do Brasil*, May 14, May 21, June 2, and July 22, 1976.) The phosphate deposits the government is beginning to work in Minas Gerais are estimated at a potential worth of $12 billion, but once again there is a substantial investment needed before large-scale production is achieved. (See *Tendência*, May 1976, pp. 92-96; *Veja*, May 26, 1976, p. 90; and *Jornal do Brasil*, April 26, 1976.)

[26] *O Estado de S. Paulo*, March 28, 1976.

[27] A political crisis of protracted duration would absorb a large part of the chief executive's time and energy—since the calculus of survival must take first priority—thus, at least temporarily, limiting the time he could give to foreign affairs and necessitating increased delegation of authority in this field.

[28] Useful on this point is Juarez Távora, *Memórias: Uma Vida e Muitas Lutas*, vol. 3 (Rio de Janeiro: José Olympio Editôra, 1976), pp. 3-58.

[29] The most current work in English on this subject is Wayne Selcher, "The National Security Doctrine and Policies of the Brazilian Government" *Parameters*, forthcoming. The current codification is in Escola Superior de Guerra, *Manual Básico 1976* (Rio de Janeiro: Estado Maior

da Forças Armadas, 1976).

[30]Created by law in July 1975, Indústria de Material Bélico, S.A. was actually established in March 1976 with an initial capital of Cr.$1.7 billion. See *O Estado de S. Paulo*, March 24, 1976, and *Manchete*, June 12, 1976, p. 26.

[31]*Tendência*, May 1976, p. 49. See *Visão*, April 19, 1976, p. 44, for a statement by Reis Velloso to this effect. Velloso was interviewed on related topics in *Veja*, June 9, 1976, pp. 3-6. MDB leader Roberto Saturnino Braga's defence of state investments and call for a new economic model based upon greater concern for the internal market can be found in *Veja*, June 30, 1976, pp. 3-6; *Visão*, July 26, 1976, pp. 30-32; and *Jornal do Brasil* and *O Estado de S. Paulo*, July 22, 1976.

[32]*Veja*, June 2, 1976, pp. 21-22, stressed that the statism issue has engendered debate which is not along party lines and that a number of political figures suspect that the multinationals are behind the campaign for "destatization." This could become an important foreign-policy issue, particularly with respect to the United States. (See also *Visão*, May 17, 1976, pp. 8-9 and 70-76, as well as *Veja*, May 19, 1976, pp. 20-25.) *Jornal do Brasil*, May 18, 1976, quoted Senator Passarinho of Arena on sponsorship of the antistatism campaign by multinational companies. A cabinet minister in both the Costa e Silva and Médici governments, this Arena leader can hardly be considered an irresponsible nationalist. Industry and Commerce Minister Severo Gomes was quoted in *Veja*, July 7, 1976, pp. 3-6, and *Visão*, August 9, 1976, pp. 64-69. BNDE president Marcos Vianna proposed some degree of privatization of state holdings in *Veja*, June 2, 1976, p. 21. *O Estado de S. Paulo*, May 25, 1976, cited Arena Senator Luíz Cavalcanti as against statism, while the official leaders of the two houses of the national Congress were quoted in the press on frequent occasions. Governors Paulo Egydio Martins of São Paulo and Aureliano Chaves of Minas Gerais—Brazil's two most populous states—have come down on opposite sides of this issue. During June and July 1976 the influential alumni association of the Higher War College (ADESG) became involved with the Commercial Association of Rio de Janeiro in joint study groups on the statism issue. (See *Veja*, June 9, 1976, pp. 85-86, and *Jornal do Brasil*, June 6, 1976.) Their reports called only for the containment of further statist tendencies in the future, rather than for the condemnation of existing activities desired by leaders of the business community. (See *Jornal do Brasil*, July 20, 1976, *O Globo*, July 24, 1976, and *O Estado de S. Paulo*, July 26, 1976.

[33]The Economic Development Council in mid-June considered the

statism issue and issued a document, "Action for National Private Enterprise," which stated that the relationship between the state and the private sector was clearly spelled out in the Second National Development Plan. (See *Veja*, June 23, 1976, pp. 84-85.) The government held that denationalization of the economy was a danger that justified a dynamic role for the state. Retired admiral José Carlos de Macedo Soares Guimarães, a businessman who was a leading columnist for both the *Jornal do Brasil* and *O Estado de S. Paulo* on the evils of statism and the need for privatization, returned to the attack with a column, "We Are in a Hurry, Mr. President,"and another entitled "Analysis of a Document," the document being the CDE paper of the preceding month. (The first of these long columns ran in *Jornal do Brasil*, July 9, 1976, and the second in *O Estado de S. Paulo* and *Jornal do Brasil*, July 16, 1976.) For having accused Reis Velloso of being of "bad character," the author was charged under Brazil's rather stringent national security law, an action which proved quite controversial. (The CDE document is discussed in *O Estado de S. Paulo*, June 16, 1976, and *Folha de S. Paulo*, June 17, 1976.) A provocative interview with Macedo Soares is in *Veja*, July 14, 1976, pp. 22-23, and a criticism of the CDE's position in *Visão*, July 12, 1976, pp. 78-88. Also relevant is *Visão*, June 14, 1976, pp. 68-72 and 78-80.

[34]For the former this meant only six months cut off his career, but the latter could otherwise have served another eighteen months before reaching age sixty-six.

[35]*Folha de S. Paulo*, May 27, 1976, and *Jornal do Brasil*, May 14 and June 7, 1976.

[36]Professor Albert Fishlow's analyses of these two school of thought, as expressed on April 30, 1976, at a conference on the external research paper from which this book developed, have been of real use in delineating these positions. Consult also Carlos Castelo Branco's column in *Jornal do Brasil*, May 30, 1976, and *Veja*, October 27, 1976, pp. 20-26.

[37]This scenario bears some relation to the "fortress Brazil" option elaborated a few years ago by Brady Tyson and H. Jon Rosenbaum and published in the latter's "Brazil's Foreign Policy: Developmentalism and Beyond," *Orbis* 16, no. 1 (Spring 1972): 55-84.

[38]*Jornal do Brasil*, May 23, 1976, placed Brazil's coffee stocks at 15.7 million sacks, or roughly ten months' supply. The 1976-1977 harvest is estimated at 6.6 million bags, and that for 1977-1978 at perhaps 13 million sacks, minimumly sufficient for Brazil to meet both its internal needs and export commitments. Actually, there is reason to believe that

supplies in private hands may be larger than official figures, perhaps about 12 million sacks as of mid-1976 in addition to the Brazilian Coffee Institute's reserves. (A useful round-table discussion of the coffee situation is carried in *O Estado de S. Paulo*, May 23, 1976.) Sugar exports from the 1976–1977 harvest are estimated at 35 million sacks or 2.1 million tons. (See *O Estado de S. Paulo*, May 25, 1976.)

[39]The first is a traditional Brazilian saying; the second is a slogan of the Médici government.

Bibliographic Essay

The study of Brazilian foreign policy has received relatively little attention from scholars in Brazil and North America. One recent treatment in English is William Perry's *Contemporary Brazilian Foreign Policy: The International Strategy of an Emerging Power;* Foreign Policy Papers, vol. 2, no. 6 (Beverly Hills and London: Sage Publications, 1976). This brief monograph builds upon the foundation of the Foreign Policy Research Institute's quite detailed research project, conducted in 1972-1973, the results of which were issued only as a two-volume research report—cited in note 4 of Chapter 1—not as a finished book. Among recent articles the most useful is Riordan Roett's "Brazil Ascendant: International Relations and Geopolitics in the Late 20th Century," *Journal of International Affairs* 29, no. 2 (1975): 139-154. Perceptive insights are contained in Brady Tyson's chapter in the Davis and Wilson text cited in note 43 of Chapter 2. Few of the general books on Brazil pay much attention to foreign policy, the major exception being Philip Raine's *Brazil:*

Awakening Giant (Washington, D.C.: Public Affairs Press, 1974). Other relatively recent efforts include Roger Fontaine's work cited in note 1 of Chapter 3 and Wayne Selcher's *The Afro-Asian Dimension of Brazilian Foreign Policy, 1956-1972* (Gainesville, Florida: University of Florida Press, 1974). These six studies provide the basic literature in the field of Brazil's foreign relations. Older works as well as sources on specific topics are fully cited and discussed in the extensive notes at the end of each chapter of this book.

Brazilian materials on foreign policy are also far from abundant. Since 1974 the Foreign Ministry has published a quarterly, *Resenha de Política Exterior do Brasil,* which contains all relevant statements by the president and the foreign minister and also addresses by foreign-government officials visiting Brazil and texts of joint communiqués, treaties, and international agreements entered into by Brazil. Brief notes on trade and cultural exchanges are also included in this publication, as well as a listing of all congressional speeches on foreign affairs. Specialized articles of a generally legal nature are frequently found in the *Revista Brasileira de Política Internacional,* and conferences of diplomatic personnel are occasionally reported in the *Revista Brasileira de Estudos Políticos. Segurança e Desenvolvimento* contains many lectures and studies from the Higher War College. Yet, in the ultimate analysis a very close reading of the Brazilian press is essential if one wishes to keep abreast of developments in the field of Brazilian foreign policy. As evidenced by their frequent appearance in the notes of this study, the most useful of the daily papers in this regard are *Jornal do Brasil, O Estado de S. Paulo, Folha de S. Paulo,* and *O Globc. Veja, Manchete,* and *Visao,* among the news magazines, are of particular value, while *Tendência* and *Comércio Exterior* are very helpful on economic and business matters.

In addition to the authors cited above, most of whom are engaged in research which will lead to further publications in this field, the reader should be on the lookout for future books and articles by H. Jon Rosenbaum, Thomas Skidmore, and Norman Gall, particularly the latter's "The Rise of Brazil." Useful annual updates on Brazilian developments include my articles for *Collier's Year Book* and those appearing in the yearly issue (generally about February) of *Current History* devoted to Latin America. Unfortunately, for the English-speaking person there are very few reliable sources for following Brazil's affairs on a reasonably current basis. The weekly London-based newsletter *Latin America* must be used with care, and coverage in even the *New York Times* and *Washington Post* is spotty at best.

Index